JOBSEARCH

REVISED EDITION

Jobsearch

REVISED EDITION

*The
Complete
Manual for
Job Seekers*

H. LEE RUST

amacom

American Management Association

This book is available at a special
discount when ordered in bulk quantities.
For information, contact Special Sales Department,
AMACOM, a division of American Management Association,
135 West 50th Street, New York, NY 10020.

This publication is designed to provide accurate and authoritative information in regard to the subject matter covered. It is sold with the understanding that the publisher is not engaged in rendering legal, accounting, or other professional service. If legal advice or other expert assistance is required, the services of a competent professional person should be sought.

Library of Congress Cataloging-in-Publication Data

Rust, H. Lee.
    Jobsearch : the complete manual for job seekers / H. Lee Rust. —
Rev. ed.
       p.   cm.
     Includes index.
     ISBN 0-8144-7750-X (pbk.)
     1. Vocational guidance.   I. Title.
HF5381.R79   1990
650.14—dc20   90-55208
                                                 CIP

Printing number

10 9 8 7 6 5 4 3 2 1

Contents

Preface

To the Job Seeker:

You want to find a job. Where should you start? Write a résumé? Contact a few friends? Answer some help wanted ads?

Don't.

You can't afford to let your search be a haphazard effort. After all, the job you find may absorb fifteen years or more of your career. It will provide the livelihood for your family and will occupy the majority of your waking hours. It can be a satisfying, challenging experience, or it can be total drudgery in an incompatible environment. It can advance your career or stunt your growth.

Whether you are looking for your first position or the one that will cap your career, your next job may be the most important move in your professional life. To find it you should use an efficient, systematic marketing plan. This is Jobsearch, your step-by-step guide to conducting your own job campaign. It prepares you to market yourself to those employers, and only those, who meet your career needs. It shows how you can be the only candidate in the race, and how you can put yourself in the enviable position of having several opportunities from which to choose. It will save you time that may be wasted on ineffective methods and will help you avoid mistakes that can impede your search or cause you to miss opportunities.

In this revised edition of *Jobsearch, The Complete Manual for Job Seekers*, I have expanded the scope to include help, examples, and search techniques for every job seeker from entry level to the highest executive. The use of personal computers in the job search has been added. "Outplacement," the newest severance benefit for employees who are laid off or otherwise terminated, has been explained. More personal experiences of other job seekers have been added, examples of individuals with problems similar to the ones you might face when looking for a new position. All reference materials have been checked, updated, and expanded. The entire book has been reviewed and revised for use during the 1990s, the decade when you can take control over your career progress and find the job or jobs that can advance you toward your career goals.

Each task, from defining your goals, writing your résumé, and contacting your job targets through interview techniques and negotiating your salary, is explained completely. All contingencies for your job campaign are covered.

Examples show you how others have solved problems, located job leads, and sold themselves in situations similar to your own.

The maze we call The Job Market is divided into its component parts with concise techniques developed to penetrate each. Although the names and addresses have been disguised, the experiences, correspondence, and people described in this book are real. They had problems or fears similar to those you may feel as you approach the job market. They used the Jobsearch methods presented in this manual to overcome these fears and problems and go on to advance or establish their careers in new, exciting positions.

You can find the job you want quickly and efficiently. But you must remember,

> *Jobs don't always go to the most qualified*
> *candidate. They go to the candidate who*
> *sells himself or herself the best.*

This Jobsearch manual will show you how to be this successful candidate.

For a number of years, I was a consultant to people seeking new jobs, people just like you with similar problems, similar backgrounds, and similar goals. I had always found it easy to find jobs for myself, jobs I enjoyed and for which I was paid well. I felt I could help others do the same by using the unique methods I developed for approaching the job market. These are the methods presented in this manual. They resulted from helping several hundred job seekers as I studied the job market, determining what worked and what didn't, refining the techniques, and expanding the most effective methods of reaching that market.

My approach, however, was not to study how people get jobs. That's the approach taken most often by job seekers and career consultants, but it seems to look at the market from the wrong perspective. Instead I looked at how companies hire their employees. By determining what motivates the hiring decision, what sparks a request for an interview, what places a candidate above others being considered, I was able to develop the Jobsearch methods. Because I've also spent a substantial portion of my career running small companies, I've often been in the hiring position. I've hired good employees and made mistakes, but I've also learned what advances one candidate's chances and what errors job seekers make when presenting themselves.

I decided to develop a complete, comprehensive program to package an individual to appeal to a specific market. This is Jobsearch. It has worked for many people before you. It can and will work for you.

ONE

Starting Your Jobsearch

1

Introduction
and
Instructions

An executive came to my office not long ago to discuss his career. David was with a well-known electric switch gear manufacturer. His position was secure; he had been with the company for seventeen years, rising to become manager of two plants with 300 employees each. But he was uncomfortable with his career and his future. At age 52 he felt his job progress shouldn't slow down. In fact, he felt better prepared to take advantage of his experience than at any previous time. Still he had not been able to move beyond plant operations. Larger plants, yes; new locations, yes; but the promotion that would put him in a position to affect the future direction of the company remained elusive. It was obvious he needed to make a change. He needed to put his career back in his own hands.

At that time I ran a consulting company to help people like David. To be precise, I helped people sell themselves. I was good at it because I realized years ago the three aspects of selling people that are of paramount importance: One, individuals have within themselves and their backgrounds a product to sell; two, the methods used to package and present this product to the job market affect its acceptance; and three, most people are ill equipped to make this sale, although it is frequently the most important sale of their careers.

Why should even a seasoned executive know how to find a job? Often his or her experience at job seeking is no broader than that of someone entering the job market for the first time. During thirty years of experience with only three job changes, David had never been required to plan and execute a marketing campaign to sell himself. Even though he had hired others, he actually knew little about the job market.

How and when do companies identify personnel needs? How do they screen and hire employees? Of perhaps greater importance, how do they eliminate the candidates who aren't hired? What is the function of the résumé in this entire process? And how and to whom does the job candidate address himself or herself?

Through my firm, Jobsearch, we helped David answer not only these but numerous other questions. We also showed him how to organize and execute a complete marketing campaign for that difficult product: himself.

We told him, however, that the sale wouldn't be an easy one to make. We explained it could not be the random effort it so often is with many job seekers. It had to be both planned and thorough. We pointed out that to make the sale, his campaign would also have to be massive, touching perhaps several hundred companies. But we showed him how this could be done quickly and efficiently. The Jobsearch method worked. David is now the vice-president of operations for one of the largest specialty steel product fabricators in the United States.

It can also work for you whether you're entering the job market for the first time or seeking an upper-level management position. If you've already attained a management role or if you have educated yourself with either schooling or experience to make a contribution in a corporate environment, you can benefit from the Jobsearch program presented in this manual.

But why should you? Why should you expend the time and considerable effort required to analyze your market, package your product, advertise its availability, and make the sale?

Perhaps you're like David, secure in your job, satisfied with your past accomplishments, but uneasy about your immediate or long-range prospects. Career advancement demands change. After you've mastered a task or made your maximum contribution to a position, you must decide whether to stay or move. If the appropriate move can be made within your present company, fine; do it. However, if it cannot, the decision—although it may be more difficult—must still be made.

Perhaps you're looking for your first job; an entire career lies before you. That first job could still be one of the most important you'll find: the first step in an advancing career or a mistake that starts you on the wrong line of development.

A change in companies or your first job may require moving you and your family. It will certainly include the risks of an unknown environment with new colleagues, new managers, and new problems. You must realize, however, that it will do little for your career to have five years of the same experience twice, even less to have one year's experience five times. Your career belongs only to you. You must guide and develop it yourself. Only you can and should make the choices. If your career becomes stagnant, staying where you are is no less a decision, even if it is not a conscious one, than deciding to make a move. Too often the refusal to make this decision turns out to be the wrong choice.

There are many other reasons to seek new employment. At Jobsearch we have worked with men and women who had a variety of motivational needs and goals. We have worked with first-time job seekers. We have helped those who were seeking an increase in compensation, often substantial. People desiring to move to another city or preferred area have used our program, as well as those who wanted to avoid a transfer. We have executed campaigns for career changes from one industry to another, from the military to business, and from private to public service employment.

In most cases, prior to these changes the men and women were adequately paid, made contributions to their organizations, and were reasonably content, but they realized something was missing. Adequate compensation and moderate satisfaction with their work wasn't enough. Call it a new challenge, a chance to improve either pay or environment, the prospect of better use of their skills—in any event, it meant a job change. Invariably the change was warranted; they and their careers benefited. Most individuals don't change jobs too frequently, they change too seldom. David, for instance, should have made his decision five years earlier.

You may not be in this situation. The decision may have been made for you. Perhaps you were fired or laid off or retired too early. Perhaps you are looking for your first job. Now a job search is inevitable. It should not, however, be executed with any less precision nor need it be any less successful, regardless of the reason.

For whatever reason, your decision is made. You are ready to apply your experience and efforts to the exciting, although perhaps initially forbidding, business area we call The Job Market. This manual will show you how. In these first pages you are starting a task that will be one of the most absorbing and interesting experiences of your entire career: the job of finding a new position, a new employer, and a new opportunity.

Let me assure you, somewhere there is a company that can use your talent and experience and pay you well for them. Not only that, it's probably located where you want to live. Your job is to find that company and sell yourself into the position you want. It can be done more easily than you think. I have done it too many times to think otherwise, and I have done it using the techniques set out in this manual.

This Jobsearch manual offers a complete, programmed approach to the job-seeking process. It was developed over a four-year period by helping individuals like you find the employment of their choice. Virtually all approaches to the job market were tried, modified, and tried again. Records were kept to determine the most effective methods of obtaining job interviews and, through these interviews, securing job offers. Ineffective methods were modified and in some cases dropped entirely. In addition, a review of available literature on the job market and the job-seeking process was used to evaluate the Jobsearch method against the approaches and suggestions from other knowledgeable sources. Used with care and judgment, the Jobsearch method can help you reach your immediate and long-range career goals.

But how long will it take? This is one of the questions I'm asked most frequently. There is no average time. At Jobsearch we had clients who used our interview techniques and secured a new position in less than a week with a prospect they already had in hand. In most cases, however, you should count on an effort that will absorb between two to four months of your time. Among other factors beyond your control, it will depend on the time you can devote to the search, whether you are employed and can work on the search only at night and on weekends or whether you can devote your full time to your campaign.

What will it cost? The expenses associated with supplies, postage, secretarial and computer typing services, long-distance telephone calls, and miscellaneous items usually run between $200 and $300. This depends, of course, on the extent of the search and on whether it is local or national. It also depends upon the extent of work you can do yourself, whether you can type and have access to a computer, and how much time you can devote to the effort. In any case, it's a small investment in your future. For the college graduate looking for his or her first job, the expenses can be decreased by doing much of the work yourself. For the person who needs to advance his or her career with a strategically chosen move, the investment in time and money may be more substantial but still small in relation to the satisfaction of a job you enjoy in a position that moves you toward your personal goals.

How to Use This Manual

The Jobsearch method is set out in chronological sequence and should be followed in the order in which it's presented. Don't try one section and then another in a haphazard fashion. Instead, by following the individual steps through your Jobsearch one by one, you will produce the maximum number of interviews within a relatively short period of time. Your objective is to secure multiple job offers, which can then be compared and negotiated one against the others.

Remember, however, that seeking a new position is a personal endeavor. Your immediate situation, your experience, and your background are different from those of all other individuals. For this reason you may find it appropriate to put additional emphasis on one or more marketing techniques, perhaps neglecting othes entirely. Use your own judgment in tailoring this program to your maximum advantage.

Before starting any actual work, look through this entire manual, review the Table of Contents in detail, and study the forms and examples in the Jobsearch Workbook section at the end of the manual. Familiarize yourself with the information included, the forms you will complete, and the marketing techniques suggested. This will give you an overview of the Jobsearch method.

Then establish a preliminary schedule of work to be accomplished and milestones to be reached. Workbook Form 1 is included in the Workbook section to record this projected work schedule. Once established, make every effort to adhere to your timetable. Be realistic, but also demand the most of yourself. The best results will be obtained with a smooth, continuous effort directed toward a specific goal.

As you proceed through the manual, or when circumstances change, your schedule should be updated. In this way you will be continually working toward realistic goals.

Discipline yourself to meet these goals. Establish a certain period each day or certain time segments during each week to work on your Jobsearch campaign. If you're unemployed, approach your campaign as you would a full-time job. Start at 8 A.M. and work five or six hours a day, five days a week. During most of your search there will be sufficient work to absorb this time. And much of the work will be both interesting and stimulating.

A specific area, usually in your home, to be used as your Jobsearch office, will prove advantageous in conducting your search. This space should include a desk (or a table that can serve as a desk), a telephone, and a place to keep stationery, reference books, and other supplies. Conduct the search from this office as you would any other well-organized marketing or sales campaign. Information must be readily available as you contact prospective employers or as they contact you, frequently when you least expect it.

You will find a standard three-ring binder most effective as a master file for your correspondence, contact lists, and other Jobsearch information. Buy tabbed dividers and label them: To Do, Résumé and Data, Personal Contacts, Ad Answers, Mail Campaign, Other Contacts, Prospects, and Miscellaneous. Filing your work in appropriate sections in this notebook will facilitate your locating them when they are needed.

In the To Do section, add a blank page of lined paper. This will be used for listing work to be accomplished or required follow-up during the current week. As items are completed they should be marked off, with new items added to the bottom of the list. At the beginning of each week, the list should be rewritten and the old one discarded.

A successful Jobsearch effort is largely determined by attention to numerous details. This requires organization. In your correspondence, personal contacts, and follow-up with potential employers, you'll be at least partially judged by your ability to organize your work. A well-organized, well-executed Jobsearch will be evident to prospective employers and will act in your favor.

Expense Records: Deduction for Federal Income Tax

In the 1986 revision to the tax code, the Internal Revenue Service (IRS) continued its practice of allowing expenses associated with a search for employment as deductions for federal income tax purposes. This deduction, however, is a Miscellaneous Itemized Deduction subject to a 2 percent adjusted gross income limitation. Deductible items include all expenses incurred as a result of the search, including fees paid to an agency or consultant, whether successful or not. Travel expenses are also deductible if the primary purpose of the trip is to secure a new job.

Expenses aren't deductible for a person seeking his or her first job or for individuals who have been unemployed long enough to create a substantial lack of continuity between jobs. Neither are they deductible for a search directed toward a different trade or business from that practiced previously.

In determining deductibility in your own case, do not necessarily consider a career change as a change of trade or business as might be defined by the IRS. If you are a manager and are seeking a job as a manager or executive, this is not necessarily a change of trade or business even though you might change industries or the type of business. If you are currently in sales, any new job involving sales or taking advantage of your sales experience will most likely be recognized as being in the same trade or business. If you have questions concerning your own case, ask a certified public accountant or qualified lawyer for his or her advice or opinion.

In order to obtain your income tax deduction, your expense records must be complete and detailed. You must be able to substantiate them if you're audited by the IRS. This means you should keep all receipts or other information that supports your expense records.

See Workbook Forms 2–5 for recording your automobile, telephone, and traveling expenses as well as a summary record for these and miscellaneous items. Record all your expenses as they occur. Include automobile travel even for short local trips. This expense can accumulate and represent a substantial amount during your entire job campaign. Record telephone calls as they are made including date, phone number, city, and person called. When your monthly bill arrives, fill in the toll charges and transfer the total to the summary page. Use copies of the Travel Expense Report for trips that aren't company reimbursed or for submission to companies that don't give you their own form.

Objectives and Approach

The largest employer in the United States is private industry, and most individuals seek jobs in this sector of our economy. For this reason, the major emphasis of this Jobsearch manual is on positions in the business world. This doesn't mean the program cannot be used with equal facility and success to secure jobs with associations, nonprofit institutions, professional groups, or government agencies. In fact, even with a former career in business, you might want to target a portion of your Jobsearch effort toward one or more of these other areas of potential employment. In such cases, use care to modify your correspondence and other information to conform to the requirements, objectives, and in some instances jargon of these groups.

One of our most successful searches was done with a career army officer who wanted to enter private business. It was difficult for him to drop twenty years of military language and tailor his résumé and letters to the business world. He did it well, however, and is now personnel director in a 500-employee company. It is not the 7,000-person military installation for which he performed similar functions, but the pay is substantially higher and his opportunity is unlimited. He gained the control over his career that he wanted.

As you proceed through this Jobsearch manual, be cognizant of the objectives of each section. The overall program is designed not simply to find a job but to secure for you a career position offering maximum compensation and job satisfaction. This dictates a multifaceted and thorough approach to the job market. By pursuing several effective marketing techniques simultaneously, you can attract a number of job offers at about the same time. Success in this effort will give you the luxury of choosing among available alternatives, of using one offer as a negotiating tool with others, and of planning your future career using all available options.

In Part One of this manual, your objective is to gather information and establish the basis for correspondence you'll use in your marketing effort. Although important, this work is only preparatory. You won't receive a job offer in response to a letter or a résumé. An offer will be received only through a personal interview. You must sell yourself to an employer face-to-face.

With this in mind, the objective of the marketing phase of this Jobsearch manual—Part Two—is to secure the maximum number of personal contacts with prospective employers and to maximize your job interviews. During the selling phase of these job interviews and the follow-up described in Part Three, the objective is directed toward attracting job offers that will give you the necessary choices to guide your future career.

The Job Market and You

In seeking a new position, or your first position, you shouldn't be concerned about the state of the economy or any comments you might read or hear concerning the availability of jobs in your field. Whether the country is in expansion or recession, whether you are looking in a broad or a narrow field, attractive jobs are available. These are created by the mobility of the work force: the death, retirement, and promotion of current job holders and the growth of companies throughout the economy. Your basic approach to the job market shouldn't be altered by the factors of supply and demand. Although they may influence the extent of your search or the emphasis placed on various marketing methods, the techniques are the same.

Just remember, regardless of prevailing economic conditions good jobs are still available. The Jobsearch method will help you identify these positions and direct your efforts to a successful conclusion.

What Employers Are Looking For

Most résumés are a litany of job titles and responsibilities. They are written as a career history of the candidate. This approach is simply wrong. They should be written instead as a sales tool directed toward the expected audience. A company will seldom hire you because of titles you held or responsibilities you exercised. It's interested in your ability to produce profits or to improve the efficiency of their organization. This is true whether you're an experienced executive applying your former experiences or a first-time job seeker applying educational skills to the job.

A company either makes a profit or dies. If a company hires you for $25,000 per year, it expects a $50,000 return. It's obviously a losing game to hire you at that salary and get only a $20,000 return. Your ability to make such a contribution can best be determined by those of your past accomplishments that relate to the profit or success of your former employer, not by your past job titles and responsibilities. For this reason, this Jobsearch manual and your approach to the job market will be accomplishments oriented.

Just because I've been the president of four companies does not qualify me to be the president of a fifth. The fact, however, that I took a losing brick manufacturer and made it profitable in two years might qualify me to run another company, but that is an accomplishment, not a job title. Karilyn Naff, whose résumé is included in Workbook Form 20, had been treasurer or controller with four companies. Did this qualify her to be a treasurer for another? No, but bringing the financial statements up-to-date and filing a Securities and Exchange Commission 10-K Report in less than three months for her last employer certainly did.

As you proceed through this manual, never lose sight of the fact that you're hired to produce profits or efficiencies and usually for no other reason. Although different words are used to describe profits, this is as true for a charitable or social service organization as for a business venture. While your career goals, job satisfaction, and personal fulfillment are important to you, they are of no importance to a prospective employer. It's up to you, not the prospective employer, to determine that your job and career offer personal satisfaction.

It is irritating to most business executives to receive a résumé that starts with a job objective stating: "I seek a management-level position affording the opportunity to broaden my background and experience while offering the potential for growth and compensation commensurate with my abilities in a self-satisfying career."

That's a quotation from a résumé in my Jobsearch files. The client quickly agreed he didn't need any of these self-gratifying platitudes. Once he analyzed his past accomplishments, he realized he had the wherewithal to sell himself into a position that would give him the job excitement and pay he wanted. He went on to do it with no reference to such a job objective.

Search While Employed or Unemployed

A popular misconception about jobs and the job market is that it's easier to get a job when you have a job. This is not true. It's based on the belief that when you're employed there's no need to explain why you left your former position. It fails to take into consideration that a similar explanation may be required for all previous job changes.

No job candidate offers ideal qualifications for any position. Explanation is a part of your entire career history. In most cases individuals interviewing you for a new position have been terminated or have made job changes during their careers. They don't expect to find candidates who have never had periods of unemployment.

There is, of course, some advantage to having continuing income when you are employed during your search. Nevertheless, most advantages of being employed during the search are balanced by the time you can devote to the effort if you don't have a full-time position. In either case the work is the same, the approach is the same, and the results should not differ.

If You Are Fired

A large number, if not a majority, of businesspeople who have led active careers have been fired or dismissed in some manner from a company. I can speak from experience; I've been fired twice in my career. Although this may create a psychological trauma, it's not the end of your career. On the contrary, it can be an exciting opportunity. You'll be free to concentrate on finding a new position. There's no reason this new position shouldn't advance your career. I've heard more than one businessperson, including myself, say that being fired was one of the best career moves they ever made. You must put the trauma behind you and get to work on the job at hand.

After losing their jobs, most people think first of taking time off to rest and decide what to do next. This is a mistake. Even a short vacation will cause you to lose momentum. Instead of relaxing and using the time to think constructively about your future, you'll worry about your next job, how you're going to find it, and whether it will be as good as the one you just lost.

Some Jobsearch clients came to us after such vacations; invariably, it was more difficult to start a search in these instances. After several weeks of worry, they were confused. They felt rejected and couldn't objectively view their past careers to identify the strengths that were their best sales tools.

You should begin preparing your Jobsearch campaign immediately after losing your job. Take a vacation after your campaign has been successfully completed and before you report to your new position. You'll then be in a position to relax and enjoy your well-earned free time.

When you're fired, for whatever reason, your new job starts the moment you are told. You must act in a businesslike manner. Don't become emotional, and don't try to talk your employer into keeping you. It never works. Simply try to determine the reasons the action was taken. It may also be important to give your side of the story just for the record, but if this seems advisable, keep it brief. Don't be drawn into an argument. You have another important item to discuss—your severance benefits—and for this you don't want a hostile atmosphere.

Negotiate your severance benefits politely but firmly. These benefits may represent a major portion of your livelihood until you are in your new job. Be realistic, but try to get more than you are initially offered, and don't forget there are numerous benefits other than cash payments. You may find the company is willing to give you free secretarial services during your job search campaign or allow you to use a company car for several weeks. These and similar items can reduce expenses while you're unemployed.

During these conversations, it's also important to determine what your former employer will say about your termination. You must know if you're to be given a poor reference in order to soften its impact when you approach a new company.

In the coming weeks you will have to tell your friends and business associates, as well as potential employers, why you were terminated. It's important to prepare your answer in advance. You'll find it helpful to write a one-paragraph explanation stating your own reasons. These may or may not be the same as those given by your employer, but they should be the truth as you see it. Your explanation should contain little negative information, preferably none. Then, once it is written down, don't change your story. Put your past job behind you quickly and start your search for an even better position.

Your Attitude

A major obstacle to success in your search for a new job or first-time job is your fear of being rejected. Particularly in the case of persons who have been fired, the fear of rejection is frequently so great they subconsciously disqualify themselves before they can be refused. This can best be overcome by conducting a thorough search and uncovering a number of good opportunities for consideration. In the process of doing this, however, you must understand a principal rule in the sale of any product. Every individual in the potential market does not represent a buyer. Some will neither want nor need the product you sell.

In a Jobsearch campaign, you are the product. You're selling your own talent, experience, and education. These may be of great value to one company and of no value whatsoever to another. Rejection is part of making the sale. After all, you want only one job, and the market is large. Expect refusals and don't let them affect your determination or your self-confidence.

One Jobsearch client frequently canceled job interviews because of conflicts that arose with her duties at the time. Another invariably showed up late for interviews, although he was habitually punctual. In both cases these clients were seeking ready excuses for the refusals they feared. Once they understood what they were doing and the reasons for their actions, they went on to secure the jobs they wanted.

Your attitude about yourself and your objectives is important to the success of your campaign. Written and verbal communications should be positive and direct in tone. You should feel self-assured, comfortable with your past accomplishments, and confident about the future. If these aren't your current attitudes, they will change as you progress through this manual. The more you work on your future career, the more contacts you make, the more interviews you have, the more convinced you'll become of your probable success.

Your best job interviews will be those you do not consider crucial. Knowing you have other options, you will be more at ease. This will be evident to the prospective employer and will work to your advantage.

You wouldn't purchase a product in a torn, dirty, or unattractive package. Now you must package yourself for maximum appeal to your potential job market. Your attitude, as well as your dress and appearance, is part of this package. Keep it positive and confident.

Professional Assistance

A large number of firms, primarily in the larger U.S. cities, offer assistance to persons seeking employment. These services proliferated during the 1980s. Although this Jobsearch manual is designed to eliminate the need for such assistance, it's advisable to understand what is available. In some, albeit rare, instances a job seeker may wish to consider some sort of specialized help or may have it extended by their former employer at no expense.

Firms that work with job seekers are of three basic types: résumé services, career counselors, and placement consultants. Of these, the professional résumé services should be avoided by virtually all job seekers. Most résumé service companies offer a standard résumé form that lists a candidate's past job titles and responsibilities. Many include information that is extraneous or even damaging. Costs for this service range from $25 to $1,000. Not only do these résumés neglect the important emphasis on accomplishments, which are the candidate's major selling points, but they're also easily recognizable by most employers with experience in the job market.

A company expects your presentation to be your own. If it's not, it will tend to discredit you. In addition, many of the résumé services urge the candidate to have his or her résumé printed in large quantities and offer to mail them out to a standard list of company presidents. This Jobsearch manual will explain why these suggestions are erroneous and will give you effective alternatives.

Generally, career counselors should also be avoided. They are expensive and are not needed by most job seekers. Typical charges range from $1,500 to $5,000. For these fees the job seeker receives a battery of psychological and vocational tests coupled with counseling to help pattern future career objectives. This may be followed by some help in turning these objectives into a job. However, if you have a well-planned Jobsearch campaign, you can do better by executing it yourself. If this campaign includes several well-considered job objectives, you will know more and learn more about your future career potential and goals than a counselor could tell you.

If, however, you feel you need professional guidance in making your immediate and long-term vocational choices, consider consulting a good industrial psychologist. For fees ranging from $200 to $1,000 these professionals offer the same type of testing and evaluation as the heavily advertised career counseling firms. Most such individuals or firms are listed in the Yellow Pages of major city telephone directories. Directors of personnel of large corporations can also recommend industrial psychologists whom they use in candidate screening processes.

Placement consultants usually offer a combination of career counseling and help in securing employment with major emphasis on the candidate's job search. Again these services are expensive in relation to the assistance provided. Fees range from $2,500 to 10 or 15 percent of the candidate's first year's salary. Although these firms relieve the candidate of the major portion of work involved in the search, their efficiency and methods are difficult, if not impossible, to judge prior to entering into a binding contract. Because a job search is a close, personal endeavor, job seekers will find they can do a better job of choosing target companies and presenting themselves than a third party who knows them only superficially.

The one exception to this is the outplacement services that might be offered by your former employer if you're laid off, retired early, or dismissed. Outplacement with expenses paid by the former employer has grown rapidly over the past decade. If this service is offered with no obligation on your part, you should certainly accept. However, do not relinquish control over your own search. Establish the parameters for your Jobsearch campaign using the suggestions in this manual. Then review these with the outplacement consultant and assure yourself that he or she will be of substantial assistance. You'll then be in a position to have the consultant take on much of the tedious or repetitive work in the campaign while you manage his or her efforts.

Conducting an Anonymous Search

Steps can be taken to keep your Jobsearch campaign confidential if you find it necessary to do so because of your current employment. In general, this will reduce the response to your campaign. It doesn't mean, however, that you will be unsuccessful; it means only that your options may be more limited than with an open search.

You must judge the extent to which your anonymity is important. If you're unsuccessful in your first campaign, you'll still be gainfully employed. You can wait a few months and begin again. At that time you might reevaluate the importance of confidentiality and its effect on the success of your search.

In only four cases out of over a hundred was a Jobsearch client's open campaign for a job discovered prematurely. In none of these situations was the person terminated. On the contrary, a mutually agreeable transition period was worked out. As a consequence, these Jobsearch clients were then able to concentrate on their future as well as use their employers as references.

In one instance a client answered a blind help wanted advertisement that had been placed by his own company. The requirements specified in the ad matched his target perfectly. He was in pharmaceutical sales with a desire to move into marketing and product management where he could use his chemistry and MBA degrees. His employer agreed with his assessment, and he secured the job he wanted without changing companies. Carefully review your need for confidentiality as well as the job prospects you might find without a move.

If your search is confidential, you'll be severely restricted in the use of personal contacts. Rather than broadcasting your availability to all business friends and associates who might help, you'll be forced to limit your appeals to a select few you can trust implicitly. If your situation is particularly sensitive or you are well known in the area of your search, you may find it necessary to eliminate all personal contacts.

You can, however, conduct an effective direct mail campaign and answer help wanted advertisements by using a close personal friend as an intermediary. This is done by following the same procedures as for the direct mail marketing letter and ad responses described in the appropriate sections of this manual (see Chapters 11 and 12). Instead of using your own name and address on the letterhead, use that of your friend, writing the letters as if they were being written on your behalf.

Look at the sample of a direct mail marketing letter and an ad response (Workbook Forms 6–7) done in this manner. Note that the reason for confidentiality is stated in the letters. Each letter ends with a disclaimer of any economic interest in an eventual agreement between you and a new employer. These are important points. The reason for confidentiality must be plausible. Otherwise it will be viewed as a gimmick and restrict the rate of response even more severely. Because on occasion employment agencies or other "finders" answer help wanted ads or send out letters similar to these, the commission or fee disclaimer is used to advise the reader that no such situation exists.

In this type of search you must use a friend to receive calls and letters at his or her own address and telephone number. Don't attempt the subterfuge of a false name over your own address. This ploy will eventually become known to any respondent and will act to your disfavor. Nor should you use a blind post office box; few companies will respond to an unnamed party. A situations wanted advertisement, blind or not, is usually an ineffective method of finding employment. The methods used to protect the confidentiality of your search must be as genuine as the reasons for it.

The choice of an intermediary in a confidential Jobsearch campaign is of utmost importance. In many cases, prospective employers will speak to this person first, and this conversation will constitute their initial evaluation of you even though you aren't speaking for yourself.

If possible, your intermediary should be a person familiar with the field in which you seek employment. He or she should be on the same level or above that of the position you seek, and must be conversant with your background, talents, and objectives. A copy of your résumé, your accomplishments list, and the mailing list for your letter campaign should be readily available to him or her. For responses to help wanted advertisements, your intermediary should have a copy of the advertisement stapled to the letter you wrote.

Even though these letters will be written, typed, and mailed by you, they should be personally signed by your intermediary. In signing each letter, he or she should check the name to be certain the salutation is appropriate. You might have addressed a letter to "Mr. Blakley" when your intermediary would have started with "Dear Bill."

Never take undue advantage of your friend during your campaign. All the work involved should be done by you including overseeing printing of the letterhead, typing, stuffing envelopes, and mailing letters. As soon as any real interest is established, the intermediary should divulge your name, offer to put you in contact with the prospective employer, and withdraw gracefully from any further involvement in interviews or negotiations.

When you consider a confidential search, think carefully about your current situation, the probability of your employer's learning that you're looking, and the effect on your job if that should occur. Most businesspeople you contact in your search will respect a simple request for confidentiality. In addition, they will want to know who is interested in their company and the identity of his or her current employer.

An employer who hears you are interested in changing jobs may still keep you until you've found a new position. This is usually the case if you continue to contribute to the company. After all, your employer needs time to find your replacement. On the other hand, if you're terminated immediately, you'll be free to devote all your efforts to finding a new job. After you have definitely decided to make a change, this may not be as bad as it first appears.

In any case, don't use your search as a bargaining tool with your current employer. You may be offered inducements to stay on, but in most cases you will have damaged your reputation with the company. Regardless of how attractive the inducements, your future with the firm may be jeopardized. When you are considered for promotions, there will be a lingering doubt about your remaining with the company.

If your search is discovered, discuss it frankly and openly with your employer. Make definite arrangements to complete the tasks you have in process for the company and offer to help in finding your replacement. You must leave on the best possible terms. Don't forget that a good reference from your employer will be of assistance in your search. But don't bargain to stay. Your decision is made and you should act on it.

2

Preliminary Work

This Jobsearch manual is directed toward four major and a number of minor approaches to the job market. These various methods are composed of numerous small details which will require your attention. Your Jobsearch campaign is a business venture. You will need organization, supplies, and services in order to conduct the venture successfully. Prior to actually working on your campaign, complete, or at least begin, all the preliminary work discussed in this chapter. You will then be assured that items you need are available at the appropriate time and that your search can proceed smoothly from this point to its successful conclusion.

Organizing Your Effort

Again, organize your effort. Set up a Jobsearch office. File materials in your notebook; don't let unfiled materials accumulate. Record on your To Do list all work and follow-up to be accomplished. Then cross off those items that have been completed. Schedule time each day or week to devote to your Jobsearch effort. The ability to organize your work will have a marked influence on the success of your campaign.

Jobsearch Stationery

For your Jobsearch correspondence, you will need a supply of stationery. Even if you now have stationery, it's probably not adequate for this use. You're conducting a business campaign and should use stationery printed in a business style and format.

It should be on a good grade of white paper, 8½ by 11 inches with matching envelopes. A 20-pound, 25 percent rag paper will offer the best appearance without excessive expense. Your name and complete address, along with your telephone number, should be printed in block letters centered at the top of the page. Use only one type style for the entire heading. Don't use a print style that is too bold or too elaborate. Workbook Form 8 is a sample of this type of stationery. You may have the heading engraved, but this is more expensive than printing. It may also appear ostentatious and therefore shouldn't be used when seeking a job below $30,000 per year. In most cases, 500 first sheets, 500 envelopes, and 100 blank second sheets will be more than adequate.

Get two or three quotations for the stationery from local printing companies. Frequently, quick-copy shops specialize in this type of small-order printing and will offer an attractive price. Printing the stationery shouldn't take more than one week. Be sure you have a firm deadline from the printer at the time of order. A few days after the order is placed, call to expedite completion. This quantity and style of stationery should cost from $50 to $75.

Photograph

Unless you're a first-time job seeker, you'll make limited use of the résumé in your Jobsearch campaign. You will, however, need one that is well-written and well-presented. To the extent possible, this résumé should show you as a real person. One way to further this objective is to include on the résumé a recent photograph of yourself. Even though it is illegal under equal opportunity laws for a prospective employer to request a photograph, it's not illegal for you to include one unsolicited. The choice, however, is up to you.

Because of the time required to locate the least expensive source for these photographs and have them made, if you decide to use a photograph, this detail should be taken care of at the same time you order your stationery. The photograph should be a glossy print, approximately 2 by 2½ inches, showing a head and shoulders view. Even if seeking a fairly low-level position, a man should wear a dark business suit, white shirt, and conservative tie. For a woman, a tailored suit and a conservative blouse are appropriate. Your hair and general appearance should be neat. Take care that the photograph doesn't make you appear too young or old, sleepy, inattentive, frivolous, or otherwise unbusinesslike.

You'll need approximately twenty-five copies. Most commercial portrait studios aren't equipped to do small multiple copies and will therefore be excessively expensive. This shouldn't be an amateur job, however, unless the amateur chosen has substantial portrait experience. As a source for these photos you might try passport photo shops or discount stores offering children's photographs. Or contact the placement office of a local university. They frequently know people who do résumé photographs for graduating seniors. You should be able to purchase these pictures for a dollar each or less.

Think carefully about your use of a photograph with your résumé. As you will see in later sections of this manual, except for first-time job seekers, you will use your résumé sparingly. In some cases, however, it will be passed on to people reviewing your qualifications who have not yet met you. At Jobsearch we felt it was wise to give these people an idea of the candidate's appearance. Then when they meet you, it's not like meeting a stranger; they already recognize you. Because, however, a photograph cannot be requested by a potential employer, there is some feeling it should be omitted. You must make the decision as to whether you feel it will be helpful in your own case.

Establishing Information Sources

Throughout your Jobsearch you'll need substantial information concerning prospective employers. In the marketing phase of your campaign this will consist primarily of names and addresses of companies that might be of potential interest to you. This information must also contain the names of individuals in these companies who would be appropriate recipients of your correspondence, the people who would be interested in you, and in a position to make a hiring decision.

Much of this information will be available to you locally, particularly if you're conducting a Jobsearch campaign limited to your current home area. In most cases, however, some of this information must be ordered. For this reason review all available sources of information at this time, and make a list of those that appear most appropriate to your search. Order immediately by telephone or letter those that must be sent to you. The following sources of information will be helpful.

Your Local Library

Most public libraries, in particular the main branch of libraries in major cities, contain extensive sources of business information. This manual includes a list (Workbook Form 9) of only a sampling of business reference books available at large libraries. Visit your local library and discuss your Jobsearch campaign with the head of the business or research section. Determine which of the books on the list are available. Look up other books and directories suggested by your librarian. Study the table of contents of each and familiarize yourself with the method of listing and the extent and layout of information. In general, these major reference books are too expensive to order specifically for your Jobsearch campaign. They will, however, include listings of trade periodicals, specialized directories, and association publications you might want to order.

The Chamber of Commerce

Most state chambers of commerce publish directories of industrial and other business companies for their entire state. These directories list companies alphabetically, geographically, and by product or Standard Industrial Classification (SIC) code numbers. Many city chambers of commerce publish similar directories for their Standard Metropolitan Statistical Areas (SMSA) and also have information available concerning local banks, wholesalers, community organizations, distributors, insurance companies, and large employers. If you're conducting a campaign on a local level, or are specifically interested in working in certain states or cities, these directories are excellent sources of information. You can buy them at your local chamber of commerce office or order them by phone or letter. Expect to pay $20 to $60 for most state industrial directories and somewhat less for local directories.

State Agencies

Industrial directories are also frequently published by state development, economic, or commerce departments. Call these organizations in states of interest to you. Ascertain the information they have available and its cost. When ordering these directories, be careful not to duplicate information available from the chamber of commerce.

Trade Journals

Most trade journals or magazines contain classified help wanted sections. For a search directed toward one or more specific industries, these are better sources of potential job information than the more general classified sections of city newspapers. *Ulrich's International Periodical Directory* and the *Encyclopedia of Business Information Sources* both list trade periodicals. These directories are available in most large libraries. Trade journals exist for almost every conceivable business. Determine which of these magazines might be of assistance in your campaign, and call or write to the publishers to request subscription information and cost. Also request a sample copy. If you subscribe, ask that you be sent the two editions previous to your subscription date.

Association Publications

Many trade associations publish newsletters or magazines that have help wanted listings. They also have membership lists that can be excellent sources of information about potential contacts. Look in the Gale Research Company's *Encyclopedia of Associations,* also available at large libraries, to determine which of these organizations might be helpful to you. Call them, explain your needs, and find out what information they have available that would be useful.

Local Newspapers

City newspapers contain more classified job listings than any other single source. Most employment agencies advertise in their local newspaper to fill positions for companies that have retained them. In addition, local businesses use classified newspaper ads to find lower-level or technical employees. Although help wanted ads in city newspapers are more effective as sources of these lower-level jobs, any job seeker interested in a specific city should review the local paper's help wanted advertisements, particularly the Sunday edition. Even if you're conducting the bulk of your campaign in a broader area, subscribe to the Sunday edition of the two or three largest newspapers in that area.

Major City Newspapers

Although most city classifieds have only local area listings, there are some exceptions. The six newspapers listed below, all with Sunday circulations of over one million, attract help wanted advertising from their entire region of the United States. They also draw advertising for higher-paid positions than those carried in smaller newspapers. If appropriate to your search, subscribe to the Sunday edition of one or more of these newspapers. In general, paying extra for first class mail delivery isn't warranted. With normal delivery you'll have sufficient time to submit your responses. In the list below, the telephone number following the address is that of the circulation or subscription department of the newspaper. When you subscribe, be sure to ask if you will receive the entire classified section. Some out-of-town editions may not include all of the Help Wanted sections you need.

Los Angeles Times
Times-Mirror Square
Los Angeles, Calif. 90053
Telephone (213) 626-2323

San Francisco Examiner & Chronicle
925 Mission Street
San Francisco, Calif. 94103
Telephone (415) 777-7800

Washington Post
1150 15th Street, N.W.
Washington, D.C. 20071
Telephone (202) 334-6100

Chicago Tribune
Mail Subscription Dept. FC 400
777 West Chicago Avenue
Chicago, Ill. 60610
Telephone (800) 874-2863

The New York Times
229 West 43rd Street
New York, N.Y. 10036
Telephone (800) 631-2500

Atlanta Journal-Constitution
Post Office Box 4689
Atlanta, Ga. 30302
Telephone (404) 522-4141

In addition to these six regional newspapers, the following two publications should not be overlooked:

1. *The Wall Street Journal:* A nationally distributed business newspaper, *The Wall Street Journal* is probably the best single source of classified help wanted ads for middle- and upper-level positions in all fields. It is appropriate, however, only if you are willing to relocate. It can be purchased daily at most large newsstands. Help wanted advertisements are published primarily on

Tuesday and Wednesday. Because *The Wall Street Journal* is printed in four regional editions, be sure you subscribe to and receive the edition for the area in which you wish to conduct your search. The regional editions are eastern, midwest, southwest, and western. Their subscription address is:

The Wall Street Journal
200 Burnett Road
Chicopee, Mass. 01021
Telephone (413) 592-7761

2. *National Business Employment Weekly:* In addition to the regular daily *Wall Street Journal* regional editions, that paper publishes the *National Business Employment Weekly*. This publication includes all employment ads shown in all regional editions of *The Wall Street Journal* for the previous week. It's published each Monday and is sold by subscription and through large newsstands. The individual issue price is $2.50. Subscriptions are $35 for eight weeks, long enough for most job campaigns. Subscriptions to this job listing can be ordered by phone at (800) 628-9320. The first issue will usually be delivered within a week of the order.

College Placement Publications

Some college placement offices publish lists of available jobs that have been brought to their attention. These lists are sent to their alumni on request and, in some cases, to local residents who did not graduate from the college. To determine if such publications exist and are appropriate to your search, contact the placement office at your alma mater or the state university nearest your preferred location. You might also contact placement offices at several other colleges or universities in your chosen area. In addition to these job listings, some placement offices also register job applicants and submit résumés and résumé summaries to companies seeking employees. The appropriate registration procedure will be discussed in Chapter 13 of this Jobsearch manual. For the present, it's sufficient that you determine what publications are available to you and secure them for future use.

Foreign and American Embassies and Chambers of Commerce

If you're interested in a job overseas with the subsidiary of a U.S. company, working in the United States for the subsidiary of a foreign company, or working for a foreign company outside the United States, embassies are an excellent source of information. The French Embassy in Washington, D.C., for instance, publishes a list of all French subsidiaries in the United States showing the name, address, and principal business of both the parent and the U.S. company. This and other such listings are available through the commercial attaché at no charge. The American Embassy and American Chamber of

Commerce in foreign countries also publish such lists for U.S. subsidiaries overseas. American embassy addresses and the names of appropriate contacts can be obtained from the U.S. Printing Office directory, *Key Offices of Foreign Service Posts,* from your local federal information center, or from your congressional representative's office listed in the blue government office pages of the telephone book. Foreign embassy addresses and telephone numbers in the United States can be obtained through telephone information in Washington, D.C., (202) 555-1212. Addresses for chambers of commerce overseas are available through your local chamber.

Special Publications

The World Trade Academy Press, 50 East 42 Street, New York, N.Y. 10017 (212/697-4999), publishes lists of U.S. companies, subsidiaries, and affiliates operating in 198 different countries. Prices range from $10 to $30 per country. It also publishes lists of foreign companies operating in the United States for forty-seven countries, as well as other special directories. It will send you prices and descriptions of these publications on request.

The American Management Association, 135 West 50 Street, New York, N.Y. 10020 (212/903-8286), publishes the *Executive Employment Guide* listing nearly 130 executive search and executive recruiting firms including a number that offer a job registering service. This is available by mail for $15 per copy. Executive search or recruiting firms are retained by companies to find and, in most cases, steal an individual with specific talent and experience from another firm. It's appropriate to advise such firms of your availability only if you are seeking a high-level position, will relocate, and have extensive experience specifically related to the job you seek. If this matches your search, order the list now. Its use is discussed in more detail in Chapter 12.

Also consider these two publications:

1. The Yellow Pages: Substantial business information is available in this ubiquitous directory and shouldn't be neglected in your Jobsearch campaign. Both your local library and your telephone company main office have out-of-state directories including Yellow Pages. In addition, they will usually be supplied to you free of charge by your local telephone company. Simply call the business office and explain that you plan to do telephone solicitation in conjunction with your Jobsearch. They'll send you the directories for your target cities, usually within a week or two. Although the information from this source does not include names of individuals or information concerning company sizes, it offers excellent listings of local companies by product categories. Frequently, additional information concerning officers' names and company size can be secured with a telephone call to the firm.

2. *Who's Who in Finance and Industry:* Available in most libraries, this

can also be a source for names of individuals in companies of interest to you. This book can be used in conjunction with other directories and sources that list companies of interest but do not show names of individuals to whom you might address your correspondence.

Computer Databases

Finally, if you have access to a personal computer with a modem and are fairly conversant with its use, you may investigate the career and employment data bases that list job opportunities and register job seekers. The *Directory of On-Line Data Bases* and the *Computer-Readable Data Bases—A Data Source Book,* both available at most libraries, list over twenty employment-related computer data services and the method to contact them to inquire about their services, scope, and cost. Although most of these are specific to one industry and others are only a registry of job seekers, you may find one or more suitable to your search.

Secretarial and Computer Services

Throughout your Jobsearch campaign you will need competent secretarial services on a part-time basis unless, of course, you can provide them yourself. These will be most useful if the service uses computers or word processors to produce multiple letters individually addressed. Although readily available, most commercial secretarial and computer services or temporary help companies are somewhat expensive. As an alternative, you may have a friend or associate who is, or knows, a secretary who will work for you at night or do typing during his or her free time. The current rate for such assistance is around $6 to $10 per hour depending upon the area in which you live. Many of our Jobsearch clients found ready sources of secretarial assistance through the offices of friends who were lawyers or accountants. As an additional benefit, all of these use word processing systems with substantial capabilities.

Of course, if you both type and have or have access to a personal computer with a letter-quality printer, you can do virtually all of this secretarial work yourself. This can save considerable time as well as money. Because you must confirm every contact made during your Jobsearch with a letter, it is particularly convenient if you can do the typing while you compose the letter. Among my recent Jobsearch clients, almost half were able to arrange access to an appropriate personal computer without going to an outside service.

The extent of secretarial work in most campaigns will include typing several résumés, answering approximately ten to twenty help wanted ads per week, typing form letters, miscellaneous correspondence, and letters confirming each interview and telephone conversation regarding a job. Depending upon the source and capability of your available assistance, this work might also include the production of several hundred letters for the direct mail campaign described in Chapter 12.

For all your typed work, it is important that an electric business typewriter or letter-quality computer printer be used. If possible, it should have a carbon rather than a fabric ribbon although some 24-pin, letter quality, dot matrix computer printers with fabric ribbons do produce adequate quality. In the case of computer dot matrix printers, avoid their use unless the letter quality print is almost perfect. The typeface should be standard typewriter characters. Don't use script, italics, or other unusual print.

The first impression you make on a prospective employer will usually be in written form. At least in part, you will be judged by the appearance of this correspondence. It should be neat, attractive, grammatically correct, and should contain no spelling errors. Much of this will depend on the secretary you use or your own skills. If you use a secretary, he or she should be chosen with care.

Copying Services

Two forms of copying or multiple reproduction will be required for your Jobsearch campaign. Except for the direct mail letters, you'll need copies of all correspondence. These can be either carbon copies or any legible, copying machine reproduction. For your résumé, plain paper reproductions on a business copying machine will be needed. It will be best to locate a convenient source of photocopying facilities such as a quick print shop. You may also have a business friend or lawyer who can make his or her firm's equipment available to you.

Computer word processing for multiple reproduction of similar letters will be necessary for your direct mail marketing campaign. This equipment will individually type and address form letters on your letterhead at a rate in excess of one every two minutes. Companies offering such services are generally available in medium-size to large cities. They can be found under the listing for Letter Shop Service or Advertising—Direct Mail in the Yellow Pages of your telephone directory. The cost of these services should range from 40 to 60 cents per letter, depending upon its length. Call several of these firms to check their rates, but again, if you can do the work yourself, do so. You'll find it easy and fast.

Financial Planning

Before starting your principal Jobsearch effort, it's always wise to do some financial planning. If you're employed, this might consist only of an estimate of the expenses involved in your search. More complete financial planning may be appropriate if you are unemployed. In this case, not only will you be required to pay for the search, but you must also support yourself and your family until you secure a position.

You should usually plan for a four-month Jobsearch effort. Although the search can frequently be completed in a shorter period, it's preferable to eliminate a deadline controlled by economic considerations alone. A careful review of your expenses, financial strength, and potential sources of income will usually disclose that you can sustain your family without a regular salary for an extended period.

If not, you may want to consider part-time employment during your Jobsearch. Whether you are looking for your first job and have little experience or are a business executive working on a career change, part-time work is often readily available. Many of our Jobsearch clients worked through temporary help agencies during their search. In the case of executives, they often did consulting for companies they knew or companies in their industry. In one case, the consulting work with an electronics firm resulted in a permanent position matching the original objective of the search.

Workbook Forms 10 through 12 are included to calculate your net worth, estimate your monthly cash flow, and appraise your total Jobsearch expense. Even though the numbers may be only rough guesses, it's advisable for unemployed individuals to complete all three forms and for employed individuals to complete the Jobsearch expense estimate. As situations change and new information is gained, the forms can be updated. This review and organization of your finances will then allow you to plan your Jobsearch more effectively and to devote more of your time and effort to this task with less concern for the immediate future.

3

Compiling an Accomplishments List

Of all the items of work involved in your Jobsearch, the accomplishments list is one of the most important. You will use it throughout your campaign. It will form the basis for your résumé and your direct mail sales letter. You'll refer to it for other written correspondence and also immediately prior to going on job interviews. Your past accomplishments are what you have to sell more than any other single item. The list of these accomplishments should be prepared with care; it should be complete. When you're ready to work on this list, reserve a morning or afternoon with three or four hours during which you can think and write without interruption.

As previously stated, you will not be hired by a new company because of your former titles or responsibilities. You will be hired to produce profits, or in the case of a nonprofit organization, to improve efficiency or provide services. The only real measure of your ability to contribute in these areas is your past accomplishments.

Use Workbook Forms 13–16 to list your career and other pertinent accomplishments. In all cases, each item should be described in one short phrase. Because these lists will be used as a reference for most of your correspondence, the phrases should be suitable for incorporation into your résumé and letters. Make them direct and action-oriented. Do not use superfluous words. The lists should be complete. To the extent possible, include accomplishments that best relate to the job or jobs which are the objective of your campaign. Before you start to write, review some of the examples of résumés and letters in the Workbook section of this manual. Note their phrasing and choice of words.

Wherever possible, quantify your accomplishments with numbers. Most people, particularly business people, identify easily with numbers. They are concrete, are readily understood, and can be related to other sets of numbers. Instead of stating that you were responsible for a major increase in sales, say you increased sales 30 percent, or by $200,000, in a one-year period. Instead of saying you substantially improved efficiencies, state that the improved efficiencies saved your company $30,000 yearly. If you managed the engineering department, indicate the total number of engineers under your direction, and the total dollar value of completed projects. If you have delivered talks to numerous professional groups, mention the total number of such groups and the number of participants.

In many cases the numbers you need will not be readily available. Leave blanks in your list and search out the information later. If the numbers can't be found, put down your best guess, making every effort to be truthful. An estimate based on your best recollection is preferable to using a loosely defined word such as "large," "substantial," or "major." In fact, your accomplishments will serve you better if most qualifying words and adjectives are left out entirely.

The majority of our Jobsearch clients complained that their accomplishments were difficult to describe, too general in nature, or impossible to quantify. Yet they proceeded to assemble impressive lists of achievements. Look at the résumé written by Karilyn Naff (Workbook Form 20). As a treasurer and controller throughout her career, she didn't believe she could quantify the daily task of accounting or point to impressive accomplishments. She was wrong. By reviewing her past career and the effects of her financial controls, she was able to compile an impressive list of accomplishments and subsequent résumé.

The only requirement is that you think about your past career as a series of objectives, tasks, and projects. Jobsearch attorney clients found, for instance, that they could describe the number of cases they handled, the total monies at stake, and even the number of cases where they were able to avoid litigation, the bane of any business executive. Then they sold these desired skills and themselves. Review Janet Parsons' résumé (Workbook Form 25). She did an excellent job of turning a mundane position with a title insurance company into a challenging prospect as head of the right-of-way department with a major utility company.

If you're looking for your first job and have few if any business experiences to list, you can still present accomplishments that relate to the job you seek. What particular aspects of part-time or summer work were relevant? What course grades in school were significant to your future career? Did you participate in case studies or other special projects that would interest a prospective employer? Is there any volunteer work or elected positions, such as an officer of a club, that were accomplishments? And even with items such as these, use numbers: the volume of newspapers you delivered on a daily basis for so many months, the number of people in a club where you were an officer, your class standing in one particularly important course.

If you are a first-time job seeker, review the résumé of Susan Abrams (Workbook Form 27) and the one used by my son, Felix (Workbook Form 28). Susan had no job experience related to the position she sought but concentrated on her educational accomplishments and used her summer work experience to confirm her ability to work hard, fast, and accurately. With few accomplishments to list, she used a more conversational style of writing but included items that should have interested an employer looking for her educational background and skills.

My son, Felix, looking for an unusual job with low demand—music composition and song writing—highlighted his musical background and accomplishments even though these had been largely personal efforts not related to any previous job. He was, however, able to quantify the extent of this work and include with his résumé recorded examples of songs he both wrote and performed.

Regardless of the position you seek, in a few weeks you'll be asking potential employers to pay you a salary to perform a job. Perhaps your desired or requested salary will be higher than an employer wants to pay. This salary and the new position itself will depend upon the return that employer expects to receive from its investment in you. Your past accomplishments, more than any other single item, will allow them to judge the probability and level of this return.

Direct Job-Related Accomplishments

The first three pages of your accomplishments list (Workbook Form 13) are to record all those items directly related to your past jobs, responsibilities, and performance in these jobs. Although all pertinent accomplishments should be recorded, each section should include several that indicate a direct contribution to the profits or success of the company or organization. Do not neglect accomplishments of your subordinates performed under your direction or responsibility.

Never fall victim to the fear that you have no significant accomplishments. Ronald Marque had never worked directly in the field for which he was educated and wanted to enter (see his résumé, Workbook Form 21). He spent hours reviewing his career, discussing it with his wife, and talking to colleagues. The result was a listed series of projects and studies he could relate to financial analysis, some of which he had done during off hours with little apparent relation to the job he was hired to do. Now Ronald is a senior financial analyst with a major shipbuilding company. An attractive peripheral aspect of this job is its proximity to water, permitting Ronald's indulgence in his favorite sport of sailing.

Also review the résumé of Jeffrey McCauli (Workbook Form 26). Jeff was an electrician who had never worked in other than residential construction for a single company. He wanted to broaden his experience with work in the commercial industrial field. Even though he never graduated from college, note his listings of electrical-related courses and certifications. He listed the level of amp service with which he had worked and the number of homes wired. He even listed the number of air freight containers he had assembled in a prior laborer's job. Jeff had four job offers and accepted a position as an electrician with Disney World. He's gaining experience with a view toward forming his own electrical contracting firm.

Look at other résumés in the Workbook section. Notice how the use of numbers and accomplishments lends credence to the abilities of the writer. Even if many of these aren't directly related to the job being sought, they display a serious approach to a job that is results oriented.

Your accomplishments should be listed by company in reverse chronological order. On the first line of each section show your title and the company name, city, and state. Under this, on the left, show the time period in years only (e.g., 1971–1976), not months. This should be done for each company. If you need additional pages, use lined tablet paper.

If you worked a long period of time with one company and acted in several different areas of responsibility or held several titles, separate these in the list as you would for different companies. Start a new section for each area of responsibility or title.

Think back over your career carefully. What was done better because you were there? What wouldn't have been done had you not been there? What do you consider your most important or personally most satisfying direct, job-related accomplishments? List them all whether you feel they are pertinent or not; you can cull the list later. For now be complete and don't be hesitant to portray your work and your results in the best light possible.

Indirect Job-Related Accomplishments

On the fourth page of your accomplishments list (Workbook Form 14) record indirect job-related accomplishments. These are those performed as a result of a specific job but that weren't directly related to the responsibilities of the job itself. If you were in sales, such an accomplishment might be teaching a sales training course for employees in another region of your company or outside it. Another example might be technical papers you wrote which weren't required but were published for the benefit of your entire industry. A service performed for a professional or trade association in your industry would qualify as an indirect job-related accomplishment.

As with your direct, job-related accomplishments, be specific and quantify wherever possible. If you conducted training classes, how many groups or individuals were involved? If you published a paper, to how many people was it distributed?

Even a first-time job seeker should not neglect indirect job-related accomplishments. If you've participated in clubs or have hobbies related to the type of work you seek, use these experiences. Think about your school activities not related to your everyday studies. Are some of these pertinent to your future work? If they are, they should be listed.

Educational Accomplishments

The next page of your list (Workbook Form 15) should show all the accomplishments related to your education which you felt to be most important or most satisfying. Don't include high school accomplishments unless you have only recently graduated or unless you attended a prominent preparatory school. The spaces provided are for college courses and activities, graduate work, and continuing education. Pay particular attention to include courses or studies taken after your formal schooling, particularly any that were related to your job or sponsored by your employer. On the first line of each section show the degree received or course completed, the name of the institution, the city, and the state. The space to the left is for the time period in years or the year the course was taken. Include both direct and indirect educational accomplishments; that is, list those relating directly to your studies and those, such as extracurricular activities, you performed while attending school.

For the first-time job seeker, these educational accomplishments will be particularly important. More than any other item, they are what you now have to sell. Think of your school career as a job. What lab work or study projects could have been used by a company? Where did your courses come closest to matching the needs of a business? Which courses were most important to your future career and what did you accomplish in them? In your future job, you will have to relate your studies to the business world and its problems. Think of this as you compile your educational accomplishments and write them as sales tools directed toward your job targets. Pick those courses and educational experiences that might be of most interest to a future employer and think of the papers you wrote, the case studies you completed, and research you did that might relate to the business world. List all of these and again, don't neglect any extracurricular activities that might be pertinent.

Personal or Civic Accomplishments

The last page of the list (Workbook Form 16) is for those personal or civic accomplishments you consider the most significant in your adult life. These might be accomplishments performed for civic, charitable, or religious organizations, or in line with your hobbies. In all instances, however, they should relate to or demonstrate your competence in some aspect of your work. If you're an engineer, for example, you might list assembling a color television kit. A major contribution to a fund raising effort can demonstrate organizational or sales ability.

After completing all four parts of your accomplishments list, wait a day and then go back and review your list. Ask yourself some questions. Do the items indicate a contribution to profits, efficiency, or the delivery of services? Do they show a willingness to work? Do they indicate awareness of what makes an organization successful? Most importantly, can they be used to sell you as an attractive investment for a new company?

4

Establishing
Your Career Goals

Prior to setting the specific targets for your Jobsearch campaign, you should establish or review your short- and long-term career goals. In your campaign you're not attempting just to find a job, you're trying to secure a career position. To do this it's necessary to target your efforts based on your career goals and, in the final stages of your search, to compare job opportunities with these short- and long-term objectives.

In reviewing hundreds of résumés and discussing careers, both past and future, with Jobsearch clients, we found the most frequent mistake made in their career development was lack of planning. Too many men and women simply find a job with no thought of its impact on their future development. These people came to us later, their résumés crowded with jobs of short duration. With each change of employment it became increasingly difficult to sell their past accomplishments and to locate the jobs they should have taken care to find years before. Don't let this happen to you.

Your career goals are composed of all the personal achievements and benefits you expect from your job efforts. These goals should be specific, quantified, scheduled, and realistic. Instead of establishing "a top management position" as one of your goals, you should define this position perhaps as "vice-president of sales." Quantify the position by stating that it will be in a company grossing at least $10 million per year. Specify the time period within which you would like to attain this position. Then judge whether this objective is realistic in relation to your background, ambitions, and time frame.

Once you've established these goals, determine what sequence of events must occur and what personal efforts or preparation you must undertake to meet them. If, for instance, your ten-year objective is to be vice-president of sales and you're now a territory salesperson, you may identify it as desirable to be the top salesperson in your area. This would put you in a position to become an area sales manager. The subsequent steps might be district sales manager, regional manager, department head, and finally vice-president of sales. Don't neglect to identify additional training you might need, either in your job or through supplementary education.

Once established in written form, your career goals should be reviewed yearly. This review will determine whether your progress is consistent with your goals, as well as whether and how these goals should be modified. As you progress in your career, your objectives will and should change. You will continually gather data about yourself, your capabilities, and your job. You'll also learn about your likes and dislikes, both in work and in private life. These and other such items will have an influence on your career objectives.

Immediate, Five-, and Ten-Year Objectives

Use Workbook Form 17 to record your career goals. When completing this form, note the following:

Position: Should include the title you wish as well as the area of responsibility, such as "comptroller" or "vice-president, finance."

Salary: Should be stated in today's dollars, disregarding inflation.

Percent equity: Refers to your ownership in the company for which you work.

Scope of authority: Might be defined as your discretion in hiring and firing a specific number of employees, the extent of your control over the profit and loss of the company, or the effect your decisions might have on the future course of the business.

Number of subordinates, direct: Refers to the number of employees reporting to you.

Number of subordinates, indirect: Refers to the total number of employees for whom you're responsible or who are beneath you on the company's organization chart.

Independence: Refers to the extent of your desire to work alone or work as a member of a team. It can be listed as strong, average, or weak.

Structured environment: Refers to your desire to work in an atmosphere of established procedures or one of a more flexible nature. It can be listed as highly, moderately, or loosely structured.

Recognition: Should indicate your desire in each of these categories as high, average, or unimportant to you, regardless of whether the job might produce it.

Procedure for Defining Goals

If you can't establish your career goals with assurance or are ambivalent about your vocation, examine yourself as well as your education, background, and work experience. This will assist you in formulating ideas. If you're young, don't be overly concerned that available data are insufficient or incomplete. Use the data available and realize that your objectives will be affected by the experiences that lie before you in your career.

The following seven exercises will begin to give you ideas about yourself and your career. They can also help you choose a vocation or evaluate available vocational options.

1. Go back to your accomplishments lists and, for each item, indicate those you enjoyed, were ambivalent about, or disliked. You'll find you accomplished more and enjoyed the work in areas where you have the greatest interest.
2. Make a list of your likes and dislikes. Include all you can think of in a general spectrum, and then star those that are work related.
3. Define yourself and your character by completing twenty sentences in response to the question "Who am I?"
4. Make a list of everything that motivates you to work, then rank the items in the list, 1, 2, 3, and so forth, the highest motivating factor to the lowest motivating factor.
5. For the perfect job, describe in short phrases its characteristics, the work involved, the relationships with people, its scope of authority, and its responsibilities.
6. For this perfect job, describe the changes that would make it still perfect in ten years' time.
7. List those jobs or tasks that your education and experience have trained you to do.

With the above information you can now go back to your career goals. Check each of these against your likes and dislikes, character, motivation, description of the perfect job, and training. If you find inconsistencies, determine what changes you need to make in your goals or in yourself.

If after completing the above work you would like to examine your vocation or investigate other vocations, an excellent source book is the *Dictionary of Occupational Titles*, stock number 029–013–00079–9, published by the U.S. Department of Labor. This two-volume set is available at most public libraries or may be purchased for $32 from the Superintendent of Documents, U.S. Government Printing Office, Washington, D.C. 20402 (202/783-3238).

To use this dictionary, turn first to Appendix A of Volume Two. This section gives an explanation of the three-digit code relating each listed job to data, people, and things. Then review the Worker Traits Arrangement of Titles and Codes Section in Volume Two. This gives the work performed, worker requirements, and clues for relating applicants and requirements as well as the training and methods of entry for 176 career fields. It also gives classifications of jobs related to each field. Volume One of this dictionary lists over 40,000 job titles showing the work performed with a six-digit code relating to the worker traits discussed in Volume Two.

Although an examination of these books might at first appear to be a monumental task, they're arranged in a convenient format that can be skimmed to quickly determine the areas of interest to you. If these books serve no other purpose, they will give you a comprehensive view of the scope and opportunities available in the job market. They can be of assistance not only in reviewing your choice of vocation and your career goals, but also in establishing the specific target areas for your Jobsearch marketing effort.

You may find the perfect job in the place you least expect. Karilyn Naff, whose résumé appears in Workbook Form 20, was an accountant and controller. She is now the legal administrator for a fifty-partner law firm, a job that includes not only accounting but control over every administrative aspect of a $10 million business. When she started her search she was unaware that such a position existed.

The scope and diversity of American industry and business are wider than you can imagine. Within these countless fields are companies and organizations that address every aspect of our needs and hopes, and within each organization are positions that have a direct impact on the goods and services delivered as well as the success of the company or group responsible. At a point of career decision in your life, you owe it to yourself to investigate new ideas, new possibilities, and new ventures. One of these might be working for yourself, discussed briefly in Chapter 5. In targeting your marketing effort, discussed in Chapter 6, you should choose at least one simply because you would love doing the job even if it doesn't relate specifically to your past experience or training. If this job is consistent with your career goals, it may be the one that puts you on a new and exciting path.

CHAPTER

5

Working for Yourself

When you've decided to make a job change and are reviewing your career goals, you should investigate all possibilities. If you have substantial business experience and an entrepreneurial spirit, one of these may be working for yourself. If you feel this should be a job option, now may be an opportune time for some preliminary investigations. This can be done at the same time you conduct your Jobsearch campaign. In addition, some of the techniques explained in this Jobsearch manual can be used as tools for this investigation.

When considering an entrepreneurial possibility, however, examine your intent carefully. If working for yourself is a way out of possible failure in the job market, don't try it. Starting a new business or taking over an existing one is risky, difficult, and time consuming. You must forgo much of your family life to spend time on the problems of inadequate capitalization, work force, and recognition in the marketplace. Review your career goals carefully. If substantial equity in the future is not one of them, assess your entrepreneurial spirit. If it's not real, running your own business may turn into an unwanted nightmare. If, on the other hand, you must try it at least once in your career, now may be the time.

Although this manual cannot include a complete prescription for starting or acquiring your own business, I've spent a substantial portion of my career in that pursuit and can make some comments that might be helpful. I have, by the way, had both successes and failures in those ventures and so have personal experience with both results.

First let me give you my two cardinal rules for entrepreneurial ventures.

1. To calculate the capital you'll need, do a complete set of financial projections in as much detail as possible; in the case of an acquisition, add the required funds for the purchase. Once this is done and you know exactly how much capital is needed, triple the number. That's the capital you'll actually need.

2. Before starting or acquiring a business, study it thoroughly. Study the markets, the products or services offered, the competition, financial results

and projections, and the types of personnel and facilities required. After all this is done, you should know the business as well as anyone could. Remember, however, the day you close the acquisition or start your new venture and sit behind your new desk, you'll open your right-hand desk drawer and a large snake will jump out and bite you. No matter how well you study the business before that moment, you will not know where the snake is, but it's there and it will bite.

These problems notwithstanding, there's nothing quite so satisfying in business as working for yourself. In pursuing this goal, there are three avenues you might consider: acquiring an existing business, starting a new company, or purchasing a franchise. Of these, purchasing a franchise is probably the easiest and has the least risk; acquiring a business is the most expensive; and starting a new venture is the most difficult and dangerous. In any case, capital sources are of paramount importance.

Review your financial resources and possible avenues for raising additional capital. Make sure you're ready to support both your family and the future business while you make substantial sacrifices and fight the high risk of failure. Over 75 percent of new businesses fail within the first few years, most because of inadequate capitalization.

Look over your personal contacts list and other sources of information you assemble for your Jobsearch campaign. Within these you'll certainly find people and organizations with whom you should discuss your entrepreneurial objectives. Some, such as lawyers, accountants, and bankers, may have not only advice but also knowledge about or contacts for locating acquisition candidates. If an acquisition appeals to you, check with business brokerage firms in the cities of interest.

Before proceeding on this course, you might also want to read *The New Venture Handbook* and *The Insider's Guide to Franchising.* Both are available from the American Management Association and can be ordered by phone through their bookstore at (212) 903-8082. Another excellent source of advice and ideas as well as a potential source of funds are venture capital firms. *Who's Who in Venture Capital* published by John Wiley & Sons is a readily available book listing over a thousand venture capital firms throughout the United States. The National Association of Small Business Investment Companies publishes *Venture Capital, Where to Find It,* a small pamphlet listing the NASBIC members in each state. This pamphlet can be ordered for $1.00 from NASBIC at 1156 15th Street N.W., Suite 1101, Washington, D.C. 20005.

For salespeople or those with that talent, another avenue of working for yourself with somewhat less risk and capital requirements is acting as a manufacturer's representative. One Jobsearch client studied this possibility as a part of her more conventional campaign and used the letter shown in Workbook Form 50 as a part of her mail marketing campaign. Although this was only one of her job targets, she found a company that did need representation in her area. Starting with this single line of merchandise, she has now built a business with five employees and nine products each from a different manufacturer. After her business was started, she continued to use the Jobsearch mail marketing techniques to locate other manufacturers who could use the services of her company.

The third-party letter in Workbook Form 51 was used by another of our Jobsearch clients conducting an anonymous search to locate a distributor or manufacturer's rep firm he could acquire. In fact, many of the techniques presented in this book can be applied to finding an acquisition candidate or starting your own business. The mail marketing campaign is only one example, as is the use of personal contacts for locating acquisitions as well as capital.

Although you might devote some of your career development efforts to the concept of working for yourself, do it only as part of your overall Jobsearch campaign. This keeps all your options open. In addition, you may locate a company that will offer equity as part of your compensation package. This might give you the potential for capital appreciation and the satisfaction of working for yourself with substantially less risk than initiating your own entrepreneurial venture.

If equity is one of your career goals, concentrate a large part of your Jobsearch on smaller companies and request an equity participation with a lower initial salary as a part of your compensation. If your background and experience place you in a position to dramatically affect the future success of a small business, locating such a company and opportunity is no more difficult than securing a job with a company not in a position to reward your efforts in this manner.

In Chapter 6, when targeting your marketing efforts, consider your entrepreneurial instincts; if they are strong, include them among your targets.

6

Targeting
Your Marketing Effort

You are now ready to define the specific targets for your Jobsearch marketing effort. These targets are the positions, locations, industries, and types of companies or organizations you would like for your next job. For most campaigns, at least three or four different targets should be pursued simultaneously. These might be similar to one another or may represent entirely different career options, either in the same industry or in different industries. They may be related to the same job responsibilities or vary widely in scope. The intent is to expand your potential opportunities by not only covering a single market as thoroughly as possible but also by selling yourself into several different markets at the same time.

In many instances clients used their Jobsearch campaign as a method of choosing between different careers or career directions. They did this by establishing each career as a separate target and then evaluating the offers received in each.

One such case involved a young medical laboratory supervisor who came to us with the desire to break out of the confining environment of standard, automated medical testing. She wanted more contact with people and a greater opportunity for advancement. Although two of her targets were related to the medical field, her third target was personnel management outside the medical industry. For the nonmedical market, she wrote a separate résumé and separate letters tying her hiring and personnel work in the laboratory environment to this target in personnel management. The job she finally chose was assistant personnel manager for one of the largest department store chains in her state, even though she had two other offers in health care.

When a person has substantial experience in one field and wishes to remain there, he or she may consider this as a single marketing target. Such a person, however, should define second and third targets by considering a different type of organization, size of company, or geographical area even though these all remain within his or her immediate background and expertise.

In these situations, targets may be identical in all respects except one.

This will be appropriate if that one difference is distinct enough to clearly define a separate set of options. For instance, your targets may differ only in geographical location. If you're limiting your primary search to one city, you may consider another even though it wouldn't be quite as attractive. After all, you might not want to live in a particular city, but if some company paid you enough, you would probably be glad to do so. If you're conducting a nationwide search, perhaps you should also choose one city that appeals to you and concentrate a portion of your efforts there. You might be pleasantly surprised to find yourself relocating to the city of your choice.

In defining your targets, do not neglect types of organizations outside your past experience. Many business skills are needed by associations and nonprofit groups of all types. Religious organizations need advertising skills. Fast-food franchisers need real estate lawyers. Large companies hire social counselors. Pulp and paper manufacturers hire lobbyists with environmental control experience. Trust departments of banks hire foresters. Improbable though it might seem, all these examples came from Jobsearch clients and the companies that now employ them. Use your imagination as they did, and don't arbitrarily limit your search.

In some Jobsearch campaigns an individual might consider as many as five different targets. While this may occasionally be appropriate, there are specific reasons why it should be an exception. Organizing a massive effort with as many as five targets tends to make the search unwieldy. Different résumés and direct mail marketing letters will usually be required for each marketing target; different responses are required for each. Thus, the effort can easily become dissipated to such an extent that it loses its effectiveness.

Within these constraints, however, the number and definition of targets are up to you, but they should all relate to your immediate and long-range objectives as well as your past accomplishments. This shouldn't limit your investigation of different careers, but for each target chosen, use your accomplishments to demonstrate your probable future success to prospective employers.

A word of caution, however: Don't try to sell yourself as a generalist. Throughout your business career, you've probably heard that companies want generalists. Although this may be true, they seldom hire them. Instead, they hire people with specific skills to do specific jobs. With the exception of entry-level positions, they expect these people to have gained enough experience to contribute in areas outside their specialized fields.

If you try to sell your general business skills, you will probably fail. Select your strongest skills or those readily saleable. Select the *specific* areas in which you would like to work, and use these to establish your targets.

If you have skills in several areas, fine. Use each to define a separate marketing target, but don't fall into the trap of offering a potential employer a shopping list of jobs for which you feel qualified. If you do this, you probably won't be called even if a vacancy exists. For each area in which you have expertise, define those target companies or organizations most likely to need those specific skills. Treat each as a separate marketing target. You will then be selling into your areas of greatest strength to the most probable audience.

Establishing Targets

Use Workbook Form 18 to define the targets for your Jobsearch marketing effort. When working on these target definitions, note the following:

• *Industries.* Be as specific as possible. Instead of simply stating "manufacturing," state the products manufactured, the raw materials used, or the manufacturing processes involved, whichever is most appropriate to your background and Jobsearch campaign. If you have chosen a single industry for all target areas, it may be wise to go from the specific to the general. For instance, your first target might be the manufacture of plastic household utensils; your second target might be the manufacture of plastic articles for consumer or OEM (original equipment manufacturer) use; your third target might be any manufacturing process using extrusion or injection molding techniques.

• *Size of company, division, or organization.* This should be stated in gross sales dollars per year or total number of employees, whichever relates most appropriately to the position you seek. In either case, indicate which is used and state the range that most accurately defines each target.

• *Type of company or organization.* This should indicate whether the company is family owned, publicly owned, stock exchange listed, nonprofit, a professional partnership, a trade association, or other type of organization.

• *Geographic area.* Again, be as specific as possible and if appropriate, go from the specific to the more general. If you're limiting your search to your home city, unless the reasons are compelling, consider at least one target in a broader geographic area. An employer who wants you badly enough may offer an increase in salary that will more than compensate for the inconvenience of moving. You can't know this until you've found the opportunity and negotiated with the potential employer. This is particularly true for individuals at a high salary level. In an industrial city of one million people, there may be only thirty or forty firms large enough to pay a vice-president of finance $50,000 a year. Adding three other large cities may increase the number of potential employers to over 200. The same, however, is true for lower-level positions: The larger the geographic base, the more opportunities available.

• *Position and responsibilities.* This should include your desired title and a short description of the responsibilities you expect to exercise. If possible, define these responsibilities by such items as the number of employees under your supervision, the territory for which you might be responsible, or the total sales or manufacturing cost over which you might have control.

• *Personal preference.* Review the targets you have defined and rank them first, second, and third, according to your personal preference.

• *Career preference.* As above, rank your targets according to their probable effect on your career goals.

When you've finished defining your targets on Workbook Form 18, go back and review your accomplishments list. Mark the accomplishments that relate best to each target area. For each separate target, consider new, more appropriate wording or a different expression of the quantifying numbers most appropriate to that audience.

It's also advisable to relate your targets to the sources of information you investigated earlier. Go back to this list and review it to be certain the information you ordered is appropriate for the target areas chosen. If you can locate new sources of information, order them, and add them to your list.

Finally, in establishing your targets, also take care that they are attractive to you. If you're considering a new industry, talk to a friend who is in that industry. From your information list, find another person in your local area and discuss with him or her the industry's environment and methods of operation. If you're considering a city away from your current home, it may be advisable to visit it and talk with real estate agents, bankers, and members of the chamber of commerce. This will also give you an opportunity to gather job information locally and purchase directories that will be needed for your search. In any case, be comfortable with your chosen targets. One of them may absorb fifteen or more years of your working career.

With your targets set, you now know the direction of your search. The targets you've established define the objectives of your job campaign. With these you can now focus the balance of your work. The information for reaching your market targets should be at hand. Your accomplishments are listed; you have the supplies and materials you will need. It is now time to package your product—yourself, your training, and your experience—to appeal to your chosen markets.

7

Preparing
Your Résumé

Much has been written about résumés, their preparation, style, layout, wording, and content. While all these items are important in a résumé, they are no more important than in any other written business communication. In addition, most of the published material concerning résumés assumes that this document will have widespread use in any job campaign and will be an important factor in its success or failure. In your own Jobsearch campaign this may not be the case. Except for first-time job seekers, you will make only limited use of your résumé.

While you might be eliminated from consideration for a job by your résumé, you'll never be hired from it alone. You will only be hired by selling yourself in person in one or more interviews. For this reason, you will use your résumé only where it can be a positive asset to your search, not a negative instrument used to screen you out.

In addition, many books on résumé preparation were written by individuals more accustomed to reading than writing résumés. These books can be prescriptions for disaster. In addition to concentrating on style rather than sales, recommendations for content can tend to merely facilitate the screening process instead of packaging and marketing the product (you) that your accomplishments represent.

How Employers Use Résumés

Some years ago when I was president of a small brick manufacturing firm, I ran a three-line help wanted classified advertisement for a plant manager at $20,000 per year. Placed for one day only in the Eastern edition of *The Wall Street Journal*, the ad attracted two hundred replies. Today a larger display ad in this paper can easily draw more than one thousand replies while local classified display ads frequently produce five hundred or more responses. Most of these are in the form of résumés, with and without cover letters.

As result of these response rates, one or a team of individuals from the hiring company or its employment agency must read these résumés. They have no choice but to organize this task into a manageable format. This can be done only by skimming each résumé, giving it no more than thirty to forty-five seconds. Even done this way, one thousand résumés would take over eight hours to review.

The reader usually establishes a set of somewhat arbitrary criteria to use in this skimming process. Because judging a candidate's job qualifications is a difficult task, the criteria selected will have little to do with the candidate's ability to perform in the desired position. Instead, for instance, the reviewer will decide not to consider anyone under 30, over 40, without a college degree, having more than two jobs in ten years, or lacking experience in the reviewer's industry. None of these is any reflection on an individual's ability to do a job. They do, however, allow for a quick culling of the candidates.

The reader picks up each résumé and consciously or unconsciously thinks, "What in this document automatically allows me to eliminate this candidate?" This is done with no disdain for the candidates. It's simply a convenient method to reduce the total responses to a manageable number. When I spent forty-five seconds each on the 200 résumés for my plant manager, it took two and a half hours reading time. If more time than this was spent on each résumé, I would have forgotten the first long before the last was read. I had no choice but to quickly eliminate the majority of the candidates.

Thus reduced to twenty or thirty candidates, a reviewer will read an entire résumé—if it is no more than two pages long. Reading two typewritten pages takes two and a half to five minutes. At best, this is still an hour and a half to two hours of reading. Again the emphasis is on elimination. The purpose is to reduce the number of candidates to four or five, whom the company will take the time and expense to interview first by phone and then in person. Once this is done, the résumé has served its purpose: It's been used to eliminate over 95 percent of the candidates responding to the company's advertisement. The hiring process will result from these interviews.

In most companies of medium to large size, all this work will be done by one or more members of the personnel department. Because their primary function in the hiring process is to screen (i.e., to eliminate applicants), they want résumés with maximum information included to facilitate the screening process. These members of the personnel department, however, rarely have the authority to hire new employees.

In general, no department manager will allow some other person in the company to hire people who will work for him or her. Instead, the personnel department will be requested to present the manager with three or four of the best candidates. These individuals will subsequently be interviewed by the department head, who will then hire the candidate he or she wants. While it's difficult to avoid personnel departments entirely, it is important to be cognizant of their function and to realize why they invariably request résumés. When sending résumés, members of personnel should be tactfully avoided whenever possible.

It's particularly important for you to remember this use of the résumé in the job-seeking process. Almost invariably it is a negative instrument used to screen you out rather than hire you. As a result, in your own Jobsearch campaign, limit the distribution of your résumé to those areas and occasions where it can become a positive instrument.

You need a résumé; it should be a good one, but its use must be closely controlled.

How You Should Use Your Résumé

In your Jobsearch campaign, the most appropriate use of the résumé is as a means of communication between someone who knows or has met you and another interested party. If, for instance, you have been interviewed by a member of a company, follow up by giving that person your résumé. Then, in talking with others in the company, he or she can give them a copy of the résumé, along with an impression of you and an expression of interest in your background, experience, and abilities. As the new reader searches for the areas of interest spotlighted by this colleague, the résumé will become a positive rather than a negative instrument.

In the early stages of your campaign you will give your résumé only to individuals and organizations who might pass it on to potential employers. In almost all such instances, this will be accompanied by a cover letter or verbal explanation showing some interest in you.

It will be appropriate for you to send a copy of your résumé to, or leave it with, all personal contacts you use in your campaign. You will also give your résumé to other individuals or companies who do not represent potential employers but who may know of organizations that might have an interest in you. These recipients of your résumé may include employment agencies or executive recruiters as well as college placement officers and some trade associations.

In the job market, these individuals and organizations are interested in offering assistance to both employer and employee. In the case of employment agencies and executive recruiters, a commission for this assistance is expected. Although not always the case, particularly with employment agencies, most of these individuals and organizations will transmit your résumé to interested firms with some indication of your ability to contribute to their company.

Only first-time and entry-level job seekers will use their résumés in answering help wanted advertisements or the mail marketing campaign. Even if a help wanted advertisement requests that a résumé be sent, do not send one except for lower-level jobs. When answering these advertisements, there is no reason to give a potential employer sufficient information to eliminate you for reasons unrelated to your qualifications for the job. Instead you will give only enough information to interest the employer in talking with you personally. For similar reasons, except for first-time job seekers, you will not send a cover letter and résumé in your mail marketing campaign. Instead you'll use the alternative of a well-executed sales letter designed to arouse the interest of the reader.

One Jobsearch client, for example, answered an ad in a large regional newspaper for a public relations director at $32,000 per year. Although the ad requested a résumé, he sent only a letter. Of the 264 respondents, he was one of the 6 who were called. He got the job. Had he replied by sending his résumé, however, he would not even have had an interview. The ad specifically requested five years' experience; he had only four. Although this would have shown up on his résumé, he did not have to mention it in a letter. He had only to describe his substantial accomplishments in the public relations field.

In the latter stages of your Jobsearch campaign, you'll use your résumé to confirm and support your discussions in personal interviews. In these cases your résumé will be given or sent to the interviewer at the end, rather than the beginning, of the interview.

Each of these uses of your résumé will be discussed in more detail in the appropriate section of this manual. In most Jobsearch campaigns, twenty-five to fifty copies of the résumé will be sufficient. The only exceptions to this might be a broad canvassing of executive recruiting firms or a large number of personal contacts for a national campaign where 100 to 150 additional copies may be required. First-time or entry-level job seekers will also need 100 to 200 copies, depending upon the extent of their search.

Layout

There are five basic approaches to résumé preparation. These are:

1. *Chronological.* Work experience arranged in reverse chronological order by employer.
2. *Functional.* Work experience arranged according to function or responsibilities exercised with little regard to chronological order or different employers.
3. *Organizational.* Work experience listed according to companies or organizations, frequently without regard to chronological order.
4. *Narrative.* Work experience written in a continuous narrative style.
5. *Creative.* The entire résumé in its layout, wording, and use of artistic or other embellishments considered as creative in style.

Although each of these formats has an appropriate use in some campaigns, in this Jobsearch manual only the chronological and functional styles of résumé will be considered (see Workbook Forms 20–28). The narrative résumé is difficult and time-consuming to read. The creative résumé too frequently becomes a gimmick which works to the disadvantage of the job candidate. The organizational résumé is a modified chronological form that in most cases is better presented in its more usual and acceptable style.

The chronological and functional résumés are by far the most common and are generally more acceptable to the recipient. In addition, the résumé will be used in your Jobsearch campaign more as a sales tool than as a complete recitation of your career history. It can, therefore, be a straightforward presentation of your accomplishments and experience that enhances your case for employment.

In most Jobsearch campaigns the chronological form of résumé will be preferred. It's easy to read and understand, and presents the job candidate's work experience in the expected order of importance to the reader. A potential employer is more interested in your accomplishments last year than in those ten years ago. This is particularly true when your recent accomplishments have a more direct relation to the job you seek than those of your earlier career. Most job seekers, in attempting to take maximum advantage of career progression in their new positions, will find this to be the case.

When your most recent experiences do not relate to the position you seek, the functional style of résumé should be considered. This style can be used effectively by those who have held a great number of jobs of short duration. It can also be used by persons who have had a long career including responsibilities over several different areas with only one or two employers. In these instances the work experience, grouped according to function, can be arranged in the order of maximum advantage to the job seeker. Several jobs with different companies can, for instance, be grouped in one functional paragraph.

In the functional résumé it's appropriate, unless reasons are compelling to the contrary, to indicate the total duration in years, not necessarily including dates, for each function exercised. The Jobsearch résumé form for your first rough draft (Workbook Form 19) is set out in a chronological format. To change this to a functional format simply list your title or function responsibilities in the space provided for the company name, and include the time period in the text rather than in the left-hand column. In some cases names of companies for whom you've worked and dates of employment are included, one line for each, at the end of the professional history section. Except for these changes, the layouts for functional and chronological résumés are identical.

The résumé layout preferred in this manual places all headings in the left-hand column. All biographical data are given first, followed by professional highlights, professional history, special items of interest, and references, in that order. The intent is to make the job candidate appear first as a human being rather than as mere words on a page. The initial biographical section will contain items to which the reader can readily relate. Children, for instance, hold a special position in most families, and the reader might remember when his or her children were the ages yours are. The reader may also relate to your age, may have known people from your home town, or may otherwise start to visualize you as a real person as he or she reads this section.

Next comes Professional Highlights, which is a summary of those career accomplishments that are most pertinent to the job you seek. For the first-time job seeker, the emphasis in this section may be on educational accomplishments. With the reader's interest stimulated by these highlights, he or she will review your subsequent professional history with more attention than it might otherwise get.

In considering the layout of your résumé, it's imperative that it be neat, well-organized, and balanced on the page. Except in the case of a first-time job seeker, it should also be two pages long. The reasons for this are simple. One page is not enough; a single page will neither offer sufficient space to describe your accomplishments nor impress the reader. Three pages will not be read; it's too long.

To lay out and balance your résumé, you may find it necessary to retype it several times in order to adjust the margins, the spacing, or the length. A word processor or personal computer, if available, is an excellent tool for doing this work. The résumé should be typed and adjusted until you feel it is correct in every respect. For the reasons mentioned in the section on Copying, it should not be typeset even if you have access to a desktop publishing system.

Photograph

The layout of the biographical data in the Jobsearch résumé form provides a space for your photograph, if you choose to use one, in the upper right-hand corner. Generally it's most convenient to staple the photograph to the page. As an alternative you might use the stick-type glues available at most stationery stores. Do not have your photograph printed as part of the résumé. You don't want a recipient to feel he is getting one of hundreds but that your résumé was prepared for him or her with limited distribution.

Because of the expense involved, résumés with your photograph should be used only for the most important contacts in your Jobsearch campaign. This might be, for example, after an interview for a job of particular interest to you or with a personal contact who has a specific job vacancy or company in mind that fits your objectives.

The extent of their use will depend, more than anything else, on your financial situation and personal preference. If they can be secured inexpensively, you may wish to put photographs on all résumés distributed. They may enhance your presentation as well as offer a different look and approach for your résumé.

Copying

Your résumé should be reproduced on a good quality, plain-paper copying machine using white bond paper. The use of colored paper is a gimmick to be avoided. In no case should your résumé be offset printed or otherwise produced in a printed, commercial form. Most processes of this type are used when a hundred or more copies are required. Again, your intent is to make the reader feel that he or she is one of only a few recipients of the résumé, not one of many to whom it has been distributed.

Draft and Wording

For most résumés, follow the Jobsearch Personal Résumé form (Workbook Form 19). Prior to beginning work on your first draft, review the job targets you established for your marketing effort. Then decide how many different résumés you intend to write. The possibilities to consider are these:

- A single résumé for the entire Jobsearch campaign where your marketing targets are similar in position and responsibilities.
- Different Professional Highlights sections for different targets with all other aspects of the résumé identical.
- A functional-style résumé with a different arrangement of the functions under Professional History and a different Professional Highlights section for each target.
- Separate résumés for each target with substantial differences in wording and, perhaps, in style.

In making these decisions, be certain your résumé is appropriate for each specific job you seek.

When you're ready to start, pick your first priority target and complete the résumé form for that job. You can then work on drafts for your other résumés using this first one as a guide.

For the first draft, do the biographical section first, from Name through Education. Then complete the Professional History section including Professional Organizations, Military Service, and Special Items of Interest. Only after these have been written, complete the Professional Highlights section. References should be added after you have checked their responses as discussed in Chapter 8.

Use no abbreviations or contractions in your résumé. Spell out the names of all states, universities, and organizations. Take particular care that any trade or professional jargon you use is suitable for the position you seek. Unless it contributes to a demonstration of your competence, limit the use of such language or avoid it completely. Do not use the word "I." Write your sentences as if its inclusion were implied. The repetitive use of "I" will make you seem overly self-centered.

Use a direct and active writing style. Keep your sentences short and to the point. Instead of saying "was responsible for supervision of the entire sales force," simply put "supervised the entire 50-person sales force." Instead of saying "cost control procedures were revised," use the shorter and more active "revised cost control procedures."

Finally, and extremely important, the spelling, punctuation, and grammar must be correct.

For each résumé, exercise your own judgment in deciding which sections should be emphasized. For instance, if your military service was short, it should be placed after the Professional History section as shown. If, however, it was a significant portion of your career experience, it should be included under Professional History with other positions held. If you are weak in education but strong in experience, relocate the Education section immediately after Military Service.

Your entire résumé should be accomplishments oriented. Prior to beginning work on your résumé, review your accomplishments list in detail. For the Professional Highlights section, pick the three or four most outstanding accomplishments of your career that relate to the job you seek. For Professional History, review your accomplishments list again and include the most pertinent accomplishments for each company or function without repeating those used in the Highlights section. If you must repeat, change the wording or expression of the quantifying statistics. Under Professional History, for instance, you might say, "cut overhead costs by $100,000 per year." In the Highlights section this could read, "reduced overhead 24% annually."

Where you show a title held or describe responsibilities exercised, also include the result. Instead of saying you were an area salesperson responsible for industrial clients in northern Alabama, go on to say that you increased sales 30 percent during this period. If you were a plant manager responsible for production costs, include the amount these costs decreased during your tenure or the fact that they increased only 10 percent while material and labor costs increased 16 percent. Among your accomplishments, find measures of your performance that indicate your contribution to the success or profit of the organization and include them.

When writing your résumé, be honest with yourself and your future employer. Your objective, however, is to cast your career in the best light possible. Do this unabashedly; be boastful. It's your career. They're your accomplishments. List them in a manner that will facilitate the reader's evaluation of your probable contribution to his or her organization and will also enhance your candidacy. The employer must decide whether to make a sizeable investment in you. Your intent is to influence this decision to the maximum extent possible.

Let your accomplishments speak for themselves, however. Minimize the use of self-laudatory words such as "greatest," "best," and "outstanding." Eliminate meaningless, supercilious adjectives such as "largest," "major," and "substantial." Do not use the word "very" in this or any other written correspondence. Because of its overuse it now tends to have the opposite effect to that desired.

Nine sample résumés, six of the chronological and three of the functional style, are given in Workbook Forms 20–28. Review these with care. Pay particular attention to the style, language, and order of presentation for each.

When completing your first résumé draft, note the following:

1. The words "Personal Résumé" should be typed near the top of the page, with the month and year immediately underneath. Both typed lines should be centered. Use the month when you'll most likely give your first résumé to a job contact.

2. *Name.* Type your last name first, written in capital letters. Given names should be written in upper and lower case. No nicknames should be used. If you are usually called by a nickname, this can best be mentioned in a personal interview. If your last name is particularly difficult to pronounce, you may wish to include a phonetic spelling of it in parentheses to the right or on the line below it.

3. *Address.* Type your house number and street on one line. Give city, state, and zip code on another. Only your residence address should be shown.

4. *Telephone.* Type your area code and home phone number. If you can receive calls concerning employment at work, give your office telephone number and indicate which is which. Include your area code even if your search is limited to your local area.

5. Under *Civil Status* include birth date, city and state of birth, citizenship if pertinent, and marital status. Write these facts in brief narrative style as shown in the examples.

6. Include information concerning your wife or husband if you think it is pertinent. Your wife's maiden name may be included if she or her family is well-known in the area where you seek employment. Her citizenship may be included if it's not the same as yours or is pertinent to a foreign position you seek.

7. In general, don't indicate you are divorced unless you feel being single at your age might raise more questions than a divorce.

8. *Children.* List number of daughters and sons, showing ages. Do not include names of your children. It's not necessary to indicate that older children are no longer living with you. This will be inferred and is of little importance. If your children have graduated from college, you might include this information because it reflects on you.

9. *Languages.* Include only those foreign languages with which you are fairly conversant. Indicate your fluency in speaking, reading, or writing. If you imply proficiency, be careful that you can demonstrate it. I was surprised on one job interview with Litton Industries to find that my interviewer was also proficient in French. Over half the interview was conducted in that language.

Even though its use was not required for the job, my proficiency contributed to my getting the job.

10. *Education.* List degrees attained in chronological order starting with high school, if appropriate, your university or college, and then graduate school. Unless you're a recent graduate, include high school information only if it's an outstanding school that might be known to the reader or if you received some honor that might be pertinent to your job campaign. Under Graduate and University, include a complete description of the degrees you received. Mention minor subjects only if they relate to the job you seek. Include any honors you received. Also include extracurricular activities that might be pertinent. Under Continuing Education, list night courses or special education courses taken during your career. If this list is long, include only those courses which were business related.

11. *Professional Highlights.* Write this section last. It should be a short, one-paragraph summary of your recent job history and most important accomplishments. Do not show company names, but include recent titles followed by accomplishments that demonstrate a contribution to profits, cost reductions, increases in sales, production efficiencies, or the success of the organization. Those accomplishments that can be quantified with numbers are most important in this section. Indications of the scope of these accomplishments and their impact on the company are also important. For first-time job seekers, you may concentrate on educational accomplishments in this section and even retitle it appropriately. Remember, a potential employer skimming your résumé may read only this far. These highlights should make the reader want to read further. Write and rewrite this section; refer to your accomplishments list; refer to your job history; refer to your recent education. Make this paragraph relevant to the job you are seeking. It's the most important paragraph in your résumé.

12. *Professional History.* For the chronological style of résumé, your career history should be listed in reverse chronological order. The first line should include the name of the company and the city and state where you worked. The company name should be underlined. If it was a large company, include the name of the division or subsidiary. On the second line, show the dates of your employment in years only. Unless you're seeking a job early in your career and have limited experience, the months are unimportant in the reader's eyes. In addition, showing only the years will eliminate obvious periods of unemployment which might otherwise require explanation.

For each company or major job responsibility, write a short paragraph. The first sentence should include your most recent title and a statement of the size and type of organization, including, for a manufacturing company, the major products produced. The second sentence can include a short description of the responsibilities exercised, ending with a result or accomplishment. The following sentences should include several other accomplishments. If you held more than one position and worked for this company for a considerable period, you may wish to include the appropriate years in the left-hand column adjacent to the beginning sentence defining each position.

Proceed in similar fashion throughout your history, listing each company for which you worked. As you go further back in time your paragraphs and descriptions should become shorter. For jobs you held in the distant past, at the beginning of your career, you may wish to include only the company and responsibilities with appropriate dates.

13. *Military service.* Show branch, rank achieved, period in the service by years, and any specific assignments, duties, or accomplishments related to private business or the position you seek.

14. *Professional organizations.* List only organizations and any official positions held that relate to your business career.

15. *Special items of interest.* List items of specific interest not covered above, such as articles you have published, special honors you received, business licenses or patents you hold, speeches you've made to professional or business organizations, and your outside activities or hobbies, but only if they relate to your business career or the employment you seek.

16. *References.* For this portion of your résumé, refer to Chapter 8 of this Jobsearch manual.

Items to Avoid

In most cases your résumé should not include information or items other than those discussed above. The only exceptions would be items directly related to your career history, your accomplishments, or the position you seek. Volunteer work performed during several years might be an example.

As already pointed out, the résumé as commonly used is a negative instrument. For this reason, you should not include any information that could be construed as a negative reference to your career or personality. These items can best be explained in a personal interview.

Other items to avoid are:

• *Salary.* Do not include any mention of past salaries or desired salary. A résumé isn't the place to indicate the salary you might expect in your new position. This is a point of negotiation which should be discussed only after a potential employer has decided to hire you for a job. In addition, you may be considered for a job with compensation that far exceeds your highest career salary. You don't want to be eliminated by showing previous salaries not in this range.

• *Reasons for changes in employment.* Explanation of such changes is frequently awkward and shouldn't be attempted in a résumé. The reasons for a change in employment may have been personal, or you may have been fired. Regardless, they have little to do with your accomplishments. The subject should be deferred for a full discussion in a job interview and even then, only if you are questioned on the point.

• *Desired position.* Discussions of your job objectives, availability, desired location, or willingness to travel shouldn't be included in your résumé. They should be part of a letter or subsequent job interview. In particular, all mention of job objectives should be avoided. Nothing will dampen the impact of your résumé more than some arrogant reference to your wanting a job "in a responsible management position that will allow me to realize my full potential while contributing to the success of the company." A potential employer is not interested in what you want, only in what contribution you can make to help solve his and the company's problems.

• *Other items.* Don't include any of the following miscellaneous, unrelated bits of information: height and weight, health status, race, sex, supervisors' names and titles, unrelated hobbies, sports interests, test scores, academic grades other than top-class standing, church affiliation, family background, home ownership, Social Security number, or driver's license number. If a company wants to hire you, do you really think it will care whether you are 5 feet 5 inches or 6 feet 3 inches tall? Leave this information for employment application forms.

In all my years working with job seekers, I've been amused by the number of résumés that include a reference to "Health." It is invariably shown as Excellent or Good on every résumé, even by people with obvious health problems. "After all," they explained, "for someone with this problem my health is excellent." Leave it out.

Handling Problems

Because in most cases your résumé will have limited use in your Jobsearch campaign, it's not difficult to handle special problems such as age, lack of experience, overly specialized experience, frequent job changes, and career changes. Notwithstanding this, you should direct some care and attention to these areas.

If you're advanced in age, your résumé should emphasize experience and, wherever possible, a long list of accomplishments and progression in your career. These should be directed toward one or two specific areas in which you can make an immediate contribution. You might find an employer with special problems who would welcome having a sixty-year-old with thirty years of experience to solve the problems within the five- to ten-year period before his or her retirement.

One Jobsearch client was well into his seventies. In his résumé, we turned his age to advantage by focusing on job targets of short duration for specific tasks with listed accomplishments that demonstrated quick success. He was hired for just this type of work. After all, while an older employee may have only five to ten years to devote to a company, he or she may be more likely to remain in the job that long than an ambitious and impatient thirty-year-old.

If you lack experience in the field you want to enter, emphasize accomplishments indicating that your intelligence and drive will more than compensate for the problems associated with a career change. Any similar changes in positions or responsibilities in your past career should be emphasized along with accomplishments which show that the change was successful.

If you have highly specialized experience in a field that is not your current target, describe your accomplishments in terms that show their application or impact in a broader area. Mention work or participation in company decisions outside your specialty. Drop all jargon used in your field and substitute general business terms.

This is particularly important when you're making a change from the military, government, or education field to private industry. Most business executives have a bias against such persons because of their presumed lack of experience with profit incentives. You can best overcome this in your résumé by stressing accomplishments that relate to cost reductions or demonstrate a concern for costs and efficiency. In addition, the use of business terms and expressions is particularly important. Review your accomplishments and ask yourself if they would read the same if your employer had been a business organization.

If you've changed jobs frequently or held jobs of short duration, it may be wise to omit all reference to some of them. These may be considered as temporary or exploratory positions that didn't work out. As such, they don't have to be included as part of your career history.

Your résumé is a sales tool and should be treated as such. Write it in positive terms. Keep it accomplishments oriented, and consider carefully how problems should be phrased in relation to your specific job targets.

Finally, remember the objective of a résumé in the job seeking process. It's not to get a job; that can only be done in a personal interview. The objective of a résumé is to secure the personal interview or, more frequently, to reinforce the impressions left by this interview.

CHAPTER

8

References

Your choice of references can be critical to your Jobsearch campaign. At some stage in considering you as a potential employee, virtually all companies will phone your references. They'll want to discuss your work habits, personality traits, and past performance. Because these responses are important to the potential employer, it's not enough that you choose your references with care. You must know what they will say about you and your performance. Their responses must, therefore, be checked, and you must then maintain close contact with them throughout your campaign.

Never include a line in your résumé stating, "References available upon request." If they're available, they should be listed. Don't force a potentially interested employer to request these names. You have nothing to hide and can expect your references to make a strong, positive statement about you. Because of the limited use made of the résumé in your Jobsearch, there is little likelihood the people you list will be inconvenienced by too many phone calls.

Once chosen, list your references at the end of your résumé, including the full name, title, company affiliation, city and state of residence, and telephone number. Because reference checks are usually made by phone, it's not necessary to show full addresses, although a fax phone number, if available, should also be shown.

You should not list your references in the order of best to worst. It can be damaging if the response becomes less favorable as more references are called. This might suggest to the caller that additional references would continue in this pattern. For this reason you should consider listing your best reference second.

You should choose and list three references. This is a convenient number to call and, with similar response from each, should be sufficient. If more are needed by any particular company, they will be requested.

Choice of References

Other than for first-time or relatively inexperienced job seekers, all three of your references should be businesspeople who've known you well in one or more of your recent jobs. If possible, their's should be jobs that relate closely to the position you seek. It's also advisable to include a reference from your last employer if it's a good one. If this cannot be done, be ready to explain why. An interested company may specifically ask to talk with your last supervisor. When you have substantially different job targets and résumés, you might consider listing different references or listing the references in a different order for each.

Your references should be persons in an equal or superior position to the one for which you are applying. If possible, it is advisable to have one reference whose position is above or similar to that of the probable caller. The only exception to these rules might be a reference who reported to you or worked under you in a former job. This might be appropriate if a major aspect of your new job would be supervision over similar employees. This exception, however, must be handled with care. In the eyes of many businesspeople, a subordinate is not always the best judge of his or her immediate superior. In addition, subordinates do not generally enjoy as close a business and social relationship with their superiors as people who are of equal or higher rank.

Do not use personal references such as your minister, neighbors, or close friends who've had no contact with you in business. Any prospective employers checking your references will expect your business associates to be as conversant with your honesty and personality traits as your friends. In addition, they are most interested in these traits as they appear in a business environment. Your references should be persons who know you well in both a business and a social context wherever possible.

For first-time or relatively inexperienced job seekers, the choice of references is often more limited. However, when possible try to list individuals for whom you've worked even in part-time summer jobs. For recent graduates, former professors should be considered. Beyond these, the best choices are businesspeople who know you well, perhaps friends of your family or others with whom you have had substantial contact. Don't use immediate members of your family or casual friends. For business references, mature businesspeople are always preferred.

Checking Reference Responses

As previously stated, you cannot choose your references on the basis of what you think they will say about you. You must know what they'll say and how they'll say it.

Too often our Jobsearch clients gave us references they considered excellent, such as old friends who would surely want to help. On calling them for the reference check, we found they did indeed want to help, but occasionally made a seemingly innocuous statement which would have destroyed the interest of any prospective employer. In one instance, an otherwise excellent reference simply wouldn't stop talking. He went on to explain how long he had known the job seeker, spoke of both their advanced ages, and went into a long explanation of visiting his friend in the hospital after a mild heart attack. None of this information was pertinent to the job at hand or helpful. We eliminated that reference and found a much better candidate.

A reference may volunteer too much information about you, your personal life, or your negative traits no matter how slight. Others, such as the above, might mention health problems that were brought under control years before. You simply can't afford to leave these responses to chance. Although checking a reference's response is not difficult, it must be done with care. It can be harmful if the reference finds you are privy to his or her impressions of you given in confidence.

Ideally, your references should be checked by a close business associate or friend whom they do not know. You should meet with this friend or associate and explain in detail the objectives of your search and your approach to the job market. He or she should understand that your reference check isn't the result of any curiosity or anxiety on your part but only one aspect of a well-planned, well-executed job campaign. You should give the person checking your references a copy of your draft résumé, typed if possible, and a description of your job targets. Immediately before phoning each reference, he or she should read this information and be familiar with its contents.

Give your friend or associate four or five references to call, and explain that you intend to use the best three. Also give your intermediary copies of the list of questions to be asked as shown on Workbook Form 29. You should request that the answers be written down. After each call, notes should also be made concerning its general aspects and tone.

The suggested list of questions for a reference check (Workbook Form 29) can be copied and filled in for each call. "He" and "him," of course, become "she" and "her" if the candidate is a woman. Because this list is general and too long for most calls, you or the person performing the reference check should edit it before or during each telephone conversation. Eliminate irrelevant questions and add questions that relate directly to your past or the position you seek.

The person performing your check should telephone each reference, introduce himself or herself using a real or a fictitious name, and state that the call is being made because you listed the other party as a reference on your résumé. The caller can then request a few minutes to ask questions about you. The reference should be given the impression that the caller is interested in hiring you. Another option we sometimes used at Jobsearch was to have the caller describe himself or herself as an executive recruiter. This precludes possibly embarrassing questions about the fictitious company that the caller may not be able to answer.

You should not be present while the reference check calls are made. Instead meet with the caller at the earliest mutual convenience after the calls have been completed. You and the person performing the check can then review responses, including not only answers to the questions but also the general impression the reference made on the caller. If you do not find three acceptable references from these initial calls, continue the procedure until you have three in whose response you have absolute faith.

In making decisions concerning your references, consider that some slightly negative information about you is desirable. It's for this reason the person performing your reference check should specifically ask about any negative characteristics or traits you might have. This negative information will lend credence to the preponderance of positive statements about you and your career. This is particularly advantageous if the negative information or trait would in some cases be viewed as a benefit. For instance, a reference might state that you are sometimes overly aggressive or that you demand too much of your subordinates or yourself; neither of these should be damaging and may be viewed by some as an asset rather than a liability.

Your best reference won't be a sugar-coated recital of the traits of a perfect worker. Your reference should know you well enough to speak of your weaknesses as well as your strengths. These, however, should not be weaknesses that would have a strongly negative impact on your suitability for the job.

Communicating With Your References

After your references have been chosen and their responses checked, contact each of them and then keep them well advised of your progress. Your initial contact should be made just prior to giving out your first résumés, as late as possible in the campaign. In this way your conversations with the references will be near the time they might receive calls.

Try to meet with each of your references personally. If this isn't possible, phone them. In this first conversation, request permission to use them as a reference. The reference may mention that he or she has already been called. You can explain that you were pursuing an initial job possibility but have now expanded your search to include a much wider range of potential opportunities.

Ask the reference to accentuate the positive and even help directly in your search, career change, or advancement, but also request that the statements be both frank and honest. Explain your approach to the job market, as well as the targets and objectives you have established. Tell your reference you'll send him or her a copy of your résumé as soon as it is completed. Don't, however, take a copy of the résumé to this first meeting. It would be presumptuous to give your reference a résumé with his or her name already listed before permission has been requested to include it.

Following this initial contact, write a letter to each of your references and enclose a copy of your completed, typed résumé. This letter should express gratitude for the assistance to your campaign, and should summarize again the objectives of your search. Tell each reference you'll keep him or her advised of your progress. (See Workbook Form 30 for a letter of this type.)

As you proceed through your campaign, phone each reference periodically to report on your progress. This will keep your search fresh in the reference's mind. It will also give you an opportunity to learn the names of the companies that have called and to again thank your references for their assistance. You might also phone them after any particularly interesting job interview, discuss the position with them, and forewarn them of possible calls.

At the successful conclusion of your Jobsearch campaign, advise your references of the new position you have accepted and thank them for the contribution they made to the success of your effort. They will appreciate this recognition. In addition, you may wish to call on them again for assistance as you work toward your career goals.

TWO

Marketing

CHAPTER

9

Marketing Yourself

You have now completed all the preliminary work, established your information sources, and prepared the basic written materials you'll need to execute your Jobsearch campaign. You're ready to begin making your initial contacts with the job market. In this phase of the program, five principal methods will be used to introduce you to potential employers. These are personal contacts, answering help wanted advertisements, a direct mail campaign, other contacts, and developing a single-target Jobsearch. Emphasis placed on each of these will depend on your individual circumstances. However, virtually all job seekers will make at least some use of each marketing method except perhaps developing a single-target Jobsearch.

Throughout this phase of your program you must remember your immediate objective is not to get a job but to secure the maximum number of personal interviews with potentially interested employers. Maximize these opportunities by being expansive. If you're in doubt about a contact, make it. If you're attracted by a help wanted advertisement but feel your qualifications might not be adequate, answer it. If a little more work is required to expand your mailing list, do it. You can't make too many contacts with the job market; you can certainly, however, make too few.

Make as many contacts with the market as the information and time available to you permit. This Jobsearch manual shows you how to make and organize these contacts with a minimum of effort. In most campaigns you should be able to make your talent and experience known to between 200 and 500 individuals and organizations.

Because these will result in a number of personal meetings and interviews, it will be convenient to keep a standard business appointments diary. These are available at most office supply outlets. As you set up appointments, enter them in the diary. You may also wish to block out certain periods during each day to devote to other aspects of your Jobsearch campaign. As with any thorough marketing campaign, organization and follow-up will be of paramount importance.

Review the discussion under Your Attitude in Chapter 1. You're about to embark on a major marketing campaign with yourself as the product. Expect but don't fear rejection. Every company you contact does not need your services. Some may need them but can't afford to pay what you're worth. You, on the other hand, need only one job among the thousands that are available at any given moment. When a company turns you down, sends a polite rejection letter, or chooses another candidate over you, it's not a reflection on you personally. Don't slow your effort, reflect on failure, or have regrets. Go on to make the sale among your other contacts. With the thorough marketing campaign outlined below, there will be plenty of these.

Confirming Letters

This Jobsearch manual stresses one cardinal rule: *Do not contact anyone concerning a job either by telephone or in a meeting without confirming your discussion in a follow-up letter.* This refers to all persons who are in a position to help you or who represent a potentially interested employer. Examples of such confirming letters and an explanation of their content are included at each appropriate point in the following chapters of this manual.

These letters are not only polite, they're often a pleasant, unexpected reminder to the recipient that you appreciate the assistance or consideration being given. They remind the recipient of the expected follow-up to your conversations and don't allow him or her to forget you and the objectives of your search.

In the business world, letters of this type are so rare they'll do more to advance your job campaign than any other single item. I've talked to directors of personnel who have interviewed thousands of job candidates. They tell me that less than 5 percent confirm their interviews in writing. Consequently, these few individuals are recognized for their thoughtfulness and effort and immediately have an edge over other candidates.

One Jobsearch client went on a full day's interview at a company's corporate headquarters in Washington state. He met individually with nine officers during the day. After returning home he wrote each man and woman he had met. The letters were short, and the wording of each was varied to avoid embarrassment if the recipients compared notes. He got the job over two other finalists who had the same opportunity but did not follow up with confirming letters.

This cardinal rule is particularly important for first-time job seekers as it establishes a habit that will serve you well for years. When I was graduating as a mechanical engineer in 1962, I had six corporate recruiting interviews during the spring semester. For each of these I not only immediately confirmed the meetings with a letter, but referred to several of the most pertinent points discussed and related my education to each point. I had four job offers, a higher percentage than my classmates.

CHAPTER
10

Personal Contacts

Personal contacts are defined as those individuals in business who are in a position to help you and would want to help. They might be close friends, customers, or former associates. For first-time job seekers, this could include family friends, professors, managers at businesses where you worked part time, or other businesspeople with whom you or your family have had past relations. Because your initial contacts with these people should be made by telephone and wherever possible, in a personal meeting, they should be limited in most Jobsearch campaigns to approximately twenty individuals. More than this number will become cumbersome and too time consuming.

An exception to this might be a campaign conducted by a well-known executive in a national firm. He or she may wish to solicit help from forty to fifty business associates spread over the entire United States. This can be handled best as a part of the direct mail campaign by writing a letter similar to that used for executive recruiters or employment agencies (Workbook Form 54) with a more personal introduction. He or she could then add a personal note at the end of each letter and enclose a résumé just as would be done with other personal contacts.

In some instances you may know of only two or three individuals who will be in a position to assist you in your Jobsearch campaign. However, even with so short a list, you should not neglect these people. They may suggest a company or send your résumé to a friend who needs you.

Because your personal contacts don't usually represent potential employers but only put you in touch with other interested parties, they should be consulted early in your campaign. Job interviews from these sources will then more closely correspond to interviews secured later through more direct methods.

Whom to Contact

Use a number of sources to compile your personal contacts list. Search your memory. If they're available, review your old business files and correspondence. Look over your or your family's Christmas card mailing list. If you were

67

married less than five years ago and had a well-attended ceremony, review the invitation list to your wedding. Talk to members of your family and close business associates. Even if you're a first-time job seeker, personal contacts should be a part of your campaign. Surely you know or members of your family know of businessmen and women who would be glad to make introductions for you. In any case, be expansive. Talk to anyone who may be in a position to help. You may be pleasantly surprised by the number of contacts you can develop in a short period of time. In general, people enjoy helping others particularly if the help is both effective and appreciated.

List everyone who might be interested in helping you. Be careful, however, not to waste your time contacting people who might want to help but are not in a position to know of potential employers matching your job targets. Your best contacts will be people directly related to the business in which you hope to be employed. This includes customers, suppliers, or participants in this industry. The next most preferable contacts would be businesspeople indirectly related to the industry of your choice. This includes members of banks, law firms, accounting firms, advertising agencies, or business consulting firms with contacts or knowledge of this industry. Finally, your contacts may include persons who are not related to the industry of your choice but might be able to suggest your candidacy to other businesspeople. This could include executives of civic organizations who are well known in their community or have an outstanding reputation in the business world.

All of these personal contacts should be entered on Workbook Form 31, giving the name, title, company affiliation, business address, and telephone number of each. Space is provided to record the required follow-up as well as any subsequent contacts generated for you by these individuals. The list should be kept in the Personal Contacts section of your notebook, followed by copies of all correspondence with these individuals.

Make as many copies of the form as will be needed for your total number of contacts. Space is provided for five on each page.

How to Contact

After you have completed your list, establish a schedule for making these contacts. Phone all individuals in your local area and request an appointment to meet with them personally. If you feel it's appropriate, tell them you're starting a job search campaign and would like to discuss it with them. At these meetings, review your approach to the job market and describe your objectives and job targets. Ask for their comments or suggestions concerning your approach. After this is done, you can request their assistance and, if possible, suggest several specific things they could do or contacts they could make for you.

Most people are flattered by requests for advice and enjoy assisting others.

Consequently, these meetings should be among the easiest and most pleasant of your campaign. During these meetings, attempt to guide your contacts into being as specific as possible, particularly in regard to the ways they might help you or the people and companies to whom they might make introductions. Write down the names of these companies and individuals. If a contact suggests that you get in touch with another party, ask that he or she call to introduce you first.

Where it's impossible for you to meet personally with individuals on your contacts list, call them and briefly review the same information discussed above. End the conversation by telling them you'll send a copy of your résumé and a description of your objectives.

In any case, make it easy for your contacts to assist you. Arm them with the information they need to consider specific possibilities, to discuss your qualifications and objectives with others, and to supply prospects with your past history of accomplishments. Even your closest business friends can do little with a request such as, "I'm looking for a job. Will you help?" They need to know specifically what you're looking for and why.

Use of Your Résumé

Your résumé should be given to each of your personal contacts. When you meet them, you may leave one or more copies just prior to ending your conversation. If you prefer, tell them you'll mail the résumé, then enclose it with your confirming letter.

In no case should you begin this or any other interview by giving out your résumé. A meeting that starts with a résumé can be awkward. Frequently you find yourself sitting with nothing to do as your contact reads the résumé. Your obvious discomfort is likely to prompt your contact to read it rapidly and not give it proper attention. This may be the only time he or she will read this important document. In addition, a résumé given out prior to a conversation can too easily become a crutch for both parties. As your contact continually refers to the résumé, the conversation becomes overly structured and dwells excessively on your past instead of your future.

If you're asked for your résumé at the beginning of a meeting, explain that you brought several copies to leave with your contact but would like to first discuss your objectives and your approach to the job market. Then go on to that discussion leading in to the help your contact might be able to provide.

When the résumé is given to your contact at the end of an interview, it is appropriate to request that it be read with care and to offer additional copies. The response to this offer may indicate your contact's willingness and ability to help.

In the hands of a personal contact, your résumé becomes a positive instrument. When passing it on to potentially interested individuals, your contact will do so with a personal note or comment about you and about his or her interest in your background and abilities. The recipient will then search for reasons behind this recommendation as he or she reads the résumé, all the while looking for your strengths rather than your weaknesses.

Follow-Up and Written Confirmation

Following the cardinal rule of this Jobsearch manual, all telephone conversations and meetings with personal contacts should be confirmed by letter. You expect their help on a voluntary basis. This help isn't a part of their job or daily routine. The confirming letter will be a written reminder of your conversation and their offer of assistance.

These letters usually contain three or four short paragraphs. The first should thank your contact for his or her time and offer of assistance. The second reviews your job objectives. In an optional third paragraph, you may mention several of your strengths and list specific accomplishments that relate to your objectives. The final paragraph contains a statement of the expected follow-up and, if appropriate, a personal note. Two examples of such letters appear in Workbook Forms 32–33.

After these letters and other correspondence with your personal contacts are filed in your notebook, it's advisable to underline in red and transfer to your To Do list any follow-up expected of you. This must then be performed on a timely basis. If you said you would check back with your contact after two weeks, do this within several days of the end of the second week. If your contact has suggested you call another individual, do so and advise him or her of the results of this effort by phone or in a note.

Your personal contacts are important in your Jobsearch campaign. Treat them with consideration and keep them advised of your progress, particularly regarding opportunities to which they introduce you. But don't be overly aggressive or take up too much of their time. They are, after all, usually personal friends. You want to maintain this friendship and may need their help again as you progress through your business career.

Courtesy Meetings

One danger in using personal contacts is that you will become trapped in a long series of courtesy meetings. On occasion a friend with a genuine desire to help will request you contact a business associate who doesn't represent a potential opportunity. This person will meet with you out of a sense of obligation to your mutual friend and may then send you to another uninterested party. These meetings can easily pyramid, resulting in a waste of valuable time.

The problem with such meetings is ascertaining in advance whether an opportunity exists. If you find interviews of this type are absorbing an excessive amount of time, you may wish to mail a résumé prior to setting up a meeting. This can be done by phoning the party and mentioning that you were referred to him or her by your mutual friend. You then outline the objectives of your Jobsearch and offer to forward a copy of your résumé for review, adding "I'll contact you after you've had an opportunity to read it." Send your résumé with a cover letter confirming your conversation, outlining your job objectives, stating several of your accomplishments, and indicating that you will call again later. Such a letter will be followed by a request for a personal meeting only if an opportunity does in fact exist.

Look at the example of this type of letter (Workbook Form 34). In this as in similar letters, the request for an interview is direct and without qualifications. If the interview is not appropriate, you will be told when you call at the appointed time. Do not, however, attempt to second guess the interest of the other party or give that person any indication that a meeting may not be warranted. If the meeting is arranged, you've found another opportunity.

Answering
Help Wanted
Advertisements

Help wanted advertisements represent a good source of potential job opportunities. However, because of their extensive use and the volume of replies, you must answer numerous ads in order to generate any significant level of response. Nevertheless, they shouldn't be neglected. Using your accomplishments list and a basic form letter you'll be able to answer a large number of ads with a minimum of effort.

Help wanted advertisements are placed by two primary sources. The first is companies conducting their own personnel searches showing their names and addresses or simply post office box numbers without their identification (called "blind ads"). The second is employment agencies listing positions with companies by whom they have been retained. These are also placed as both blind ads and showing the name and address of the agency but not the company.

Occasionally employment agencies will list fictitious positions in an attempt to collect fresh résumés for their files. Although you cannot entirely avoid responding to such ads, your method of response can frustrate the objective of the agency and prevent an unwanted broadcast of your résumé. In addition, there are always classified help wanted ads, which are little more than solicitations for an investment in a sales scheme or simply misleading in their content or description of the position offered. It can also be difficult to eliminate these, although again the Jobsearch method of response will be helpful. Several Jobsearch clients who responded to help wanted ads, particularly in the sales field, went on interviews, and suddenly found themselves in a room with fifty other candidates listening to a direct-sales pitch. If this happens to you, leave. It would be rare that one of these would offer much more than a method of having you pay for your job or selling a product in an overly saturated market to an unreceptive audience.

Sources of Ads

One of the best sources of classified advertisements for most job campaigns is trade magazines. These are more directed than newspaper classified ads, rarely contain "come-on" ads, and are preselected for an industry of interest to you. On the basis of your initial review of information sources discussed in Chapter 2, you should have already subscribed to any that are suitable. If you requested several editions prior to your subscription date, you will now have a backlog of advertisements that fall within your job targets.

In addition, get appropriate city newspapers and the Tuesday and Wednesday editions of *The Wall Street Journal* or its *National Business Employment Weekly.* Your contacts with national associations and college placement offices may have also supplied you with additional listings of available positions.

If you haven't already done so, carefully review all these advertisement sources. Read each ad and compare those of interest with your objectives and targets. Cut out the ads you intend to answer and note on each the name of the publication and the date the ad appeared.

If publications you ordered haven't yet arrived, call the publisher and expedite delivery. Explain your purpose and request that one or two recent copies be put in the mail to you immediately.

Answer all the ads you cut out, even those a month or two old. The company may not have found a suitable candidate. In addition, the fact that it is searching for employees may mean the company is expanding or needs someone with your talents in another department or division.

Even if only a few ads are attractive to you, answer these and continue to examine your ad sources throughout your campaign. Respond to all ads of interest until you have actually accepted a new position.

Choice of Ads

In answering help wanted advertisements, be both liberal and expansive. Answer any advertisement in which you have an interest, even if the interest is based on curiosity or a flight of fancy. If you're interested in a specific company, answer its ads even though you're not strongly interested in the position advertised.

Although you should have at least some of the qualifications requested in advertisements you answer, remember that no job candidate will present the ideal background and experience for any position. For this reason, the company will have to compromise in making a final choice. It may be sufficiently interested in you to hire you as a subordinate to the person who gets the advertised position. It might also expand the advertised position to include other responsibilities in order to hire you if you're more qualified than intended.

Don't worry about the pay scale mentioned in the advertisements. If the figure is too low, it will be open for negotiation. If you're qualified and are the person the company wants, it won't hesitate to pay you the salary in the advertisement even if it is substantially higher than your last salary level.

Answer all ads in which you have any interest whatsoever and as many of these as you can find. Each may represent another potentially attractive opportunity. Because the Jobsearch method of answering ads is an easily executed program using a series of similar letters, the time required to answer a large number of ads over the duration of your job campaign is not excessive.

Reply Letters

Except in the case of a first-time or lower-level job seeker, all your responses to help wanted advertisements should take the form of a one-page letter without a résumé. In rare instances, such as a situation with a long list of requirements, two pages may be needed. In no case, however, is a third page warranted.

If a company's name is shown or if the information contained in the advertisement makes the company's identity easy to obtain, your reply letter should be personally addressed. Unless someone else is specifically mentioned in the ad, address the letter to the head of the department or the corporate officer responsible for the position by name, not by title. If the advertised position is for a salesperson or a district sales manager, this officer would be the vice-president of sales or sales manager. If the position is at the vice-presidential level, this person would be the president or chief executive officer of the firm. For a data entry or secretarial position, it would be the appropriate department head.

For most medium-size and large national companies, the names of these officers are listed in the Dun & Bradstreet *Middle Market* or *Million Dollar* directories. For local companies, chamber of commerce directories may list the chief executive and other officers of each corporation. In addition, executives of competing or supplier firms will often have the names of company managers and department heads. Of course, the easiest method of acquiring the appropriate name is to simply call the company and explain to the telephone operator that you wish to address a letter to the head of the appropriate department. You'll be given the name you want.

Unless specifically instructed in the help wanted advertisement to do so, you should avoid addressing the letter to the director of personnel or to a person in this department. Although, as mentioned earlier, personnel departments are to be avoided, this is one instance where following directions will be best. If you respond to an ad showing a personnel officer's name and send the letter to a department head, he or she will certainly follow company policy and turn the letter over to his or her colleague in personnel. In any case, however, a letter addressed to a person by name is always more highly regarded than one addressed simply to a company or to an unnamed department head. If the ad asks that the letter be sent to the director of the appropriate department or to the director of personnel and a name is not given, do some research and find that person's name.

In all cases, your letter should be accomplishments oriented. In addition, it must respond directly and specifically to the qualifications or requirements mentioned in the ad. Before drafting the letter, carefully review the entire ad and your accomplishments list. Underline the qualifications requested in the ad, then select your single accomplishment that most nearly corresponds to the qualifications or responsibilities of greatest importance to the position advertised. This accomplishment should be included in the opening sentence of your letter. Your objective is to immediately attract the attention of the recipient and make him or her interested in reading the rest of the letter.

The second sentence in your letter should explain your reason for writing. It should refer to the advertisement and lead into a further listing of your accomplishments.

Then pick out four or five accomplishments that also relate to the position and the specific qualifications requested. List these with a double space between each accomplishment. If appropriate, a qualification mentioned in the ad can be repeated immediately before the accomplishment that responds to it. If necessary, rewrite the descriptions of your accomplishments to make them more responsive to the ad. It's usually wise to mention the names of companies that have employed you. This adds credibility to your accomplishments.

The next one or two sentence paragraph of your letter should contain just enough biographical information to put the reader's mind at ease about you. It should include some reference that indicates your age. If you do not wish to put your exact age, you might suggest it vaguely by referring to your years of experience or the ages of your children.

If your educational background is attractive or important to the advertised position, it should be cited. Do not mention education, however, if the specific degree requested in the advertisement is one of the few qualifications you don't have.

You may wish to include the fact that you're married or are willing to travel or relocate. There should be no reference, however, to salary or any items relating to your personal objectives or job goals. Neither should there be the slightest indication that you might not be qualified for the job. The entire letter should point to the fact that you are. There should be no negative information or negative connotation in this letter. It is a sales tool and should be treated as such.

The final paragraph of the letter should request a personal interview. It must be direct and to the point. Indicate that you will be able to expand on your qualifications and background in the interview, then ask for it.

For the first-time job seeker or those looking for an entry- or lower-level position, the ad response letter will be similar although somewhat shorter. It should also include a copy of your résumé. Where you lack career experience and cannot point to a specific list of related accomplishments, your résumé will be helpful and appropriate. It can't contain much, if any, negative information. What you have to sell is your educational background and the perhaps unrelated work experience you can demonstrate with the few jobs you might have had. You should, however, respond to the requests in the ad as described above using your educational accomplishments to support your qualifications for the position. (See Workbook Form 40.)

In any case, all such letters should end with a statement indicating the follow-up expected and explaining how you can be reached. Except in cases where an ad specifically says "No calls," if the company's name is shown, maintain the initiative and state you will phone a week to ten days after the letter is mailed. This is often an effective means of ensuring that your letter isn't discarded with little or no consideration. In addition, it will allow you to gather useful information about the job, plan your approach, and assess your chances. This will be important to your follow-up not only for this prospect but for subsequent opportunities as well.

A Jobsearch client making a phone call on an ad follow-up found himself talking to the secretary of a vice-president who was out of town. In the process of asking the secretary a number of questions about the job, he noticed her accent and asked where she was from. She was a native of Chicago. He told her he had lived in that city for several years. At the end of the conversation, she assured him she would put his letter on top of the pile with a note that he had called. Suddenly he found himself number one among the hundreds of respondents.

Unless otherwise advised in the ad, don't worry about bothering the company with your phone call. Had it wished, the company could have remained anonymous with a blind ad or asked candidates not to call. Also, few candidates make such calls. It will demonstrate your interest and aggressive approach. You may even produce unusual and helpful results such as those mentioned. Introduce yourself to the person you reach. Explain that you want to be sure your letter was received. Ask if the company needs more information. Ask how many replies to the ad were received, how many candidates the company intends to interview, and how and when the candidates will be chosen. Be sure to request an interview. If the interview is not granted, discuss the appropriate follow-up, while, if possible, keeping the initiative. State that you'll call back again at an appropriate date.

Review the six examples of help wanted advertisements and letters responding to them (Workbook Form 7 and Workbook Forms 35–40). Pay particular attention to the format and order, the choice and listing of accomplishments, and the use of biographical data. If you are a first-time or entry-level job seeker, pay particular attention to the letter from Susan Abrams (Workbook Form 40) and her use of the résumé.

After you've answered a number of help wanted advertisements, it will become easy to develop a system to facilitate drafting these letters. Number the entries on your accomplishments list. Copy and then number sample paragraphs and sentences from your response letters. Use this information to develop a master list of paragraphs, sentences, and accomplishments. You can then compose a letter by simply indicating the numbers of appropriate items and have the letter typed directly from the master list. When doing this, however, review the wording to be certain it is appropriate for the specific advertisement. For most letters some sentences will have to be individually written.

This work is particularly easy if you or your secretarial service has access to a personal computer and word processing program. The individual accomplishments and paragraphs can then be stored in files and called up to compose an individual letter quickly.

File all your responses to help wanted advertisements in chronological order in the Ad Answers section of your notebook. Staple the advertisement in the upper right-hand corner of each letter. When you receive a telephone call in response to one of these letters, explain that you answered several advertisements and ask to which the call refers. This will allow you to find the appropriate letter and have it and the advertisement in hand before starting the conversation.

Don't attempt to carry on a conversation of this type without having these copies. If you can't find them immediately, say you would like to return the call in a few minutes when it would be more convenient. These calls are too important to waste. Having all the appropriate information available will allow you to respond more readily to the caller's questions and to elaborate on your accomplishments without excessive repetition.

Remember, in any such conversation your objective is to secure an interview, not get a job. Do not discuss salary. If possible, don't respond directly to questions soliciting negative information about you. You might respond to such questions with a partial answer and explain that you can elaborate when you know more about the position, the objectives of the company, and the specific problems that need to be addressed. In particular, don't volunteer any information that could be used to eliminate you from consideration.

But do ask for the interview. Don't forget that you're making a sales presentation, which is not complete until you've asked the customer to buy. Be aggressive, suggest that you could elaborate more on the points discussed in a meeting, explain that you would like to learn more about the position and the company. Offer to meet your contact at his or her convenience and ask him or her to suggest a time. You won't get a job offer until you've met personally with one or more members of the company. Your objective is to obtain this meeting.

Request for Résumé and Salary Information

Most help wanted advertisements larger than single-column line ads request that a résumé be sent. Ignore this request unless, as discussed above, you are looking for your first job or an entry-level position. After all, the company placing the ad wants the maximum information about each candidate in order to facilitate its screening process. Your interest, on the other hand, is to provide the company with only enough information to provoke an interview. In most cases, you cannot tailor your résumé to the specific requirements of each advertisement. In addition, your résumé may include information the company would consider negative. The letters described above, however, do not have these drawbacks. They're written and phrased for each individual ad.

In some advertisements the request for a résumé is emphatic. The ad may state that you will not be considered if you do not send a résumé. In such cases, mention in your reply letter that you don't have a current résumé available. The company can easily assume you are not actively seeking new employment but responded to its advertisement because of its particular interest to you. Such an assumption can frequently work to your advantage.

I recently hired a vice-president of sales and marketing for a small consumer products company I headed. Of the hundred or so responses I received from a trade magazine ad, the man who got the job had written an eight-line letter and no more. There certainly wasn't enough information in that letter to eliminate him. His former position, however, was well suited to the position we had vacant. He was one of the ten I called and the five we interviewed. My ad, by the way, requested that a résumé be sent.

Many help wanted advertisements also request your salary history or an indication of your desired salary. As with the résumé, this request should be ignored by all job seekers including entry level. In cases where the request is emphatic, you may wish to include a sentence stating that your salary requirements are open and will depend on a more complete definition of the job, the responsibilities, and the potential.

There is one exception to this. When answering an ad for a federal government position or a job with a quasi-government agency, you should respond to a salary request. Salaries for these positions are not open to as much negotiation as positions in private industry, and the screening process for ad responses is more rigid. Do not give your salary history, but state an acceptable salary range using the government salary scale code. The range for the position and the appropriate code numbers can be determined by calling your local government information office or the agency which placed the ad.

Response to Expect

When answering large display advertisements in national publications for positions of management responsibility, your rate of response can be as low as

1 to 3 percent. When answering local advertisements requesting specific technical expertise that is in high demand, your rate of response can be as high as 100 percent. These are the extremes with lower rates of response occurring more often. The point is that you should answer as many help wanted advertisements as practical and then expect a response rate of only a few percentage points.

A company's answer can come in the form of either a telephone call or a letter. Letters will either express a polite refusal, a request for additional information, or a request for you to call to set up an interview.

Again, it's particularly important that you're not discouraged by refusal letters. You only want one job, and rejection is a part of making any sale. The larger the market you reach, the greater your chances for rejection, but also the higher your chances of success.

Should additional information be requested, respond immediately and supply the information even if it includes a résumé or salary history. In these instances, your letter will have attracted sufficient attention to cast your résumé in a more positive light. Send it with a cover letter expressing your interest in the position, referring to accomplishments in your résumé that reinforce your qualifications, and requesting a personal interview. If appropriate, keep the initiative and state a time you'll call to discuss the position. Then again request an interview during that call. In all cases when drafting such letters, review the ad and your original response to it before writing your cover letter.

If salary history or information is also requested, include this in your cover letter (see Workbook Form 41). For desired salary, always state a range and emphasize that your salary requirements would depend on a number of factors which could best be discussed in a personal interview. Also, review Chapter 18, of this Jobsearch manual before responding.

If the only request made is for salary information, respond by telephone. This will allow you to ask pertinent questions and also explain your salary range and the importance of other aspects of the job in establishing a final salary. You can then ask for an interview to discuss this matter in more detail.

Most telephone replies to your classified ad letters will be to set up a personal interview. In some instances the caller may wish to discuss several matters concerning the job and your background. This may constitute an almost complete job interview by telephone. Such calls are discussed in more detail in Chapter 15. Respond to all questions asked, while also indicating your desire to meet personally with the caller. You can sell yourself better in a meeting than by phone and should make every effort to set up an interview.

Situation Wanted Advertisements

Most help wanted classified sections of newspapers and trade journals include situations wanted columns. These are advertisements placed by individuals seeking employment. They are usually a waste of money, as they generally elicit responses only from companies or organizations that want to sell you a service or some franchise scheme.

In most instances, the individuals and companies you want to reach in your Jobsearch campaign don't read situations wanted advertisements. If they're read by companies at all, the task is usually delegated to junior members of the personnel department, people whom you specifically want to avoid. In addition, a short advertisement cannot possibly include sufficient information and accomplishments to seriously interest a potential employer. Your approach must be more direct and more thorough than such an ad allows.

The only exception to this would be an ad you might place in a specific trade journal or newsletter related to the position you seek. These types of trade journal ads, if they're effective at all, are usually best when seeking a position with a relatively small company, one in which the executives or department managers might read the ads themselves. If this fits your job objective, find the best trade journals or newsletters in your industry, the ones you read yourself, and place an ad. Then treat any responses just as you would a response to your other contacts. Review the situations wanted ads placed by Jerrold Brooks and Janet Parsons in Workbook Form 42.

12

Mail Marketing Campaign

One of the most effective methods of finding job opportunities is a massive mail marketing campaign. Although it sometimes surprised us, over 80 percent of Jobsearch clients secured their jobs through their mail campaigns. This direct contact with executives in a large number of firms uncovers job opportunities for positions that are not advertised and would frequently never be advertised. On occasion companies were interested in these letters from our clients when no vacancies existed. The resulting interviews convinced the companies to create new positions in order to add our clients to their organizations.

Executives in business and in other organizations plan months ahead for additions to or changes in key personnel. A growing company may plan to add a department or divide one department into two sections, thereby creating the need for a new department head. It may plan to open a new territory, thus creating the need for additional salespeople and sales managers, or it may recognize a weakness in its organization and decide that a change in personnel is warranted. Large companies hire college graduates on a regular schedule each summer.

Not long ago a large truck-body manufacturer acquired three other divisions. Although the organization had a corporate staff of only nine, every discipline was covered except personnel. At about the time that company started discussing its needs in this area, an industrial relations manager came to Jobsearch. Neither Ed nor this company knew of each other, but the company was on Ed's mailing list. After two interviews with no competition for the position, Ed had the corporate human resources job he wanted. It was interesting that six months before coming to Jobsearch, Ed sent résumés to over 400 executive recruiters resulting in interviews with only two companies. Neither had the job he sought.

During the last year, we helped a young bookkeeper who was seeking a part-time job while her children were in school. Because she had experience in the construction industry, this was her primary target. For part-time work, she felt smaller companies would be more inclined to need this type of sporadic assistance. Using the Yellow Pages, she picked 175 potential companies and then called each to get an individual's name for her mail marketing campaign. Because she had a home computer with a letter-quality printer, she was able to produce her own individually addressed letters. The results included twenty-five phone inquiries and nine interviews. On four of these the company representative asked, "How did you know we were thinking about hiring a part-time bookkeeper?" There were no other applicants. She found the job she wanted and a schedule that fit her needs.

Situations similar to these represent potential job opportunities for you. If an unexpected letter arrives from a candidate who appears qualified for an immediate or future position, that person will be interviewed. If you then sell yourself as the one to fill the vacancy or solve the impending problem, you'll be hired even though such a move might be considered premature.

Hiring good people is a difficult, time-consuming, and expensive process. When a well-qualified candidate appears, a company would rather hire him or her than advertise for, screen, and interview numerous applicants or pay an agency or recruiter to perform only a portion of this work. Your job is to find the companies that might need you to fill a position of this type. A mail marketing campaign can help do this.

Of course, the other major advantage to this Jobsearch method is the frequency with which you find yourself interviewing for a position against no other applicants. It's also exciting and stimulating to receive calls from companies genuinely interested in you. This improves your feeling of self-confidence and makes the interview process a pleasant, more productive experience.

Sources of Information

One of the most important items of information for a direct mail campaign is the name of the appropriate recipient for each letter. Just as a letter addressed to "resident" is frequently discarded unopened, a letter addressed to a company without the name of a specific individual seldom finds its way to the appropriate person. Your objective is to have your letter read by a company executive who would be interested in you and also have the authority to hire you if he or she wished to do so. Your source of information must provide the name of this person.

In addition to these names, the information source you use must disclose enough about the firm, its size, and its products or services to allow you to evaluate your interest in working there. You must also be able to determine the company's potential interest in someone of your experience or someone requiring your level of compensation. A manufacturing firm employing twenty-five people cannot afford to hire a vice-president or treasurer earning $50,000 a year. On the other hand, you may prefer working for a smaller organization where you would be called upon to exercise a broader range of responsibilities. To the extent possible, your sources of information must allow you to exercise these judgments.

For each of your job targets, find a listing of appropriate companies which includes as much of the following information as possible:

- Name and address of the company
- Name of the chief executive officer
- Names of other officers in the corporation
- Description of the firm's products or services
- An indication of the firm's size
- Number and location of divisions and subsidiaries

A number of suitable information sources were mentioned in the preliminary work section (Chapter 2) of this Jobsearch manual. If you've visited your public library and contacted appropriate chambers of commerce and other organizations, you should be ready to make specific choices concerning these sources. You will find that the chamber of commerce publications and state industrial directories are excellent for a Jobsearch campaign limited to a single or a few specific geographic areas. For a broader search, the Dun & Bradstreet *Million Dollar Directory* and *Middle Market Directory* are good sources. For specific industries or targets outside of industry, trade association publications or membership lists should be investigated.

Other possible sources of information can be found in the *Encyclopedia of Business Information Sources* and the *Guide to American Directories* (see Workbook Form 9). If your library doesn't have the directories you need, it may order them for you. Some may be inexpensive enough for you to order yourself.

To give you an idea of the specialized directories available, *The Advertiser's Red Book* lists most agencies in the United States. In addition to the information already described, this book also lists each agency's major clients. The *Martindale-Hubbel Law Directory* provides the names of all private lawyers and law firms. The *Polk Bank Directory* includes the information needed to choose and contact these financial institutions.

Vast amounts of information are available on American business and industry in every imaginable form. It may take imagination and effort to find what you need, but it can be done. Ask for help at your library. If you have a personal computer with a modem, check data base listings in the *Directory of On-Line Data Bases* and the *Computer-Readable Data Bases—A Data Source Book*. Call association offices; talk to executives and others in industries that interest you. Tell them what you're doing, what information you need, and why. From these contacts you'll find the directories or lists that suit your purpose.

Finally, don't neglect the Yellow Pages for local campaigns. Although this directory doesn't list all the information you need, it does have virtually every company in a city area listed by product or service. If additional information, particularly the name of an individual for addressing your letters, is needed, you can call the companies of interest. You'll be surprised how easily such a name can be found by talking to the receptionist or some other person through a blind call. Ann, the young part-time bookkeeper, did it with 175 calls made over a two-day span.

Choosing Target Companies

When choosing specific firms to include in your mailing, match the industry, size, and geographic areas of your job targets as closely as possible. Once again, however, be liberal in your choices. It's better to list too many firms than too few.

When your list is complete, most of the work is done. The cost or effort to type and mail additional letters is minimal. For these reasons, you should include between 200 and 300 companies for a local campaign and between 300 and 500 for one of broader scope. Except in special circumstances, if your initial list isn't at least this long, expand it. Go back and review both your information sources and your target definitions. Expand them in one or more areas even though these might rank lower in your job preferences. Using these expanded targets, review your sources and increase the number of entries on your mailing list.

Throughout this process you'll find it convenient to keep your written target definitions in front of you. You can then refer to them as you review information on companies and information from various sources.

When making up your mailing list, don't neglect medium-size and small companies. Mailing lists are available from commercial list brokers for the top thousand U.S. companies. These companies are, therefore, inundated with letters and résumés mostly addressed to the president or chief executive officer. Therefore when listing these firms, avoid the president; instead, try to address an appropriate vice-president. The majority of your list, however, should consist of firms that are not in this group. If you use the Dun & Bradstreet directories, take a larger proportion of the names, if not the majority, out of the *Middle Market Directory*. Regardless of your qualifications, write to firms where you will not be in competition with numerous other job seekers.

If your campaign is directed toward one city, be particularly thorough in your choice of companies. Check your mailing lists from the chamber of commerce and other directories against the telephone Yellow Pages for that city. Be sure to include manufacturers' representatives firms, consulting firms, and other organizations in the city that might be interested in you or know of companies that would be.

Whom to Address

The recipient of your letter should be the individual in the company to whom you would report if hired. The next best choice is the person to whom that individual reports. One of these people will usually be an officer of the company or the head of a department. In any case, it's preferable to address the letter to the lowest-placed executive holding responsibility over the position for which you are applying.

This is the individual most interested in having strong people working with him or her. This person will readily identify with your accomplishments and relate them to his or her daily problems. In addition, he or she will know of vacancies or weaknesses in his or her department which may not be known to higher officials.

Many sources of information list only a single name for each company, usually that of the president. Where other officers' names would be particularly difficult to obtain, addressing the letter to the chief executive is both sufficient and appropriate. This is always preferable to addressing an unnamed department head. You should, however, attempt to find a more precise target. *Who's Who in Business and Finance* may include some names not shown in other company directories. For companies in which you're most interested, call the office and get the information you want.

If for certain companies you absolutely cannot find an appropriate name, as a last resort address your letter to the appropriate department head with the salutation, "Dear Sir." This is better than not contacting the firm at all.

Mailing Lists

Make up a separate mailing list for each of your job targets. Usually these will have enough dissimilarities to require some differences in the wording of your marketing letters. You can then give each letter to the typing, computer, or direct mail service with the list of names and addresses corresponding to it.

Your lists must be written legibly and should contain the addresses with the same information and in the same format as will appear on the envelope. Include:

- The name of the individual
- The title of the individual
- The name of the company
- The street address
- The city, state, and zip code

If you plan to follow up any of your marketing letters with a telephone call, also list the phone number for your own use.

If your mailing list comes from a directory you own, it's not necessary to copy out all the names and addresses by hand. Simply put a bracket around the appropriate company name, using a red pen, and underline the name and title of the recipient.

Because you won't keep copies of each letter, it's advisable to file a copy of each mailing list with the appropriate letter at the end of the Mail Campaign section of your notebook. If you haven't written out the addresses, you can ask the typing service to prepare a list as it types the letters or create one as you type. The names and addresses should all be placed on the left-hand side of the paper. The right-hand side can then be used for notations of response and required follow-up. Any subsequent follow-up correspondence, notes, and records should be grouped by company and filed in the Prospects section of your notebook.

For your mail marketing campaign, it's important that all letters are mailed on the same day. When you're performing the laborious task of hand copying your mailing lists, you may want to spread out the job by doing one list or section each week, then mailing these letters and continuing the effort week by week. However, this is not advisable. One objective of your Jobsearch campaign is to secure multiple job offers simultaneously. If your mailing period is extended, you may find yourself in initial interviews with one firm while you are in final negotiations with another.

The Marketing Letter

As was the case with your responses to help wanted advertisements, send your mail marketing letter without a résumé unless you are a first-time job seeker or looking for an entry-level position. Your letter for each job target should be carefully organized and worded to respond to the probable interest of the recipient. It must also contain a specific statement of your immediate job objective.

Even if you have had a broad range of experience, each letter must be directed toward one job target that is well defined. It should be a job title or job description familiar to the recipient and one that is realistic. Indicating that you will accept any of several positions will dissipate the effect of your letter and severely lessen your rate of response. Business managers have specific, not general, problems. Job responsibilities are usually well-defined even for high-level positions. People are hired to solve these special problems and exercise the responsibilities of one job. They are not hired to motivate their subordinates in a general sense, or to exercise broad responsibilities encompassing several departmental functions.

Your letter should not allude to any unanswered questions concerning you or your career. Do not include any item that could be construed as negative or interpreted as a weakness. Do not refer to any aspect of your career that is not self-explanatory. All sentences in this letter should be short and to the point. Eliminate any extraneous words. Use as few adjectives as possible, and do not include gratuitous references to yourself or your career.

Study the ten examples of marketing letters shown in Workbook Form 6 and Workbook Forms 43–51, paying particular attention to the following descriptions of layout and wording:

- *Date.* All letters should show the date on which they will be mailed. If you are not producing the letters yourself, check with the typing service you intend to use about its workload and the time required to complete the letters. Add several days to this or the time you will require to produce the letters. This will give you time to sign, stuff, and mail them. Date them for the following Thursday or Friday but before deciding on a date, read the section in this chapter on When to Mail.

- *Address.* The address on both the letter and the envelope should show the name and title of the recipient, the company name, its address, and the zip code. Use abbreviations for Company (Co.) or Incorporated (Inc.) only if that designation is so given in your source of information. Use no other abbreviations in the address.

- *Salutation.* The salutation should read "Dear Mr. _____" showing the last name of the recipient. Do not use the salutation "Dear Sir" or "Gentlemen." If the recipient is a woman, the form "Ms." is usually preferable except in situations where the person has specified either "Mrs." or "Miss."

- *The first sentence.* Your first sentence should attract the attention of the reader. As with your responses to advertisements, it should include the single accomplishment of your career most indicative of your competence in the targeted job. In most cases this sentence should contain a reference to the title you held at the time of the accomplishment. It should also contain some reference to the company either by name, if that would be known to the recipient, or by definition of its industry and size. Before writing this sentence, review your accomplishments list again. Write several drafts. Study each of them, placing yourself in the position of the reader and then choose the most effective. If possible, the accomplishment used should be one that is quantified with numbers and has a direct relation to the profitability or success of the organization for which you worked. This is the most important sentence of your entire letter. It must make the recipient want to read what follows. Again, study the examples in the Workbook Form 7 and Workbook Forms 43–51. First-time job seekers should pay particular attention to Workbook Forms 47 and 48. After this review, write this first sentence with particular care.

- *The second sentence.* The second sentence acts as a bridge between your opening statement and the remainder of your letter. It should indicate why you're writing to the reader. It should also state that you might be able to respond to one of the reader's needs or help solve a problem he or she has. Finally, it should introduce a listing of your accomplishments. Study the second sentences in the sample letters in the Workbook section. Again, write several drafts for each of your letters. Then check each to be certain it responds to the above criteria.

• *Accomplishments*. In this section list an additional four or five accomplishments that best relate to your job target. Each should be complete, stating what you did and the results of your actions. Wherever possible, the accomplishments should be quantified. Use of the word "I" is optional. Base this decision on your personal preference and the number of times the word is used in other parts of the letter, but do not start your description of each accomplishment with "I."

• *The third paragraph*. This should contain biographical information similar in scope and intent to that used in your advertisement response. If the second sentence of your letter is not sufficiently descriptive of the job you seek or if you wish to qualify your job objectives, add an appropriate sentence at this point in the letter. It should relate, however, only to the job you seek. Do not include any reference to your personal objectives or career goals. Don't state that you're looking for a position that would use your talents to the maximum extent, or that you want to find a challenge or a pleasant working atmosphere. The reader doesn't care; he or she wants someone to help solve their problems or improve the performance of their department. Make them think you are that person.

• *The final paragraph*. The final paragraph should state your desire for a personal interview and whether you expect to be contacted by the company or plan to phone it. For a short list of companies or those in which you are particularly interested, it's wise to say you will phone. Then block out one or two days and telephone as many contacts as possible, setting up as many interviews as you can.

If your search is directed toward one or two cities far from your current home, it's particularly effective to state that you plan to be in the city during a specific period, usually three to five days about three weeks to a month after your mailing. You will then have to pay for the trip yourself but will find companies responding which would otherwise not have done so. Then make the best possible use of your time in that area for interviews, follow-up, and other local contacts that might produce job leads.

One Jobsearch client needed to relocate to Kansas City where he had inherited some property. He had never visited that city but used a mail marketing campaign to contact 220 Kansas companies. In his letter he mentioned a trip to that city. When he went to Kansas for one week, he had fourteen interviews all scheduled in advance, and came back with three job offers.

Computer Typing and Mailing Services

Once you've completed the final draft of each sales letter, they should be typed with a sample name and address, all using the identical format, spacing, and line length you want in the ones to be mailed. Indicate on each letter the target for which it's intended. These typed drafts and each mailing list should be taken to the computer typing or mailing service you've chosen and reviewed in detail with the person who will do the work. Pay particular attention to spelling, punctuation, and grammar.

If you're producing the letters yourself, making a sample for each target is still necessary. You'll need this to file with your list as well as use as a model as you type or run off the computer generated letters.

If you use one, the typing or mailing service will prepare your letters and envelopes and, if you have requested it, a copy of the mailing list. You'll then need to sign each of the letters and make sure you place each in the correct envelope. When stamped, the envelopes will be ready for mailing on the date indicated in the letter.

One small note of caution, however. Some mailing services will also fold and insert the letters after they're signed by you and will stamp the envelopes. Check to see how this will be done. It's best to use postage stamps for this mailing and not a postage meter, and certainly not bulk rate mail. Although the envelope may never be seen by the recipient of your letter, if it is, you want he or she to think they have received a personal letter from you, not one from a mass mailing.

When to Mail

The job market is somewhat seasonal and is also affected by holidays and vacation periods. The market is most favorable just after the first of January when businesspeople are beginning to act on their planning for the year. It falls off slightly during the summer vacation period, increases in the fall, and declines again with the approach of Thanksgiving and the Christmas holiday season.

For most Jobsearch campaigns you will have neither the luxury of time nor the inclination to delay your mailing for several months as you wait out summer vacations. Furthermore, the drop in hiring activity during this period is not sufficient to warrant such a wait. It is advisable, however, not to mail your letters during the period from the first week before Thanksgiving to the first week after New Year's Day. The letters should definitely not be mailed during the period from December 15 through January 5. Also, avoid mailing your letters during the week of any holiday, particularly if the holiday results in a long weekend.

It's best if your letter arrives on a Monday or Tuesday. This allows the recipient time during the week to respond without the break of a weekend. For this reason date the local letters on a Friday and put them in the mail on either Saturday or Sunday. Date and mail out-of-state letters one day prior to mailing your local letters.

Response to Expect

The first responses to your mail campaign will come in the form of telephone calls. These will all be positive indications of interest and will usually come within ten days of your mailing. A discussion of these calls is included in Chapter 15.

Following receipt of these initial calls, you will begin to receive letters. The total response to your mailing will greatly exceed that of your replies to help wanted advertisements; usually it will be over 25 percent. A large proportion of businesses will answer a personal letter even though the replies are negative. Therefore, the great majority of the letters you receive will be polite refusals. Do not become discouraged by the volume of rejections. They are a normal and expected part of any large direct mailing.

One Jobsearch client sent out as few as 157 letters that resulted in seventeen interviews. Another client, looking in a narrow speciality, sent out 600 letters in three successive mailings that resulted in only one interview. In both these cases, however, the jobs secured resulted from the direct mail campaigns.

Among your responses, some letters will be positive. Either they will request that you call to set up an interview or that you send a résumé or other information, or they'll show interest but be vague concerning follow-up or the availability of an opening. These should all be answered in the same manner as described in the section on Response to Expect in Chapter 11.

If the additional information requested is to be given on an employment application, fill out the form even though it may be designed for use by employees at a lower level than you seek. Mail it back with a cover letter expressing your interest in the job. If the application doesn't adequately cover your experience and accomplishments, attach a copy of your résumé. Even if you do this, however, fill out the application completely. Where negative information is required, such as the reasons for past job changes, be truthful but positive. Show that you are cooperative and follow instructions. Follow the sample letter given in Workbook Form 52.

Regardless of the response you receive, don't be discouraged. Responses to the mail campaigns of our Jobsearch clients came as much as three months after the letters were mailed. Many companies keep such letters pending future openings or changes. In large companies, the letter may be circulated for some time between divisions and subsidiaries. In most cases, however, you will have received most, if not all, of your responses one month after your mailing.

If your response rate is disappointing, consider continuing with a second mailing to different firms. The Jobsearch client mentioned above who mailed 600 letters in three groups had an advanced mathematical degree so esoteric there were only a few companies in the entire country that could use his talents. He found the one he needed, although it took an exceptional amount of effort. This, however, is a rare instance. The job you want is available. You only need to find it and then sell yourself into that position.

CHAPTER

13

Other Contacts

So far this Jobsearch manual has concentrated on the three most effective methods of finding job opportunities: personal contacts, answering help wanted advertisements, and conducting a direct mail marketing campaign. In most job campaigns, however, there are other avenues that can and should be explored. These consist primarily of contacts with other organizations or individuals that can often be of help. The effectiveness of these contacts will vary widely depending on your job targets and individual circumstances. It's not suggested you make all these contacts. Review them. Do enough research to determine which ones might be helpful and proceed with those that appear most attractive to your situation.

Just as with your personal contacts, it will be appropriate to give your résumé to all the contacts discussed in this chapter. These individuals would not normally represent organizations with job opportunities for you; instead, they can be a conduit to these opportunities. When passing your résumé on to potentially interested parties, they will generally include their own positive comments.

Employment Agencies

For entry- or lower-level jobs, employment agencies can be good sources of leads. For many Jobsearch campaigns, however, particularly those with targets at an executive level, employment agencies will be of little assistance. In some cases they may even be detrimental. These agencies are retained by companies to find applicants for specific job vacancies. Applicants are subsequently screened and interviewed by the company. If one of them is hired, the employment agency is paid a commission ranging from 10 to 15 percent of the first year's salary. For most jobs at the supervisory level or above, this commission is paid by the company. For lower-level jobs, the fee is frequently paid by the job seeker.

The employment agency's incentive is to provide as many applicants as possible for any vacancy. It has little incentive to do substantial preliminary screening of candidates. It has virtually no incentive to assist persons seeking employment by doing anything except distributing their résumés and sending them on as many interviews as they might accept. In your Jobsearch campaign, these interviews can be time consuming. Too frequently they're for jobs that match neither your targets nor your career goals. In addition, you may not want your résumé distributed to a large number of firms, many of which you might contact yourself in a more appropriate manner.

In spite of these negative possibilities, employment agencies can be of use in some campaigns. If you're conducting a geographically dispersed search in a narrow field, you may find there are employment agencies that specialize in your particular area. Robert Half International, Inc., for instance, specializes in the accounting and finance industries with offices nationwide. If you're conducting a campaign in one or more specific cities and are looking for a lower-level supervisory, technical, or administrative job at $15,000 to $25,000 per year, there are usually one or two employment agencies in each city that may be helpful. Finally, if you're looking for your first job, employment agencies may be a good introduction to companies in your field. In any case, employment agencies must be chosen with care.

Register with no more than two or three agencies for any specialty or in any city. If you're looking in a specialized field, employment agencies whose efforts are concentrated in your profession will be listed in small display ads in the help wanted sections of trade journals. If you find more than two agencies listed, phone and talk to the chief executive. Inquire about the number of people in your specialty the agency places per year and ask about other fields the agency covers. Request a listing of ten companies by whom the agency has been retained in the past six months. From answers to these questions you should be able to choose the two or three agencies that would be most effective for your campaign.

For a local campaign, choosing employment agencies is more difficult. Of the large number available, only a few will do substantive work with management-level personnel. For lower-level jobs, it is best to concentrate your efforts on the largest agencies, those most likely to be retained by a large number of companies. Phone the directors of personnel of four or five large companies in your target city. Ask them for the names of employment agencies and the individuals in these agencies whom they use for the type of position you seek. Define what your specific targets are, and explain your reason for asking.

From these conversations, you should be able to determine which agencies would be most appropriate for your search. Then register with them. To do this, phone the agency and ask for one of their agents. If you are seeking an executive-level position, get the name of the chief executive or the manager of the agency. This is the person with whom you should register.

If the agency is local, arrange a meeting with the person to whom you spoke. During this interview, you must be as specific as possible. Define your job targets. Explain the methods you're using in your Jobsearch, and ask the agency executive to define how he or she anticipates helping you. You must request that your résumé not be mailed out for jobs that do not match your targets. Also, explain that you don't want your résumé sent to firms that have not registered an appropriate vacancy with the agency. Specify a minimum salary on the high side of your range and state that you would prefer this subject not be discussed with a potential employer.

At the conclusion of this meeting, give the agency executive one copy of your résumé. Immediately following the meeting, write a polite confirming letter reviewing each of the points covered in your conversation.

If possible, for distant employment agencies, call one of their agents or the agency manager depending upon the level of position you seek and introduce yourself. Briefly explain the reason for your call and ask if it would be appropriate for you to register with the agency. Then confirm the call with a letter and résumé. As in a personal meeting, the letter must be specific regarding your targets and the use of your résumé by the agency. Look over the sample letters (Workbook Forms 53 and 54). With minor modifications, these same letters can be used as the confirming letter for a meeting with an agency.

When registering with employment agencies for positions other than lower-level jobs, do not fill out application forms unless they relate to the level of position you seek. Because these forms are primarily designed for use by administrative and office staff, they require information irrelevant to a job campaign with higher-level targets. They also frequently require information you might not want divulged to a prospective employer. If you are asked to fill out such an application and feel it is not appropriate to your search, explain politely that you prefer only to use your résumé and point out the items in the form that are not pertinent. If further demands are made, register with another agency. Also, avoid signing contracts that might bind you to paying the agency a fee or might result in fee disputes if you secure a job through other contacts with a company the agency suggested.

Executive Recruiters

Executive recruiters are firms or individuals who conduct employee searches for high-level positions. In most cases they look for a person with direct experience in their client's industry and attempt to steal such a person from another firm. It is because of this practice that executive recruiters have attracted the nicknames "headhunters" and "body snatchers." Their fees are 25 percent or more of the first year's salary and are always paid by the company. Because of these high fees, they are usually retained only by large and medium-size companies.

Although most executive recruiters are always looking for specialized talent, the larger agencies have high-level contacts with a number of companies who are clients only on a sporadic basis. If you're conducting a national search for a position at the district manager's, general manager's, vice-president's, or president's level with a company employing more than 500 people, you should register with executive recruiters.

The American Management Association (AMA) publishes a list of these firms. It includes each firm's address, its telephone number, the kinds of positions it handles, the minimum salary of each position, and the firm's willingness to review résumés and interview candidates on an unsolicited basis. There is also an alphabetical code indicating the type of services provided. Individuals' names are not given; however, it's sufficient in this case to address a letter to the firm only.

In choosing firms with which to register, use only those providing executive search, code "A" in the AMA list. Do not use licensed personnel agencies, code "D," unless they are appropriate as discussed in the section on employment agencies elsewhere in this chapter. Otherwise, firms can be chosen according to the kinds of positions they handle and the location of their offices. Register with between seventy and one hundred firms by using a computer-generated letter similar to one you might use with an employment agency (Workbook Form 54) or your mail marketing campaign. This letter should include a short summary of your qualifications and state your job objectives along with any limitations or restrictions such as geographical location. Salary should be mentioned in the same manner as in a letter to employment agencies. There is no risk these firms will distribute your résumé indiscriminately, and so this need not be discussed. Enclose one copy of your résumé with the letter.

College Placement Offices

In your preliminary work you will have determined if there are appropriate college placement offices that will submit your résumé to firms that have registered vacancies or subscribe to their listing service. For a job campaign covering a large geographic area, the placement office of your alma mater should be investigated. For a local campaign, register with all nearby colleges and universities that accept résumés from individuals who are not their alumni. Your cover letter should be personally addressed to the director of the placement office and should be similar in format and wording to that shown for employment agencies.

Trade Associations

Some trade associations provide services similar to those of college placement offices, for example, the Association of MBA Executives. For a minimal monthly fee this association will print a short summary of your background and job objectives in a booklet it submits to over 500 subscribing firms. On request from a subscriber, it will send the firm your complete résumé.

Again, from your preliminary information sources and the *Encyclopedia of Associations,* find out which of these organizations might be of help. Register, using another letter similar to the one shown in Workbook Form 54.

Accounting Firms

Accounting firms are frequently in a unique position to know of vacancies in or points of weakness at the managerial levels of their clients' organizations. Because of this and their close relationship with their clients, many of the larger CPA firms in major cities have placement officers. If you're seeking a job at a high-management level or any job in accounting or with management information systems, it would be appropriate to call the major accounting firms in the city or cities in which you are concentrating your effort. Ask if they have a placement service or officer. Talk to the person in charge and follow the registration procedure indicated.

When you have a personal contact with a CPA firm, make sure he or she has a copy of your résumé and knows of your search. Follow the procedure for other personal contacts.

For other local job campaigns, particularly those directed toward a job target in the financial area, register with the top 10 to 20 accounting firms, using a computer-generated letter similar to that for your mail marketing campaign. If possible, address the letter to the managing partner of the CPA firm by name. A quick phone call to the firms will give you these names.

You might also consider a mass mailing to a larger number of accounting firms in your preferred geographic area. Such a mailing was successful in a recent Jobsearch I conducted for a treasurer in Orlando, Florida. She sent a letter to the managing directors of seventy auditing firms in Orlando asking that they refer her to any appropriate client firms. Her job resulted from such a referral.

Chambers of Commerce

For campaigns concentrating on one or more major cities, advise the director of the local chamber of commerce of your availability and search. These persons are knowledgeable about the area, local businesses, and local business leaders. After determining the name of the appropriate individual, you can meet with or phone him or her and then send a letter and résumé.

Banks and Lawyers

Commercial loan officers of banks and lawyers specializing in corporate work also, on occasion, know of job openings with their client firms. These persons, however, do not participate in the job market as actively as others I've mentioned. For this reason, contact them only if you know them personally or have an introduction.

In my own career development, I've been referred to two troubled companies seeking presidents by friends of mine who were lawyers. In both instances, the lawyers had worked with me on other turnaround situations and knew of my work in that specific area. I secured the jobs I wanted with no competition from other candidates. The referral from those companies' lawyers was as good a reference as I could have found.

Employment Conferences

From time to time, advertisements for employment conferences appear in large-city newspapers. These are mass meetings designed to put job seekers and companies seeking employees into contact with one another. They're most effective for individuals in technical, rather than management-level positions. Even so, this can be a humiliating experience. You may find yourself in a group of from 500 to 1,000 job seekers all trying to arrange ten to fifteen minute interviews with overworked personnel representing fifteen to twenty major corporations. This kind of atmosphere is seldom conducive to a discussion in which you can sell your talent and experience.

For this reason, we've seldom found these conferences to be of much value. However, for technical jobs, particularly those in high demand at any given moment, a specific job conference can introduce you to a large number of companies quickly. Following these quick introductions, you can then take the initiative for follow-up using correspondence suggested for other methods in the Jobsearch manual. Once you have the introduction to these firms, the purpose of the job conference is complete.

Another form of job conference is the mass interview, usually conducted by high-pressure sales organizations and promoters of self-employment schemes. They recruit prospects with "come on" ads in the classified sections of local newspapers. The respondents find themselves in a room with fifty to several hundred job seekers listening to a series of men and women selling the job or "opportunity." This is done, for instance, in recruiting salesmen and women for time-share real estate projects, an industry known for both high-pressure sales and high turnover in their sales personnel. These types of conferences should be avoided completely. They're not even needed to get such a job, as these companies will hire virtually anyone who calls. If you find yourself inadvertently attending one of these meetings, leave and go back to work on more productive aspects of your search.

Employment Computer Data Bases

Over the past decade there have been numerous attempts to use the accessing and screening capacity of computers to match job seekers with job opportunities in large data bases. Many of these have failed for lack of use or the ability to match the cost of the system to the price charged for its service. There are, however, several data bases in operation that offer this form of job-to-career matching service.

If you have a personal computer with a modem connection for data base use, you should have reviewed, while establishing your information sources, the *Directory of On-Line Data Bases, Computer-Readable Data Bases—A Data Source Book,* or other similar directories available at most libraries. In these books you'll find listings of such career related data bases and methods of contacting their publishers. Where these can be used for reasonable cost and relate to your search, they should be considered.

There are, for instance, several job opportunity or employment registry data bases with a relatively narrow scope which could produce interesting contacts. There is one designed for scientists and professional engineers and another for library research personnel. For jobs of more general scope, Career Placement, Inc. of Alexandria, Virginia (703/683-1085), offers a Career Placement Registry carried on the Dialog Information Services data base. For a fee of $12 for entry-level positions to $45 for jobs paying over $40,000 per year, job seekers can enter their objectives and highlights of their résumés in the data base. The data can then be screened and accessed by any corporate subscriber to Dialog Information Services for a fee of $95 per hour plus $1.50 per record. This data base recently contained the résumé highlights of some 2,500 job seekers.

Another interesting data base is *Corporate Jobs Outlook* carried by Newsnet, Inc. (800/345-1301 or 215/527-8030). Although this service does not offer a job registry or matching service, it does publish current career and hiring information on 500 of the largest employers in the United States. These corporate profiles are updated at the rate of one hundred per year and include such information as comparative salary levels, employee benefits, training programs, company growth plans, and a ranking for employee career development. If your search includes these large employers, scanning this data base may prove helpful.

In most cases, these computer data bases are appropriate only if you have the required equipment and enjoy its use. For job seekers who fall into this category, it will require little time to find appropriate registries and enter your personal data. It can also be interesting to scan information such as that published in the *Corporate Jobs Outlook* and to compare your search objectives with those of others registered in the various data bases.

Networking

Another recent development in the job market is networking, which often involves clubs or associations for job seekers that offer contact with others in the job market and, on occasion, help in the form of speakers or industry-specific gatherings for the exchange of information. The oldest of these is The Forty Plus Club, a national organization for job seekers over forty years old. In Florida, the Professional Employment Network is sponsored by Job Service of Florida, a state agency. This is an organization for unemployed professionals and college graduates.

In each issue of the *National Business Employment Weekly* published by *The Wall Street Journal* there is a Calendar of Events, which lists by geographic region the meeting times and places for these organizations as well as job and career seminars. Over eighty such organizations and seminars were listed in one recent edition of this weekly. Although these groups have grown in popularity and number, they tend to lack the most important element for the job seeker—contact with the job market. By grouping unemployed people for an exchange of information, the scope becomes somewhat one-sided.

While you may find the emotional support of others with problems similar to your own beneficial, you may otherwise find these associations take a disproportionate amount of time from your search. You would be better served by organizing and executing a thorough Jobsearch campaign directed toward the available market for your services. Then if you want to meet to discuss your situation with others who are seeking jobs, these meetings may be appropriate.

14

The
Single-Target
Jobsearch

A single-target Jobsearch occurs in a campaign when there are one, or at most, two specific companies or organizations for which you would like to work. You should have definite reasons for this preference. Perhaps you've been particularly impressed by the company's history or its method of doing business. You might have close friends who work there and would be willing to assist you. You may know this company not only has a special need for your talent but also represents attractive potential for your career development.

John Fenner was one of our first Jobsearch clients. He wanted to join a new firm set up by three former colleagues. He was excited by their entrepreneurial spirit and knew he could work well with them as he had before. He did not, however, know if they needed his talents in their new venture. After pursuing this as a "single-target Jobsearch," he moved into the new company with the job he wanted.

For whatever reasons, however, be sure your preference for the specific company chosen merits the time and effort required to approach it as a separate target. Because a single-target campaign is time consuming, in no case should you devote this amount of effort to more than two companies. In addition, this Jobsearch method should only be conducted for managerial-level positions and always in conjunction with the other, more conventional methods discussed in this manual. After all, the single target chosen may not be in a position to hire you at the time you need the job. However, as John Fenner found, the method can be effective.

Identifying Single-Target Situations

The most important criterion for identifying a single-target company is your reason for wanting to work with that organization. Beyond this, you must be able to secure information, preferably from both inside and outside the company, which will allow you to completely develop your case for employment. Finally, you must have physical access to the company to gather this information and then present your case.

Prior to starting your Jobsearch campaign, you might have several such companies in mind. You may uncover others during your search. In either case, pursuing these situations should be only one part of your overall Jobsearch effort, except in instances where you'll be able to keep your current employment if you don't secure a job with the one or two preselected firms. However, if you feel that several specific companies or organizations offer particularly attractive opportunities for you, gather preliminary information concerning the companies and complete the "Single-Target Jobsearch" form (Workbook Form 55).

Compiling Information

In pursuing an individual company as a job opportunity, you need to secure two types of information. The first is a general but complete history and description of the company, including the department, division, or subsidiary for which you want to work. The second is the information you'll need to develop a thorough and convincing case for your employment. Both of these will involve substantial time, detailed research, and careful planning.

The company history should be accumulated and kept in outline form for your own use and reference. In the preliminary phase of gathering this information, don't divulge your reasons. You may explain to those you consult that you are doing a study of the company, its industry, or its markets. With this explanation, most people will divulge a surprising amount of information about their company.

If the firm is publicly owned, get a copy of its latest annual report. The company will send this on request. You might also ask for copies of annual reports for the previous five years. Request the latest 10-K and 10-Q financial reports on the company from the Securities and Exchange Commission, 500 North Capitol Street, Washington, D.C. 20549, 202/272-7450. This will include more complete financial data than that included in the published annual statement. You might also request copies of recent 13-D, 8-K, and Proxy reports. The 13-D will report recent changes in stock holdings by owners of 5 percent or more of the company's securities. The 8-K reports recent corporate developments, while the Proxy contains detailed information about the company's directors and officers. Copies of these reports are all available to the public at a cost of about 10 cents per page, or around $5–$10 each. They can be ordered by phone or with a letter addressed to the attention of "Public Reference." Ask to be billed the correct amount when the report is sent.

A commercial firm, Disclosure, Inc., will also supply these forms at slightly higher cost but with more rapid service. To contact Disclosure, call them at 301/951-1300.

Whether the company is publicly held or not, you can phone their public relations or administrative officer and request copies of all recent news releases. Also, ask if a company history has been published or if any other historical information is available to the public.

An officer of a bank can usually order a Dun & Bradstreet report on the company for you. This will provide information concerning the company's financial condition and credit rating. It includes a description of the products and services offered, a short history of the company, and short biographical data on the principal owners or officers. These reports are available on private as well as publicly held companies. They are also frequently available for companies with as few as one or two employees.

For large companies, go to the public library and look up the name of the company and the key words describing its products, its markets, or particular activities of interest. For this you can use the directories and sources found for other parts of your Jobsearch.

In this information search, be sure to include the *Business Periodicals Index*. This will give you sources of business magazine articles about the company, its markets, and its competitors. Order those you want from the publishers, or make copies of them from past issues in the library.

For local companies, look up these same items in the index of newspaper articles available at the main office of the paper. Finally, secure a listing of the officers and major department heads of the company or subsidiaries in which you are interested. If this isn't available from published sources, phone the company's competitors and suppliers. Obtain any names you can't get in this manner by calling the company's receptionist.

From all these data, write an outline history of the company. Pay particular attention to accumulating a concise record of gross annual sales, net profits, cost of goods sold, general administrative and sales expenses, total assets, total liabilities, stockholders' equity, and stock prices over the past ten-year period. You'll find it convenient and instructive to draw graphs showing the movement for each of these important financial indices. Use this information to calculate, record, and graph the return on sales, the return on stockholders' equity, the ratio of total liabilities to net worth, the stock price to earnings ratio, and the ratio of current assets to current liabilities.

Additional financial data of a similar type relating to your specialty, division, or department should also be accumulated, recorded, and graphed. For example, if you are interested in research, determine the total research budget and calculate its ratio to sales and earnings. If you're interested in sales, separate total sales expense and compute its relation to sales and earnings.

In as complete a form as possible, draw an organization chart of the company and the department, division, or subsidiary for which you wish to work. Gather as much information as you can about the individuals on this chart. Write short biographical sketches of them. Include any personality traits mentioned by others.

All the above information should give you a good working knowledge of the company with particular emphasis on the area of your intended job.

Developing Your Case

Once your history of the company is complete, concentrate on the information you'll need to develop the case for your employment. If possible, you will find it helpful to identify and cultivate within the company a close contact who can supply you with information. Because the target firm for John Fenner was formed by former associates, he had several lower-level employees in the company who were friends. These people gave him information of particular interest about the department and its staffing.

Because you will not want to divulge your objective prematurely, however, these contacts must be developed with care. They should not be persons whom you might replace or whose performance you might criticize when presenting your case. The ideal contact would be on the same level as your desired position, but someone who wouldn't feel threatened by your presence. It should be someone who has an interest in the same area of company activity as you and, if possible, someone who might benefit from your presence. You'll have to use your own judgment in deciding how much you can confide in this person and whether you should advise him or her of your objective.

In some cases, an inside contact as intimate as that just described is impossible to secure. This, however, shouldn't deter you from pursuing a single target. You'll simply have to rely on other contacts, either inside or outside the company, and on data more incomplete than you wish.

In developing your case for employment, concentrate exclusively on the contribution you can make to the company. Do not mention your personal objectives, your career objectives, what the company might offer you, or the satisfaction you might gain from your contribution. Address yourself to a need the company has or should have. Demonstrate how your fulfilling this need will contribute to the performance or success of the organization. Finally, show from your past accomplishments how you're suited to fulfill this need, perform the required duties, and achieve the projected results.

John Fenner was an expeditor in the purchasing department of a large construction company. He wanted to head that effort in his target firm and felt this new venture had grown to sufficient size to warrant such an effort. He was correct in this evaluation. After developing and presenting his case, the owners of the new company felt they needed and could support his talents. He was in a position to readily show what he could bring to the organization. Also, because he had worked with several of the owners in his prior position, they were familiar with his abilities. They were, however, not looking for such a person when John began his efforts. He found the job he wanted by demonstrating the need to the company owners.

For instance, you might be a salesperson who could open a new market or territory for the target company. Use your accomplishments to demonstrate your knowledge and effectiveness in this new market. Relate the cost of developing the market to the expected profits that could result and demonstrate how penetration of this new market will contribute to the continued sales growth and objectives of the company. If you're an engineer with particular experience in computer applications, demonstrate how these techniques might affect the scheduling and cost of the company's current engineering work. Relate the cost effectiveness of work you have performed in the past to the results expected for the prospective employer.

Your case should be developed fully in outline form for your own use. It should then be summarized in a concise, written report suitable for submission to the company.

Initial Interviews

After the prep work is completed, you'll be ready to present your case for employment. Your initial contact should be with the person who has direct responsibility over the functions you intend to perform. That person should also have the authority to hire you if he or she wishes.

In regard to your request for a job, the initial contact can be either direct or indirect. Use your own judgment in deciding which is more appropriate. For an indirect approach, you might present your case as an independent study or a portion of a larger study you are undertaking without any suggestion you are seeking employment. The objective in this approach and the subsequent follow-up is to induce the prospective employer to originate the idea of hiring you.

Another indirect approach is to have your case presented initially by a third party. It is best if this person knows both you and the company representative you wish to contact. Depending on the situation and your intermediary's knowledge of you and your contact, this can vary from a simple introduction of the work you have done to a complete disclosure of your objectives. Make this decision and review with your intermediary his or her entire presentation.

In the direct approach, present your case and your request for employment simultaneously. In most instances the direct approach is preferable. It cannot be construed as a subterfuge and explains the reason for and extent of your investigation. Finally, a direct approach also eliminates the possibility that a job will never be discussed.

Even though you may disclose your objective, the purpose of the initial meeting is primarily to exchange information. You shouldn't dwell on your desire for employment. Instead, concentrate on the company's needs, the methods of answering these needs, and the expected results. As an outsider who has developed his or her case without the benefit of complete access to company records, you should readily admit that your facts and assumptions may be incorrect.

Avoid being presumptuous and egotistical. No matter how thoroughly you've prepared your case, your contact knows more than you about the company, its problems, and its objectives. Question your contact carefully. Delve into the areas of weakness in your plan. Ask your contact if more study or further consideration of additional information may be warranted. Your intent is to stimulate the imagination and curiosity of your contact. Although you should not expect an offer at this first meeting, you don't want a refusal either.

Before going to this meeting, review Chapter 16. Pay particular attention to the sections on Managing the Interview and Questions to Ask.

If at the end of this initial meeting, your contact is convinced your plan may have merit and has agreed to provide you with additional information to develop your assumptions and projections, you will have succeeded. In John Fenner's case, his contact asked him to develop a department budget and job descriptions for the expediting function in the new company. To do this, he was given more complete access to the purchasing department.

Following the Jobsearch cardinal rule, confirm your initial meeting with a letter. Thank your contact for his or her time and interest and describe the work you intend to do as a result of the meeting. State the expected follow-up and its timing. Use the sample letter (Workbook Form 56) as a model.

Soliciting a Job Offer

In subsequent meetings, continue to expand both your case for employment and the idea that you are the best candidate to produce the projected results for the company. Gradually become more aggressive on these points until you receive a job offer or, at an appropriate time, request employment and instigate negotiations yourself.

If possible, do not accept an initial refusal. Ask instead if you can study the question further. Review your interest in the company. Be aggressive about the contribution you can make to the profits and success of the organization. Once again, until your contact has accepted the idea of your employment and you're negotiating for your position, don't mention benefits that might accrue to you or conditions you might wish to impose.

If you receive a definite refusal, however, be cautious as to your subsequent approach. It will be difficult to appeal to a higher authority in the company without requesting permission to do so from your initial contact. You should, however, make this request. You might also explore with your contact other divisions in the company that might be interested in your proposal. In addition, request information about or introductions to competitors or other companies with a possible interest in you or your proposal. If you've done your work thoroughly and have made a convincing case, you might find a more receptive audience in a company completely unknown to you.

Continue to pursue your interest until you have reached a successful conclusion or have investigated every possible approach. If your facts are right, if your case is convincing, and if you sell yourself, you will succeed.

THREE

Selling Yourself

CHAPTER

15

Telephone Interviews

A wide audience of potential employers is now aware of your career accomplishments and job objectives. Companies and organizations with an interest in you will begin making their initial contacts. The first of these contacts will be telephone calls. Virtually without exception they will be positive. Companies that do not wish to consider hiring you will respond by letter, if they respond at all. For this reason, you must be prepared to accept these calls and stimulate the initial interest of the caller.

Don't take a telephone call from a prospective employer at an inconvenient time. It's preferable to explain that you're about to leave for a meeting or are otherwise involved at the moment. You can ask to return the call at a specific time. If at all possible, the call should be returned the same day and as quickly as convenient for you and the caller. Return or accept the call at a time when you can sit down, concentrate on the content of the discussion, and remain undisturbed by extraneous noise or interruptions.

Preparing for the Initial Contact

For these phone calls, you must have your complete Jobsearch file arranged in your notebook and readily available. It's imperative that you know what you wrote to the caller, and in the case of help wanted advertisements, in what points or areas of expertise the caller is most interested.

If the caller is responding to your mail marketing campaign, determine which of your letters was sent to him or her. You might ask several questions that will relate the caller's company to the appropriate letter. Then open your notebook to that letter and have it in front of you throughout the conversation. Be careful, however, not to allude to your having sent letters to more than a small number of firms.

If the call is in response to a blind advertisement, tell the caller you answered several help wanted ads and ask to which he or she is referring. If the ad specified the company name, this single piece of information will help you find the letter.

The calls you receive will be of three types. The first is a simple request for an interview. The second is a request for additional information. The third is a conversation which can range from several questions to a nearly complete job interview by telephone.

It's easy to respond to the first two types of calls. If a company asks you to come for an interview, simply arrange a convenient time. If the interview requires travel, you can assume the expenses will be paid by the company. Unless the caller says something that leaves doubt in your mind, it is neither necessary nor advisable to ask. For instance, if the caller expresses a wish to see you when you are in the area, you should expect to pay for the trip yourself. If you don't plan a trip that would make the interview convenient, explain this. State your interest in the company and ask if it would bring you to their city for an interview.

If the caller wishes additional information, it should be forwarded in a letter or cover letter with résumé, as suggested in Chapter 10.

If the caller wants to discuss your background, respond to the questions asked. In doing so, however, remember your objective is to secure a personal interview. For questions that might require an in-depth discussion, give a brief response and tell the caller you would like to discuss the matter in greater detail when you have an opportunity to meet him or her personally.

This can be a particularly effective method of not responding directly to questions concerning salary. Unless you are pressed by the caller to state a definite salary range or give your salary history, you can explain that your salary requirements will depend on a number of factors including the scope of the job, its future potential, and the cost of living in the particular city. Tell the caller that salary should not be a major problem but that you would prefer to discuss it after you've had an opportunity to visit the company and find out more about the position.

It's important for you to take notes during this conversation. You should have a record of all questions asked by both you and the caller including a brief outline of the responses. This will give you a good indication of the items of major concern to the caller as well as the elements of your background and experience that are most attractive to him or her. You will then be able to elaborate on these points more effectively in a subsequent interview.

During the telephone conversation, be sure you get the complete name of the caller, spelled correctly, and his or her job title. For a difficult name, make a note of a phonetic spelling. This will assure your correct pronunciation later.

For each call you receive, start a file in the Prospects section of your notebook. Include a copy of your original letter, the notes from your telephone conversation, your confirming letter, and all subsequent notes and letters.

Questions to Expect and Ask

Review the sections on Questions to Expect and Questions to Ask in Chapter 16. Depending on the scope and length of the telephone conversation, you may discuss several of these questions briefly or be asked to elaborate on some of the points in your letter. Be prepared to discuss your background and experience and explain the contribution you expect to make in your new position.

If appropriate, you might also explain why you wish to make a change or left your last job. This is a question that will usually arise at some point in the interview process. In most cases it can be answered in a positive fashion, which will reinforce your qualifications for the new position. However, in cases where the answer could be construed as a negative, it's best to introduce the subject yourself and eliminate any negative connotations that might impede the progress of your subsequent interviews.

Although the focus of this type of telephone call will be primarily on you and your background, you should also question the caller. Your questions should not match the scope or number you would ask in a personal interview. They should, however, enable you to adequately determine the primary concerns of the caller, as well as demonstrate some of your qualifications and increase the caller's interest in you. Ask about the responsibilities of the job, the authority the jobholder would be granted, and the particular problems that need immediate attention.

The caller wants to know if you're sufficiently qualified to warrant the time and expense required to bring you to the company for a personal interview. Your objective is to stimulate his or her interest and prepare yourself for the subsequent meeting. Do this by concentrating on aspects of the job most important to the caller and most relevant to the problems needing attention. You can then relate your past accomplishments to these problems.

Don't be boastful or unctuous; stick to your accomplishments. These are self-explanatory facts. Don't be pretentious. The caller knows more about the company and its problems than you do. Never allude to the possibility of your being a panacea or that you could handle the position with unusual ease. Keep in mind that you can be eliminated for being overly qualified as well as for not having adequate qualifications.

Once again, don't ask questions concerning salary, benefits, working conditions, or your own personal goals. All these items should be discussed only in a personal meeting after the interviewer has decided in favor of you for the position.

Arranging a Personal Interview

If near the end of your telephone conversation the caller has not brought up the subject of a personal interview, you should do so. Explain that you would like to have an opportunity to meet him or her personally and perhaps meet other people in the company. If any portion of the physical facilities would fall under your responsibility, also mention that you would like to visit the plant or office and look over the production equipment and see the material or process flow.

Such questions relate to your evaluation of the current situation as well as the contribution you can make to the company. They're directed toward securing a personal interview but should also allude to benefits the caller might get from this interview. The caller needs to feel the interview will facilitate evaluation of your ability and perhaps introduce new ideas. The caller should also be able to anticipate an interesting discussion.

If the caller doesn't wish to set up an interview until a later date, maintain the initiative for the required follow-up. If the caller expresses a wish to talk to other candidates first, ask if you might check back about an appropriate date. Then call at that time and again request a meeting.

Initiating the Call

If you've stated in your letter that you will call the recipient, do so on the appointed date. If that person is interested in you, the content of your call will be similar to that already discussed. If not, use the call to gain as much information as you can. Ask the recipient how he or she felt about your letter, its content, or your background. Ask for the names of any other companies you might contact and for an introduction to them or the name of the person you should call. Even though that particular company may not have a suitable position for you, the call could be helpful to your Jobsearch.

If you don't get a satisfactory response to your mail marketing campaign, choose five or six firms to which your letter was sent and call them. Determine if they received and remember the letter. Question them about your approach, other companies you might contact, or the current demand for people with your qualifications. If you can spark their interest, ask if you might meet with them, but get as much information as you can during these calls.

Use each call to its maximum advantage. Gather information that will help you in your campaign and always try to set up a face-to-face meeting.

Confirmation and Follow-Up

Unless you've arranged for an interview within one week of the date of your telephone conversation, this initial call must be confirmed with a letter. If a date has been set, the letter need only confirm the date, time, and place of the meeting. It should briefly express your interest in the job and in meeting the caller and his or her associates.

If an interview date has not been set, the letter should again confirm your interest in the job and recite several of the points discussed that were of primary interest to the caller. Include several of your accomplishments that relate to these points. End the letter with a note of appreciation for the caller's interest and state your intention to follow-up with the date you expect to call.

Even if the result of the telephone call has been negative, write a confirming letter. If you're not interested in the job, this will be a simple thank you note. If you are interested, but the company does not appear interested in you, the letter should restate your desire for the job and indicate you would like to talk to the company again if it is unsuccessful in finding a more qualified candidate.

Look at the examples of these types of letters in Workbook Forms 57–59 as well as similar letters confirming meetings (Workbook Forms 64 and 65).

When placing follow-up telephone calls, you may find your contact is hard to reach. He or she may not return your calls or may be in meetings continually. Don't let this affect your determination or interest in the company. Too many busy executives, or those who think they are too busy, simply do not return calls. Keep trying. Leave messages with your contact's secretary and remember it's always to your advantage to have this person on your side. Make sure the secretary knows why you are calling, and chat with him or her if you have an appropriate opportunity.

If you can't reach your contact after repeated calls, send a fax message (see Workbook Form 60) if possible or a letter if not. But be careful not to let any anger or anxiety show through. The fax or letter should be a polite statement of your desire to talk with the recipient by phone, explaining your inability to reach him or her. If appropriate, refer to your earlier correspondence.

Throughout this procedure maintain the initiative, be positive, and remember your objective is to get an interview. If it isn't offered, ask for it. You'll never get a job without an interview during which you can sell yourself. Don't be overly aggressive but be polite, assertive, and confident.

CHAPTER

16

Initial
Personal Interviews

The initial personal interview will usually be a major determining factor in whether you receive a job offer. In many cases this will be your only opportunity to sell yourself to the prospective employer. It may also be your only opportunity to gather sufficient information about the job, the company, and the people to properly evaluate an offer when made.

You must be prepared for this interview, which means doing research and recording pertinent facts about the company. You'll prepare questions to ask and review questions that might be asked of you. You'll also prepare yourself to manage and structure the interview to your own advantage.

If you've been invited to a company for an interview, it's because your earlier correspondence created an interest in you. Your first meeting will be your best opportunity to reinforce this interest and turn it into a job offer.

Objectives for You and the Company

Your first and primary objective in a job interview is to convince the prospective employer that you can make a contribution to his or her organization, and that the company's investment in your salary and the time required to train you will produce a positive return.

This alone, however, is not enough. In many cases you'll be in competition with other individuals for the same position. You must then convince the employer that you're the best candidate or that your contributions would surpass those of other candidates.

You must also show the prospective employer that you'll be a compatible member of the organization. A company has character traits just as an individual does. These are formed from the predominant attitudes, lifestyles, and interrelationships of its employees, particularly those in its highest management. A company, for instance, may have a highly aggressive, extremely hardworking president who has attracted an aggressive group of employees.

114

Over a period of time the company itself begins to take on these character traits. A more conservative man or woman with an active family life would quickly feel ill at ease in this organization.

It's of equal importance that you gather sufficient information about the company and its members to evaluate the job in relation to your own qualifications, character, and objectives. Even though you may be able to sell yourself to a prospective employer, if you're not convinced your contribution will exceed the company's investment in you, you'd be ill advised to accept an offered position. Not only would you become frustrated by your lack of success, but you might also find your employment to be of short duration. The identical problem exists if you're incompatible with your colleagues, or if the potential of the job is not consistent with your career goals.

The primary objective of the company in an initial interview is an in-depth evaluation of you. It's as interested in your ability to contribute and your compatibility with its group as you are in selling yourself. It also wants to sell you on the company and the job. If it makes you an offer, it wants you to accept it.

Thus both you and the company are selling and evaluating. This similarity of objectives should facilitate discussion in the interview. Realizing that neither your objectives nor those of the company place you in an adversarial position should put you at ease. Use this similarity of purpose to strive for the maximum exchange of information. This will likely result in a smooth and pleasant interview. You'll be in a position to sell yourself without an obvious attempt to do so.

You should not be nervous. In fact, there's no reason to be nervous in an interview. Don't forget you're in a position to reject any offer made and will have other opportunities to evaluate. You're as much deciding if you want them as they are evaluating you. In addition, you'll prepare yourself for the interview with information about the company and questions to ask. This combination of preparation and options should give you a feeling of control and help you simply be yourself.

Dress and Personal Appearance

Regardless of what might be appropriate for wearing on the job you seek, go to an interview dressed conservatively. You'll never be faulted if your dress is somewhat more formal than that of the person interviewing you. You will, however, find yourself out of place if you aren't dressed at least to the interviewer's standard. For a man, a business suit with white shirt and tie is always appropriate no matter what level job you are seeking. For a woman, a conservative suit or dress, blouse, and jacket would be suitable.

If you're a man, don't wear shirts, ties, or sports coats with loud colors or prints. Your hair should be neat and well groomed. If you normally wear your hair long or have had a beard for a substantial period of time, don't change your appearance for a job interview. Make certain all other aspects of your personal appearance and grooming are neat and appropriate. Cut and clean your fingernails. Don't wear rumpled or soiled clothing. Have your shoes polished. Don't wear white socks or athletic shoes.

When Jeffrey McCauli (Workbook Form 26) interviewed for an electrician's position with Disney World, he dressed in a coat and tie. He kept his beard, even though he knew it would have to be removed for a job with Disney. He got the job, shaved off the beard, and now wears a Disney uniform to work.

All these guidelines for men should be translated into the appropriate style and grooming for women. In particular, women shouldn't wear overly bright colors. Nails should not be excessively long. Nail polish, if used at all, should be a muted color. Wear minimal jewelry. Shoes should be of a moderate heel height that doesn't make you appear awkward or ill at ease. Don't dress provocatively or appear overly sexy. Although this might attract some men, in a job interview it will be for the wrong reason. As with men, women should not drastically change their appearance for a job interview.

Maintain good posture in your interview without appearing stiff. Look up; look the interviewer in the eye as you speak or are spoken to. This will contribute to both your appearance and self-confidence. Don't chew gum, bite your fingernails, or adopt other mannerisms that make you appear nervous or ill at ease. If you wish to smoke, first ask if it will disturb others in the room. Don't even ask, if there are no ash trays or smoking materials in sight. In many companies smoking is out; if you smoke, now might be a good time to consider quitting. You may well find the job you want in a no smoking environment.

What to Take With You

For all job interviews take an 8½- by 11-inch note pad or clipboard, several copies of your résumé, a written list of questions you expect to ask, and an outline of the information you've gathered about the company, which should include all your past correspondence concerning the job.

Don't take your Jobsearch notebook or information or material you've prepared for other interviews. If your schedule necessitates your taking this material with you, leave it with your coat or in a briefcase in the reception area. You should appear well-organized and prepared. Don't place yourself in a position that would cause you to fumble through numerous materials to locate information you need.

What to Expect

Most job interviews will be similar to any other business meeting where the objective is an exchange of information. If you've followed the Jobsearch manual procedures thoroughly, you'll have a number of these interviews during the next few weeks. For this reason, no single interview will be crucial to the success of your campaign. More than anything else, this should help put you at ease. You'll have your best interviews when you are not quite convinced you would accept the position even if it should be offered. In this atmosphere you'll be genuinely interested in evaluating the company as well as selling yourself.

In most interviews you will meet with one or two members of the company. Sometimes additional people will be asked to join the meeting. If you feel outnumbered, diffuse this impression by commenting on your minority position, saying you don't want to be overpowered by their questions. They should understand that the questions you have to ask are as important as theirs.

On rare occasions, an interviewer may try to embarrass you or otherwise force you into a compromising position. Don't fall victim to this ploy. Simply use this information in your evaluation of the company and maintain your composure. If an interviewer persists in being offensive to such an extent that you would refuse an offer of employment, politely terminate the interview and leave.

The person facing you may know less about interview techniques than you. In addition, he or she may not be as well prepared. Use this to your advantage putting both yourself and the interviewer at ease.

Be punctual, but do not wait over 45 minutes to be seen unless you had to travel a long distance for the meeting. After you've waited this long, explain that you have another appointment and ask if you can reschedule the interview at a more convenient time.

Don't start the interview with an extraneous comment about something in the room or an unrelated subject. Introduce yourself. If you start the conversation, do so with an expression of your interest in the job or company. Your research will have uncovered facts about the firm which can be used to substantiate this. Because the interviewer is also interested in the job and the company, the meeting will then flow smoothly.

You may be asked to have lunch with one or more members of the company. If you have the time, accept graciously. The luncheon conversation will usually be more general than that in a formal interview. This will give you an opportunity to assess the people with whom you might be working. Order a drink only if others at the table do so; then limit yourself to one. When ordering food, follow the example of your host in quantity and price. Don't start eating until everyone is served, and maintain good manners; you're still being judged.

Finally, expect to be rejected. Every interview will not result in a job offer. Don't let rejection affect your self-confidence or determination. You'll have other opportunities. In any case, carefully evaluate all interviews after they're completed. Turn each one into a learning experience evaluating your performance and that of the company. This can be particularly helpful in future interviews with the same company or others.

Research Prior to an Interview

Prior to a job interview, gather pertinent information about the company and, if possible, about the person with whom you'll meet. This information should be recorded in outline form and taken to the interview. If the company is a large national firm, go to the library and look it up in Dun & Bradstreet or other appropriate directories. Consult *Who's Who in Finance and Industry* for the names of the people you might meet and check for recent magazine or newspaper articles concerning the company. The information you need is similar to, though not as complete as that described in Chapter 14; review this chapter.

If you and any of the people you'll meet have a mutual acquaintance, speak with this third party. Explain that you're going on a job interview and would like some background information. There's little need to fear that your inquiry will be reported to the company. Most people will guard such requests in confidence. Even if they don't, this knowledge will only emphasize your thorough approach and, in most cases, will be viewed as appropriate. Do not, however, ask questions of a personal nature or those that might be resented if repeated to your interviewer.

As minimum information about the company, for higher-level jobs you should know its gross annual sales and total number of employees, as well as its major products and services. You should have information about its profitability and financial strength and a record of its growth over the past several years. For lower-level jobs, this extent of information is not necessary, but more specific information about the department in which you might work would be helpful. In any case, be as conversant as possible with the company's history and specific aspects of its performance in the area of your expertise.

Managing the Interview

Although you can and should manage your job interviews, this does not mean you should take charge, initiate all discussions, or overpower the interviewer. Simply guide the questions and discussion in a manner consistent with your objectives as well as those of the company.

In a job interview, it's to your advantage to be on an equal status with the interviewer. If you do nothing except sit and respond to all questions asked, you will automatically be the interviewer's subordinate. This is the nature of a relationship between superior and subordinate: the superior asks questions, the subordinate answers. If, however, you ask enough questions to keep the interviewer talking at least half the time, you'll be his or her equal.

This means you must be prepared, have reviewed questions that might be asked of you, and come to the interview with a list of questions you expect to ask. You must be alert and sensitive to the reactions and feelings of the interviewer. Don't persist with questions the interviewer cannot readily answer or dwell on subjects that are obviously uncomfortable for him or her. Guide the discussion into areas where you can use descriptions of your past accomplishments to reinforce your case. Although you should not introduce numerous extraneous subjects, it's wise to break a lengthy interview with a discussion of items that don't require continual concentration or mental effort.

Introduce any negative information about yourself or your background in such a way that it will do you the least harm or can be most easily explained. For instance, if you have a bad credit rating because of your own company's failure, ask about the financial strength of the interviewer's company. Explain that your interest is based on personal experience with your own undercapitalized firm that failed and the affect this had on your credit. If you've held too many jobs, explain that you are asking a large number of questions to avoid making another mistake. Stress that you are looking for a career position and describe your approach to the job market.

If there's a possibility of negative information becoming known to the interviewer, it's best to bring it up yourself. Show you're not ashamed and have your future under control. Indicate that any negative aspects of your background are behind you and won't affect your contribution to a new company.

Most people speak approximately 150 words per minute. You can think at a far more rapid rate. Don't use this free time to allow your mind to wander as the interviewer presents questions or continues the discussion. Concentrate on the subject at hand. Pause if you wish to think before responding to a particularly difficult question. Use your mind's free time to consider the direction of the conversation. Then guide it with your responses and questions.

Over the past few years, role playing has become a widely used technique for training salespeople and others who are exposed to interview situations. As Jobsearch we gave all our clients a mock interview using these techniques. Everything from the introduction to the conclusion was kept as close as possible to a true job interview. We were as frequently surprised by clients who did well as by those who needed substantial coaching. In all cases, these interviews helped in structuring content as well as presentation.

If you have a close business friend who will take the time to give you a complete interview on a *pro forma* basis, this exercise can also help you prepare for job interviews. To do this effectively, define for your friend the position to be discussed and the type of company with which you might have an interview. Ask him or her to prepare their questions in advance. Then prepare yourself as thoroughly for this interview as for any other. At the appointed time, go to the meeting and conduct yourself exactly as you would in a job interview.

Continue the session to its logical conclusion before any comments or criticisms concerning your performance are made. When you've finished, your friend should give you his or her suggestions and criticisms on a completely frank basis.

Questions to Expect

Most of the questions you will be asked in a job interview will concern your past career and its relation to the job being discussed. If you're a first-time job seeker, these questions will concentrate on your educational background. You'll also be asked questions about yourself, your personal background, your likes and dislikes, and your motivation. On occasion you may consider a question too personal or inappropriate to the interview. If so, state your feeling about this and tactfully avoid responding.

Over the past twenty years, a substantial body of law has developed concerning what is legal to ask a prospective employee. A company, for instance, cannot ask your age or race. This does not mean, however, that some illegal questions will not be asked. They frequently are, and many interviewers don't know in detail what they can and cannot ask. If you believe that the questions asked infringe on the law or propriety, you have two good options. If the question does not bother you in any way, simply answer it. If you feel there is some compelling reason not to answer, state that you prefer to leave that subject aside. The interviewer should not persist. If he or she does, you can state that the answers to such questions are not required.

You may also be asked to explain some portion of your past career that offered you some difficulty, such as reasons you left past employers. Don't forget, some portion of every job candidate's background requires explanation. This is one of the purposes of a job interview. When offering a required explanation, don't show any embarrassment or undue defensiveness about your past record. If you believe you're qualified to perform the job, concentrate on the factors that demonstrate these qualifications. When negative matters are introduced, explain how they don't relate to the job in question or how the lessons learned better equip you for your future career.

An accomplished interviewer will ask questions that are open-ended, that cannot be answered with a simple "yes" or "no" or with a short statement. Rather than asking if you liked your last job, the interviewer will say, "Tell me about the aspects of your past job you particularly enjoyed." Be ready to field these inquiries with a short description or discussion, but be sensitive to its length. Don't dwell on any subject that does not seem to interest the interviewer. Be ready to ask a question of your own to guide the conversation into another area.

The list of general questions that might be asked in a job interview (Workbook Form 61) will be useful. Review these questions and think about the responses you might offer. You should add to the list, in the spaces provided, 15 to 20 questions relating specifically to your background or to the jobs for which you might interview.

Regardless of the questions asked, tell the truth. Elaborate only when it's to your advantage to do so, but don't be repetitious. Answer all questions directly and maintain a mutual exchange of information throughout.

Questions to Ask

The questions you ask in an interview are frequently more important than your answers to those asked of you. You can show a person more about your knowledge and the contributions you can make to an organization by asking the right questions than by answering his or hers. Your questions can also guide the discussion into areas where you can appropriately comment on your past accomplishments to maximum advantage. Finally, by asking questions you'll get the information you need to evaluate the company and the job.

Prepare your questions in advance of each interview. Write them legibly or type them, leaving spaces to enter the responses. The questions should be taken to the interview on your clipboard or note pad. As you receive answers, write a quick outline or several key words that will help you recall the response later. Although taking notes is unusual in a job interview, it is not impolite. Doing so should impress the interviewer with your thorough and organized approach. This will also reinforce the impression that you're there to evaluate the company and the job as well as sell yourself.

Your questions should be asked throughout the interview. They should be interspersed at appropriate points among questions from the interviewer. Don't divide the meeting into two distinct periods, one for the interviewer's questions and the other for yours. Instead you must maintain the atmosphere of a mutual exchange of information.

The questions you ask should all relate to the company and the performance of the job under discussion. They should be a preview of the types of questions you might ask during your first several days at work. They should also give you information that will help you sell yourself, write your confirming correspondence, and prepare for subsequent meetings.

Check the list of general questions appropriate in any job interview (Workbook Form 62). In addition to queries of this type, you should add those that relate only to the particular company or job. Your complete list should contain approximately twenty questions. Some of these will be answered in the course of the interview and therefore need not be asked. But attempt to get answers to all the questions you prepared.

An interview record (Workbook Form 63) is provided for your use during job interviews. It contains information you can fill in prior to the meeting as well as space for your questions. Make a copy of this form for each interview. You'll find it to be a convenient method of organizing your information.

When going on a job interview, try to arrive in the area 30 to 45 minutes early. Go to a nearby restaurant, order a cup of coffee or some other nonalcoholic beverage, and read the list of questions you expect to be asked, the list of questions you anticipate asking, and your accomplishments list. Think about each of these. You'll then be ready for the interview.

Subjects to Avoid

This emphasis on questions and answers doesn't mean that portions of the interview should not be composed of general discussion. Some of this will not be related to you, the company, or the job. For instance, you may find that you and the interviewer have a common interest. It will be both pleasant and productive to briefly discuss this subject. Do not, however, devote too much time to these unrelated subjects. Keep the main discussion directed toward the primary purpose of the interview, and be sure you have adequate time to sell yourself and ask the questions you prepared. It's also advisable to avoid some subjects entirely. Politics, religion, and other topics often considered controversial are not appropriate for a job interview.

Early in a job interview, you'll usually be questioned about your salary requirements. As in telephone interviews, this subject should be politely avoided until you're actually negotiating your salary and benefits package. In a meeting you might elaborate somewhat more than in a telephone conversation. Explain that salary is important to you, that you must work in order to gain your livelihood. Tell the interviewer, however, that it's not the only factor, and in some cases it may not even be the most important factor, on which you will base your decision. You can explain that you have a range of salary in mind, and are sure the company has also considered a possible range. Explain that when you know the company better and have received answers to a number of questions you wish to ask, you would hope a mutual interest would be established. At this point both the company's and your salary range will probably have narrowed and a discussion of salary would then be more productive. With a response of this type, you will usually not be pressed further. If you are, state a range you consider reasonable and one you would accept.

In most job interviews you'll meet the interviewer before he or she has seen a copy of your résumé. In such cases, the interviewer may request one at the beginning of the meeting. As previously explained in Chapter 7, you should tell the interviewer that you have prepared a résumé, but tactfully suggest you would prefer to leave it at the conclusion of your discussion.

People to Meet and a Tour of the Facilities

If an initial job interview has been positive, it's appropriate for you to ask to meet other members of the firm. These would include persons in superior positions or in a position at the level of the job under discussion. Such meetings should be short. You'll be introduced by the person who interviewed you. Briefly state that you are impressed by the company and are interested in the possibility of joining it. Any initiation of further discussion should be left to the other party. It may vary from a short, polite exchange to a summary of your entire interview. In any case, carefully judge the time these people have available for you. Don't continue the discussion if they seem pressed or occupied with other business.

Usually it's inappropriate for you to request to meet people who would be under your direct supervision in the new job. This can produce awkward situations as they try to prejudge their potential new boss. In some instances, they might not yet be aware of the changes that will bring you to the company. Also, remember that you might not be the candidate finally selected. In this instance, meeting subordinates would be premature.

If your new job would make you responsible for any portion of the physical facilities, you might request to tour them after the interview. Exceptions would be instances where plant facilities are prohibitively distant from the location of the interview, where a secret process or proprietary equipment is used, or where visitors to the plant are not permitted for reasons of safety or cleanliness. Make the suggestion only if the interviewer seems to have the time and if you feel the tour would be appropriate. If your interest in the facility is not genuine, don't ask. You may damage the positive impression left by the interview.

Expense Reimbursement

At the conclusions of an interview that required you to travel, ask if you should use the company's expense report form for reimbursement. If this is not necessary, purchase a standard form at an office supply company or use a copy of Workbook Form 5. When completing these expense records, be sure to enclose all appropriate receipts. Never send loose receipts with no recorded and totaled summary of expenses. This small detail is one more reflection of your businesslike approach to the job market and your sense of personal organization.

Employment Applications

Many companies require the completion of employment applications regardless of the position. Because most hiring is done for lower-level personnel, these forms request information that might be irrelevant to the job you seek. However, if an employment application is a part of the normal hiring process at a company with which you interview, fill it out completely. If the form is sent to you prior to an interview, complete and mail it or take it with you to the meeting. If taken to the interview it should be treated like a résumé and, if possible, not be given to the interviewer until the end of your discussion.

Avoid completing application forms in the company's office. Ask that you be allowed to do it at home after the interview, and state you'll mail it back to the company. It should then be completed with the same care afforded a résumé. Where work experience is requested, it should be accomplishments oriented. Although the applications must be filled in completely, avoid giving negative information, if possible.

A good practice with applications is to make a photocopy. Fill in the copy by hand and then use a typewriter to fill in the original. This will prevent messy erasures and improve the appearance of the completed application. If it's to be returned to the company by mail, do so promptly with a covering letter that can also serve the purpose of confirming the interview.

Psychological Interview and Testing

Some companies hiring for high-level positions may request that you undergo a psychological interview or test as part of their hiring and evaluation procedure. In today's world this may include a polygraph or drug testing as well as simple company physicals. Don't attempt to avoid such tests or psychological interviews, but look on them as potentially helpful to both you and the company. This is an additional effort by the company to ensure it makes the best possible decision in hiring its personnel. This kind of testing can also prevent you from making the mistake of joining an incompatible group or perhaps undertaking a job for which you're not suited.

After the tests are completed, it's appropriate that you request copies of any reports or test results. In the case of psychological testing, you might also ask to discuss the results with the psychologist even if you are not offered the position. These reports or discussions can be both interesting and enlightening. They can give you clues that are applicable to your career goals. If you're not offered the job, they can also help you direct the remainder of your Jobsearch campaign.

An interview with an industrial psychologist will usually occur during a meeting that can last two or three hours. The atmosphere will be cordial. The discussion will center on your past work experience and your family life with emphasis on your likes, dislikes, and motivations. This meeting is different from the job interview; you shouldn't be trying to sell yourself directly nor should you be trying to impress the interviewer. Your objective is to state as frankly and thoroughly as possible who you are and why you're that way. In doing this, however, you'll find it wise to again concentrate some portion of the discussion on your accomplishments. Use those that show your imagination, ability to work under pressure, or other personality traits. The psychologist will not try to judge your technical capabilities, but is primarily interested in you as a person.

Although you should ask fewer questions than you would in a job interview, the industrial psychologist can usually provide insight into the personalities and motivation of the individuals who make up the company's management. You may question the psychologist about this and let him or her know you are as interested as the company in finding associates with whom you fit.

There are two basic forms of psychological test. The first requires answers to questions. Usually of the multiple choice type, these can be graded right or wrong. The second form asks you to describe yourself either with written phrases or by checking or ranking descriptive words. Make every effort to tell the truth when taking these tests. Don't try to second-guess the intent of the test or to create an overly favorable impression. These tests have been developed over a number of years and given to thousands of job applicants. Because they contain questions that will indicate your sincerity, you will do yourself a disservice by not being frank.

Hundreds of different tests exist to measure virtually all items of personality and intellect. They can be roughly divided into five types.

1. *Tests that measure ability.* These can be used to judge both intelligence and academic skills. At best, they predict readiness for academic work. They don't, however, measure either drive or determination, both of which have an influence on the ability of a person to perform an assigned task.

2. *Tests that measure temperament.* These tests define character traits such as aggressiveness, sociability, passivity versus activity, and dominance versus submissiveness.

3. *Tests that measure personal values.* These tests indicate an individual's likes and dislikes. They can also measure personal values such as honesty, loyalty, empathy, and desire for recognition. Both the temperament and the personal value tests can be used to determine suitable directions for job choices. They also give an indication of compatibility with a job and with another group of individuals.

4. *Tests that measure areas of interest.* These tests offer some measure of vocational interest as well as basic interest areas in the individual's life. Several commonly used tests measure the relative interest of an individual in working with his or her hands, with money, on artistic endeavors, in social services, at investigative tasks, and at administrative or conventional office tasks. One of these tests correlates the likes and dislikes of an individual with those of a large number of people who have been successful in specific fields. This can give an

indication of motivation, probable success, and compatibility in a chosen area of work.

5. *Tests that measure mechanical aptitude.* These tests measure such items as the recognition of spatial relations, the understanding of things, and the ability to work with one's hands.

None of the above tests should place you under undue strain or pressure. They're easy and in many cases enjoyable to take. Approach them with a sense of interest and curiosity. They'll serve both you and the potential employer well.

As already mentioned, there are other types of tests used by some companies in the hiring process. One of the more difficult tasks at any company is hiring and keeping good people. There's always an effort to improve or simplify this task with some form of test that will forecast results. Testing fads come and go including handwriting analysis, ink blot reaction tests, and forms of IQ evaluation. While some of these may help, it is unfortunately impossible to forecast a person's ability to perform a specific job, but it's important to attempt.

If testing is a part of the hiring process you encounter, approach it positively. It will probably be a help to both you and the company. Although the law on testing is murky, we had Jobsearch clients who took most of the types mentioned. Regardless of the legal connotations, don't refuse to take any test requested. It will be a learning experience for both you and the company.

Confirmation and Follow-Up

Every job interview, whether positive or not, must be confirmed within three days by letter. If you have not received a definite offer, use the notes from your interview to pick out several of the major problems of concern to your contact. Repeat these in your letter along with your corresponding accomplishments. If you've received an offer, express your appreciation and interest, confirm the offer, and then state when you will respond.

For all pending prospects, your letter must conclude with a statement of the expected follow-up. If it can be done tactfully, maintain the initiative or indicate you will phone if you have not heard from the company by a certain date.

Even in cases where you've been turned down, make every effort to leave the door open for future discussions. There may be a change in the company or in your Jobsearch, which would create a renewed interest.

There are examples of these types of letters provided in Workbook Forms 64–67.

After each interview, add the notes and your confirming letter to the Prospects file in that section of your notebook. The follow-up should be put on your To Do list.

CHAPTER

17

Subsequent Interviews

If a company asks you to return for a second interview, it either plans to offer you the job or has narrowed its choices to you and one or two other candidates. If salary and benefits have not been discussed earlier, this will be an appropriate time for negotiating these items as discussed in Chapter 18. This second interview will also afford both you and the company additional opportunity for evaluation and for exchanging more information.

For the male candidate applying for higher-level positions, your wife may also be invited on the trip and to the interview or a dinner meeting. If a move is part of the new job, this will give her a chance to see the city, perhaps begin gathering information for her own Jobsearch, and do preliminary house hunting. For high-level positions, many executives want to meet the wives of key employees prior to offering them a job. Make every effort to have her accompany you if she is invited. The cost of child care, should this be necessary while you are gone, will be a reimbursable expense and should not be difficult to arrange.

For the high-level female candidate, being joined by your husband on a second interview has become increasingly prevalent. Many husbands are following as their wives move up the corporate ladder. Just as with the wife's trip, an appearance by the husband gives him an opportunity to evaluate job possibilities for himself in the new city and to begin gathering his own Jobsearch information.

In today's world of two-career families, it is also a frequent practice for high-level positions requiring relocation for the company to offer some assistance to the spouse in finding local employment. If you are in this position, at an appropriate time you may want to discuss with your potential employer the position held by your wife or husband, opportunities in the local area, and what assistance they might offer. Of course, once you know your decision, your spouse can immediately start his or her own Jobsearch directed only toward that city. Suggestions or contacts supplied by your new employer should be an excellent start for that search.

A second job interview is not unusual even for relatively low-level positions in the local area. As the position sought rises in the corporate hierarchy, a third interview may be requested. In only one instance, however,

127

did a Jobsearch client have to go on more than three interviews prior to receiving a job offer. In that particular case Harry was called back seven times, gradually working his way up the corporate ladder from the division interviewing him to the headquarters office. It all took three months and substantial stamina. Two other candidates got discouraged and dropped out, but Harry finally received an offer he accepted and has had two promotions since. That company was unduly cautious, but they did choose well.

Additional Research

From the information gathered in your initial interview, you should be able to judge the probable scope and content of subsequent meetings. This is the time to do additional research. If specific problems were explored in your first meeting and you believe they will be subjects of future discussion, ask for information that might assist you in reviewing the questions and possible solutions.

I once decided to make a radical career change into investment banking. Although I had experience in finance, skills in writing, and a project orientation, all of which related to investment banking, I knew little about the business. After securing initial interviews with two small, local companies, I found three books at the library on investment banking and its development in the United States. Over a four-day period I read all of these and took copious notes. For the second and more intensive interviews, I was ready. I spent twelve years in that business before financing a company I then decided to run.

You might also go to the library and check for that background information on the industry or aspects of the job that may be unfamiliar to you. Call friends or associates who have handled jobs similar to the one you discussed. Question them about their problems, solutions, and results.

Review your notes from the initial interview. Try to pick out areas where additional discussion will further establish your competence for the job. Develop more specific questions concerning these areas and note which of your accomplishments best reflect them. Review, and if possible expand, your sources of information about the company. You might now make calls to competitors or others in the industry that were too time-consuming or expensive earlier.

You're now ready to finalize a job offer. Show you were interested enough to do some work on your own; the company will be impressed that the time between interviews was not wasted.

Managing the Interview

Once again, tactfully manage the interview to your own advantage. In meeting persons for the second time, you will find the atmosphere more relaxed and the exchange of information freer. Your questions can be more specific. You can delve into company problems that might not have been appropriate subjects for your first encounter.

Meet additional company officers and key personnel to whom you were not introduced originally. For higher-level positions, if you didn't visit important company facilities because of location or other reasons, suggest such a visit when setting up your subsequent interviews.

Try to gauge the interest and commitment of the company to both you and the position. If a job offer is not forthcoming and you feel the company has adequate information to make a decision, review the status and schedule of your Jobsearch with them. Reiterate your interest in the job and the company. Then set a time with the interviewer when you will need a decision. Remember, however, this must be done tactfully. If you have no other offers immediately pending, do not force a decision.

Confirmation and Follow-Up

Again, a confirming letter is required. It should, however, be friendlier in tone and shorter than previous letters. Vary the content sufficiently to prevent the appearance of a stereotyped approach. Unless a specific problem was discussed, it's not necessary to repeat your accomplishments. If you've received a job offer, confirm it and indicate when you'll respond. If you expect a future offer, state that you look forward to receiving it. Be positive and direct. You have sold yourself and now must take the time to evaluate this and other opportunities. Look over the example of a short confirming letter shown in Workbook Form 68.

18

Salary and Benefits Negotiations

In any interview or sequence of job interviews, there will be a specific time when it's to your advantage to negotiate the salary and benefits package to be included in a job offer. The time for this negotiation is when the interviewer has decided he or she wants you to join the company. You are no longer selling yourself; your services are being bought.

It's not difficult to determine when this point arrives. The interviewer will begin to talk about you as if you were already a member of the group. The pronoun "we" will begin to be used instead of "you." The interviewer will speak increasingly in the future rather than the present and past tense.

This is not, however, a signal for you to begin the discussion of salary. It's only an indication that you can approach the negotiations directly when appropriate. In most cases the subject will be introduced by the interviewer. If that doesn't happen and you need the information for your own evaluation, simply state that you're interested in the position and would like to discuss the salary and benefits package. An interviewer who has decided to hire you will be glad to talk about these matters.

Source of Comparative Salary Information

Before you begin negotiating your salary and benefits package, you must not only have a feeling for what the company might pay but also have information on competitive prices for your talents and experience. For the first-time or entry-level job seeker, you may be able to find someone in the company who can give you an idea of the starting pay rates. In addition, you should call several companies in the local area to inquire about their salaries for comparable positions. This information can usually be found by speaking to the Personal Director or someone in that department. Simply explain that you're discussing a position with another firm and need some basis for understanding the pay rate you might expect.

Except for a career change, for higher-level positions the first and most obvious source of salary information is the past record of your own earnings. What were you worth to your last employer and what has been the size and frequency of pay increases during your career? In most cases you can expect an increase with a change of position. This may even be one of your primary reasons for seeking a new job. If you have a past record of success, coupled with a history of increases in responsibility, use this record in your negotiations for higher pay.

Another source of salary information for such positions also comes from the company itself. If you've answered an advertisement, a salary or salary range may have been mentioned. In your initial meetings, the interviewer may have given you an indication of the salary. If you have a close contact or friend in the company, you can ask that person about salary levels. Even without knowing the salary range for the position you seek, your contact or friend can probably give you some idea of the benefits package offered by the company, and can also tell you whether the company pays higher or lower salaries than others in the industry or in the same geographic area.

Other companies with positions similar to the one you seek are also good sources of salary information. If you're being interviewed for a job as senior accountant or controller, call a firm of similar size and type and ask to speak to the treasurer or vice-president of finance. Introduce yourself; explain that you're negotiating a position with another firm and would like information on comparative salaries. Describe the job briefly and name the company with whom you are negotiating. Several calls of this type should prove fruitful. It's advisable, however, not to call companies having close contact with your target firm.

In addition to these direct sources of salary information, published data are available concerning pay scales in almost all positions and industries. One of the best sources for this information is trade associations. Many of these conduct salary surveys periodically and publish the information for salaries in low, medium, and high ranges by area of the country and by different company sizes. As an example, the Society for Human Resource Management publishes a biannual survey of salaries paid to personnel directors. Available for eighteen regions of the country, this information also includes length of experience, age, scope of responsibility, years in present position, and level of education. With telephone calls to several associations in your field, you can quickly determine if such information is available and order a copy.

Trade journals occasionally publish salary surveys. Call the editorial offices of journals in your field and ask if they compile such studies. If they do, request the latest issue of the magazine in which the survey was reported.

Another excellent source of comparative salary information is help wanted advertisements in newspapers. In your ad answering campaign you will have gathered a number of clippings from various newspapers listing salary along with job titles and responsibilities. You might also review advertisements you didn't answer.

The directors of employment agencies are usually well informed about salary levels in their area and generally will be glad to discuss them with you. In the case of agencies that specialize in one field, some publish salary data. Robert Half International, for instance, which specializes in the accounting and finance industries, publishes an annual Salary Survey which is available free through any of their offices. Calls made to several such agencies can be useful and productive.

The American Management Association (AMA) also publishes a number of salary surveys. These are listed nationally and for five regions of the country. Although the entire survey for any group is too expensive for your needs, the AMA will give you data by telephone (212/586-8100) at no charge for any one position. Their surveys and the prices for them are:

Top management	$300
Middle management	250
Professional/scientific	220
Supervisory management	165
Sales personnel	165
Technician	120
Office personnel	120

The AMA information is particularly useful for comparative salaries at the highest levels of management, which are difficult to obtain from other sources.

In addition to your research on salaries, if your new job will require moving your family, you should review the relative cost of living in cities where you may receive an offer. Real estate agents in these cities are good sources of information concerning housing costs and can sometimes give you comparative cost-of-living data. A cost-of-living index by city is also available from the chamber of commerce and the U.S. Department of Labor, Bureau of Labor Statistics.

All the information you receive from these various sources, however, must be interpreted with care. The salary the company is willing to pay and the salary you're willing to accept will depend on numerous items, the majority of which are intangible. Among these, you should take into consideration the following:

- Living cost in the area
- Current supply of your specific talents in the job market
- Current demand for your talents
- Size of the company
- The industry in which the company participates
- The type of company or organization

- How well you have sold yourself for the position
- The trade-off between salary and benefits
- The financial strength of the company
- The future potential for increased earnings
- The trade-off between salary and potential equity
- The company's ability to alter pay scales set by policy

From an evaluation of this information, you should be able to establish a realistic salary range equitable to both you and the company. Prior to the start of negotiations, write down this range together with the factors and data on which it is based.

The Negotiation

Just as you do, the company will also have a range of salary it considers equitable. Although it's not always possible, it is to your advantage for the person with whom you are negotiating to disclose the company's range or offering salary as an introduction to the negotiations. If this salary is not compatible with your expectations, state that it is close or a little lower than what you had in mind. Then proceed to a discussion of benefits. In most cases the company will pay somewhat more than the initial salary offered although their flexibility will decrease as the level of the job decreases. For jobs above entry level, however, you should leave the door open to take advantage of this possibility.

If the offered salary is acceptable, say that it is consistent with or quite close to your objective. Do not, however, indicate immediate acceptance of the first offer. After you've received other offers, you may want to ask for more.

If you're placed in the position of having to disclose your desired salary before knowing what the company will offer, don't give a range but state a definite figure at the high end of what you expect. If this is acceptable, it will immediately become the basis for your starting salary. If it doesn't appear to be acceptable, you can then discuss the reasons and the data supporting your request. Indicate some flexibility and suggest both you and the company consider the matter further. In any case, state that you're not in a position to accept an offer immediately as you have other possibilities to evaluate.

Regardless of whether your starting salary is definitely fixed during these conversations, don't accept the job until you have had time to properly evaluate all its aspects and to conclude negotiations with other interested companies.

If you've sold yourself well and the company would like to have you join their organization, don't let a salary discrepancy completely rupture negotiations. Even if the offered salary is substantially lower than what you want, indicate you are interested in the position. Explain that the salary is lower than what you expect, but you would like to consider it for a few days or weeks.

Request that the company review your qualifications and potential contribution in relation to the salary offered. Depending on other offers you receive, you may wish to accept the position at a lower salary than you expected or subsequently convince the company to increase the starting salary or include other benefits that might make it acceptable.

A Jobsearch client interviewing for a position as senior vice-president of operations for a bank holding company found every aspect of the job and offer acceptable except salary. The two parties were close to agreement but the salary offered was not quite what he wanted. He was, however, an unknown quantity for the bank since he had no prior banking experience. He used this point to his advantage by getting the bank to agree to a salary review after four months instead of one year. All he needed was a little time, he explained, to prove his value. Four months later, he had the salary he wanted.

Salary negotiations should result in your getting all the information you need to evaluate the offer. You will then be in a position to call the company at a later date and say one of the following:

"I would like to accept the position offered."

"I will accept the position if we can agree on a starting salary of $_____."

"I will accept the position if we can agree on a starting salary of $_____ together with _____."

The completion of this last sentence might be an expanded benefits package, additional perquisites (perks), or a guaranteed salary review after a shorter than customary period of time.

In a salary negotiation, don't forget that a company's initial offer is just that—an offer. In many cases, you can get the company to increase it. Although you cannot afford to appear unreasonable, you naturally want to be paid as much as you are worth to your new company. If it pays you less than this, you will be unhappy. If it pays you more, your new job may be one of short duration. The negotiation is used to arrive at a point that is equitable for both parties.

Employee Benefits and Perquisites

An immense range of employee or fringe benefits is offered by American businesses. Except at the highest levels of a company, the benefits package isn't usually open to much negotiation. Nevertheless, you should discuss all benefits offered and gather enough data to evaluate the monetary equivalent of each.

If certain desired benefits are not offered, you can discuss them with the expectation of their being provided in your case or of your receiving a compensating salary increase. However, because fringe benefits are offered equally to all employees at a certain level, companies usually have more latitude in setting salaries than benefits.

Following is a list of fringe benefits generally arranged in the order of most common to most rare with some indication of, or sources of information about, their monetary value.

• *Vacation and holidays.* Although all companies offer both these items, policy and extent differ widely. In a job change you may find you lose your vacation privileges until you have been on the job for a year. Be specific when discussing this question. Vacation policy for new employees is frequently flexible. If you've planned a summer vacation that isn't consistent with company policy, mention this and see if the vacation waiting period might be modified in your case. Don't do this, however, if you would not have a minimum of four months on the job prior to your vacation. Convert your yearly salary to a daily rate by dividing by 240. Use this figure to determine the monetary value of vacations and holidays.

• *Group insurance package.* Most companies offer a standard group insurance package to employees. These frequently provide different coverage for different groups, although there have been some recent efforts to standardize this through legislation with a new law passed and then repealed. In many companies today, these differences still exist. Of course, the most extensive coverage is offered to top executives. A different package is available for middle management and other salaried personnel. Insurance for hourly paid personnel either is determined by union contract or is again a separate plan. When discussing the company's program, be careful to determine whether it's a contributory program requiring a portion of the premiums to be paid by the employee or whether it's fully company paid. In contributory programs, the employee portion is usually deducted directly from the salary at each pay period. Ask the exact amount of these deductions for each type of insurance offered. Also determine the extent of coverage for each type of insurance. With this information you can call a local insurance agent to check the cost of similar coverage on an individual basis. In the order of frequency offered, these group plans will cover medical, life, accident, major medical, disability, dental, and legal expenses.

• *Sick leave and pay.* As with vacations and holidays, determine the sick leave policy of the company, including the number of days of salary continuation. If it's a standard number of days per year, convert these days into their salary value.

• *Automobile.* This company benefit can be of substantial monetary value to an employee. Depending on the amount of travel for both business and pleasure, the value to you of a company car will vary between $2,000 and $6,000 per year. Although IRS tax rules now require computing nonbusiness use of a company car as taxable income, for the employee, a company automobile can still be an attractive method of compensation. It's equally attractive to the company because its monetary value doesn't become part of the salary base for payroll taxes, pension benefits, and other fringes. A company car should be evaluated with care. It can frequently make an otherwise low salary both attractive and competitive. This is particularly true for sales positions where extensive travel by car is a part of the job.

• *Expense account and travel reimbursement.* Ask about the expense account and travel reimbursement policy of the company. Except for the highest level of executives, these perquisites will generally include reimbursement only for expenses incurred on company business. Policies vary widely, however. Some companies pay a standard per diem for travel, room, and board which may not be adequate to cover your normal travel expenses. If this is the case and much travel is required, it will have the effect of a straight reduction in your pay. Also be careful about the income tax considerations, if you can understand the extremely complex set of rules recently enacted. The IRS has decided to tax certain expense account reimbursements which were formally not considered ordinary income. If you will travel extensively in your job, you might want to discuss the company's reimbursement policies with an accountant.

• *Retirement and pension plans.* Although you may be years away from retirement, these plans are still important to your job evaluation and future security. As with insurance programs, they are sometimes contributory. If this is the case, determine the amount that will be deducted from your salary. Also inquire about the company's contribution in your specific case. If you're young, it's of utmost importance to ask about the vesting provisions of the plan. After you have served a certain number of years with the company, it provides for payment at retirement age of a portion of the benefits, even though you might leave prior to normal retirement. Also determine if the plan is of the "defined benefits" or the "defined contribution" type. Defined benefits provide you with retirement pay on a calculated basis known in advance. Defined contribution plans relate your retirement pay to the performance of an investment made by the company over the years as well as your salary history. Most companies today are using or converting to defined contribution plans.

• *Profit sharing and bonus.* If these are offered, determine if they are paid yearly or become part of a deferred earnings pension plan. They will work to your best advantage if they are cash payments calculated on the basis of an established formula. It's also preferable for you to be in a position of direct influence over the portion of profits included in the formula for your position. These plans are least attractive if they're based only on the discretion of a company management group of which you are not a member. In either case, ask about past bonus levels for the position you seek.

• *Stock options.* In a small company this can be an excellent method of gaining future equity and building your net worth. In larger companies these options represent a form of deferred earnings payments with favorable tax consequences. If stock options are a major portion of your benefits package, check with an accountant to determine the tax implications when the options are granted and exercised. The accountant can also estimate the monetary value of the options, if it's not evident from the plan or company contribution.

• *Educational opportunity.* Many companies will pay all or a portion of the cost of continuing education for their employees. If you intend to make use of this benefit, determine if your curriculum is consistent with the reimbursement policies of the company. This can be an attractive fringe benefit.

• *Sabbaticals.* Some professional groups and companies offer periodic sabbaticals to technical or high-level management personnel for study or research. If you work in an area of rapidly changing technology, this can be indeed attractive. When sabbaticals are offered, ask if your salary or a portion of it will be continued while you are off.

• *Personal time off.* Determine the policies of the company in allowing time off for necessary personal business, deaths in the family, or other items that might require your attention during regular business hours.

• *Country club memberships.* These are generally offered only to the highest-level executives or to those who must entertain extensively in the local area. If such a perquisite is offered, ask about the choice of clubs and learn something about their membership and status. Call the club to ask what the dues are. Be careful in evaluating this benefit, however, as the dues may be taxable income to you unless the club is used only for business purposes.

• *Medical payment plan.* These plans pay all medical expenses for select groups of company executives and their families, including doctors' visits and prescription drugs. For a large family these plans can represent substantial monetary value. Review the medical deductions on your income tax forms for the past several years to determine their value to you.

• *Education for children.* A few companies offer college scholarships for dependent children of their highest-level employees. Although this benefit is rare, the monetary value of such a plan is substantial.

Moving Expenses

When a new job requires you to move, discuss moving reimbursement in detail. If you've received a job offer as a result of a response to a national help wanted advertisement, it's customary for the company to cover the moving expenses for your family. If, on the other hand, you search out your new company, it may not have assumed it would incur these costs. This can be a major expense, which might affect your willingness to accept a new position.

You must not only ascertain the extent of the moving cost to be reimbursed, but also determine the company policy concerning temporary living expenses while you're searching for a new home.

Of equal importance is the company's policy concerning the sale of your present residence. Most companies will not indemnify you for costs or losses incurred in the sale of your home. Some, however, will pick up mortgage payments if the sale entails a prolonged period of time. Some will pay the real estate commission and closing costs on the sale. A few will actually buy your home at an appraised value, allowing you to immediately purchase a new residence and begin your job with the least inconvenience.

There are also income tax considerations in moving expense reimbursement. Some moving expenses are deductible for federal tax purposes, but these are limited to a maximum amount. If you're reimbursed for an amount exceeding this maximum, the excess may be taxable income. Ask an accountant about these expenses. If the company intends to indemnify you for all moving costs, try to have it include the estimated tax liability on reimbursements classed as income.

Salary Reviews

As already discussed, salary reviews can also be important in your negotiations for a new position. At the very least, determine the company's policies on salary reviews, including both cost-of-living adjustments and merit pay increases. If your negotiated salary is somewhat lower than you expected, you might compensate for this by having the company agree to a salary review after a short period. This would be before the normal review period but after you've had sufficient time to demonstrate your contribution. Four to six months is usually a reasonable period.

Opportunity for Promotion

This point is appropriate for discussion, particularly if your career objectives require a number of increases in job responsibilities or elevations of job status. You might briefly review your five- and ten-year objectives with your future superior. Discuss how you expect to reach these goals. Determine the past promotion practices of the company, the ages of your immediate superiors, and the ages of others in the company who have attained the levels you seek.

However, don't give your future employer the impression you will leave if not promoted after a brief period. On the other hand, unless you are only a few years from retirement, your employer should understand that you will not sit complacently in your new job for the rest of your career. The potential for advancement is an appropriate factor in most job evaluations. I would caution the first-time job seeker, however, to approach such discussions with particular care and perhaps eliminate them entirely. At an entry level the company is sensitive to high turnover and does not want a cadre of impatient, young employees. After all, you will have a substantial period of learning—one of the major tasks and joys in an early job.

Employment Contracts and Termination Agreements

Employment contracts are normally given only to seasoned executives in high positions. In today's litigious world, however, they are more frequently used than in the past. Usually their purpose is to compensate an employee who leaves a stable job for one of higher exposure and risk. A younger person should be more willing to let job and future remuneration depend on his or her own capabilities and contributions. If you're in the latter situation, discuss employment contracts only if one is offered by the potential employer.

If an employment contract includes a "noncompete" agreement, consider it with care. This can prevent your working for a competitor or entering the same business as that of your employer for a specified number of years after you leave or are terminated. You may wish to have such a clause reviewed by a lawyer. Don't sign it perfunctorily. Years later it may cause problems for your career.

A friend of mine signed such an agreement in 1965. Twenty years later, at age 72, he wanted to do some consulting work on a new product development. The old agreement surfaced and ended his employment.

Termination agreements, often called "golden parachutes," are used to protect both the employee and the company in the event the job does not work out or internal changes in the company eliminate the position. They serve to set the conditions of termination for both employer and employee. Termination agreements are also included in employment contracts for jobs involving high professional risks. Such a position might be a top executive's job with an unprofitable or failing company or a management position that historically has been subject to high turnover. These agreements stipulate the termination provisions or severance benefits if for any reason the employee is dismissed from the new position. Such agreements are appropriate but should be discussed only if mentioned by the company, or if other circumstances lead you to believe they may be important. You certainly don't want to give the impression in these negotiations that you are immediately concerned about termination.

Confirmation by Letter

After you and the potential employer have reached agreement on all aspects of the offer, it should be confirmed in writing. If you think the potential employer might normally do this, ask whether you should confirm the offer or whether the company would prefer to do it. If you write the letter, again express your interest in the job and indicate a definite time by which you will accept or reject the offer. An example of such a letter appears in Workbook Form 66.

Timing for Acceptance

Depending on how far along you are in your Jobsearch campaign and on additional offers you expect to receive, the time during which you can appropriately consider an offer will vary from a few days to a month. Except in rare circumstances, don't expect a potential employer to wait more than one month for your reply. In most cases, you should limit this maximum time to three weeks. Your objective is to gain only sufficient time to expedite and evaluate additional offers. To do this, immediately advise other companies that showed an interest in you that you have an offer to which you must respond by a specified date. This tactic should not be used, however, unless you are definitely interested in the initial offer. If the other company isn't ready to make a decision, it may turn you down prematurely.

Record of Offers

Keep a record of each job offer by filling in Workbook Form 69. For each offer, combine this record with all correspondence in your Prospects file. Then use this information in your evaluation of the jobs offered and your next career move.

CHAPTER

19

Evaluation of Job Offers

After you've received all the job offers you expect, thoroughly evaluate them individually and in comparison with the others.

Even if you've received only one, it will be necessary to evaluate it and review all other responses from your search. This evaluation will concern three possible options: to accept the offer, to delay acceptance and re-contact other companies that indicated a future interest, or to reject it and return to your Jobsearch campaign with a new and expanded effort.

An evaluation form (Workbook Form 70) is provided, which includes both concrete and abstract criteria for job evaluation. These relate to the job targets and career goals established in Chapters 4 and 6, with additional items concerning the company and the job. Several blank spaces are provided for other criteria that might be of particular interest to you.

When using this form you may rank each item first, second, and third for different job offers. You may rank each item on a scale of one to ten individually. Or if you prefer, simply enter "good," "fair," or "poor." Some items will be more important to you than others.

In addition, your final job decision must include intuition as well as preference by rank. Because of this, do not total the columns and then choose a job based on the highest numerical score. Rather, consider each point carefully and then consider the total job. Your decision will establish the next step for your entire future career.

Renegotiation

After you've finished your first evaluation, you may find one job or company that you prefer but would reject for one specific reason such as salary or scope of responsibility. In such a case, consider phoning your contact or making an appointment for a meeting at the company. Tell your contact why you prefer the company; then review the deficiencies in its offer. In the case of salary, you might ask if the company would match or perhaps come closer to that offered by another firm.

This form of renegotiation should not be used, however, unless your preference and the competing offer are genuine. You must be prepared to disclose the name of the other firm as well as the specifics of its offer. If this renegotiation proves fruitful, be prepared to accept the new position immediately. If it's not successful, you will have compromised your position with the preferred company and will find it difficult not to accept the offer from the competing firm.

Advising the Offering Firms

After you have accepted an offer and established a starting date for your new job, confirm this acceptance in writing. Refer to the earlier written confirmation of the offer, but repeat only the specifics that were later modified (see Workbook Form 71).

In addition, write to each of the other firms that made you an offer. This letter (Workbook Form 72) should politely thank the firm for its consideration and advise it you have accepted a position elsewhere. The firm will then know it should consider other candidates or return to its search to fill the position.

20

The Move

Ronald Marque needed to change careers in order to use his educational training. He went from a line job in mortgage banking to a senior staff financial analyst's position. Karilyn Naff started out looking for a controller's position; she is now a legal administrator for a law firm. Carter Harlen is executive director of a new natural history museum that needed his combination of fund raising ability and business administration background. Susan Abrams is now a junior design engineer with a turbine generator manufacturer. Other successful Jobsearch clients have been mentioned throughout this book. You can join them. It takes only hard work, good judgment, and perseverance.

My father was an executive with an international engineering/construction firm. When asked the secret of his success, he replied that it was a combination of luck and hard work. "But," he added, "it's the strangest thing. The harder I work, the luckier I get."

With your successful Jobsearch campaign now complete, you must prepare to take your new position. If you're currently employed, it will, of course, be necessary for you to resign. The starting date you establish for your new job should permit you sufficient time for an orderly completion or transfer of unfinished work with your old company. During this period, take care to maintain good relations with your former employer and to avoid adversely affecting the morale of your colleagues. Sometime in the future you may need the help of some of these people.

When you resign, do so politely but decisively. Don't try to bargain with your old employer before resigning. If you use your offer as a tool to gain concessions in your current job, you may succeed only at the price of severely damaging your credibility and future chances for promotion. Your old employer will know or may learn the new job did not just come to you. It's likely he will discover you sought the new job with the intention of leaving your current one and may be afraid you will do this again in the future.

Even if your old employer makes an unsolicited counter-offer, don't acquiesce. You have accepted employment with a new firm and must honor your commitment to it. If you wanted to stay with your old company, you should have had a frank discussion about your job and its conditions before you began your search.

Relations With Your New Employer

Your new employer will be anxious to have you join the organization. You'll also be excited about the change, the challenge, and the opportunity. If it seems appropriate, you might request preliminary information for study during the transition period. You might also meet on occasion with your new associates. You should not, however, act as though you were on the job until you are there on a full-time, salaried basis.

If your new employer is a long distance from where you now live or if you don't have occasion for contact during the transition period, don't show up on your starting date unannounced. Call several days in advance to remind the company that you will report for work at a specified time.

During the period of transition and your first few days on the new job, don't concentrate on insignificant matters that relate to your own comfort. Don't worry about your office, desk, or other facilities. Concentrate on learning about the job at hand, and probe for the problems that need your initial attention. This is what you were hired to do.

Your new job was found by dint of a thorough and concerted effort. You've had an opportunity to investigate employment possibilities with a large number of companies. You have evaluated and accepted a job offer that should be consistent with your initial objectives. You must now give your new employer your best effort.

Final Correspondence

Throughout your Jobsearch campaign you received the advice and assistance of a large number of people. As a courtesy, write to each of them informing them of the results of your search and thanking them for their help. Follow the sample letter shown in Workbook Form 73. Compile the mailing list for these letters by going through your entire Jobsearch file. Write a short note to everyone who offered real assistance. At some future date, you might again need the help of these people.

The Final Word

You've succeeded at a long and difficult task, but one that I hope was both interesting and exciting. It should have been, for you've now set your career on a new path with a new job in a new company. I've enjoyed all the jobs I've gotten for myself; I also enjoyed working with hundreds of people like you, helping them achieve their career goals. As you progress through your career, you may once more find yourself in the position of seeking new employment. Keep this book as a reference for the next time. Then perhaps I can help you again.

The Jobsearch Workbook

You'll work better against a schedule, even a tentative one. Use this form to establish that schedule for all your Jobsearch tasks.

Work Schedule

Name: _____   Date: _____, 19___

Item	Scheduled Completion Date	Modified Completion Date	Actual Completion Date
Start date			
Order stationery and photographs			
Establish information sources			
Complete accomplishments list			
Establish career goals			
Define marketing targets			
Draft résumé			
Check reference responses			
Type and copy résumé			
Complete personal contacts list			
Draft help wanted reply letters			
Start answering help wanted ads			
Draft direct mail letters			
Complete direct mail address lists			
Type direct mail letters			
Send direct mail letters			
Complete personal contacts			
Complete other contacts			
Examine single target Jobsearch			
Complete single target information			
Contacts for single target			
Complete job interviews			
Evaluate job offers			
Accept new job			
Report to work			

You'll need this as well as other expense data, on Forms 2 through 5 for your income tax records. Fill them in as each expense occurs with a cumulative total. You'll know the cost of your search as you progress. When your Jobsearch is completed, file these data with this year's income data.

Summary and Miscellaneous Expense Record

Name: _____

Date	Item	Expense	Cumulative Total
	Jobsearch Manual		

Automobile expense record for all auto use involved with your Jobsearch. Record your mileage with each trip, even to the copy center; deductible mileage adds up fast.

Automobile Expense Record

Name: _____

Date	Location	Person Seen	Mileage	@ 26¢/Mile	Total

Telephone expenses can be extracted from your monthly bill. Complete the first three columns of this form at the end of each Jobsearch related call, then add the toll charges when your bill arrives.

Telephone Expense Record

Name: _____

Date	City Called	Person Called	Toll Charges	Add 10% Tax & Service	Total	Date Paid

Use this travel expense report when you will not be reimbursed by the interviewing company or when that company doesn't supply its own form. In any case, keep a copy for your deductible expense records.

Travel Expense Report

Report No.: _____

Name: _____   Date: _____, 19___

	Date					
	Itinerary from					
	To or at: Item					Totals
Transportation	Personal car					
	Airplane					
	Rental car					
	Limousine or rail					
	Taxi					
	Parking					
	Lodging					
Meals	Breakfast					
	Lunch					
	Dinner					
	Telephone					
	Miscellaneous					
	Total					
	Purpose of trip					

Signature _____

Third-party mass mail marketing letter used in conducting an anonymous search.

H. LEE RUST
3404 East Briarcliff Road
Birmingham, Alabama 35223
Telephone (205) 967-9728

February 15, 1990

Mr. William F. Blakley, President
Southeastern Manufacturing, Inc.
2200 Fifth Avenue, North
Birmingham, Alabama 35202

Dear Mr. Blakley:

I have a business associate and friend who, as controller for a large food distributor, designed and implemented an inventory control system which cut losses and credits by $2,500 weekly. Because you may need a controller or financial executive with this kind of talent, you may be interested in a few of her other accomplishments.

As treasurer or controller of four companies ranging in size from $5 million to over $43 million in annual sales, she designed and implemented systems for converting all accounting functions to computer operations, including work with microcomputers, service bureaus, and large systems.

She recognized the need at a franchise operation and set up a buyer's guide showing inventory movement, source, and delivery information. This allowed a 50% reduction in purchasing department personnel.

She designed installment sales accounting procedures including an automatic delinquency notice system which reduced average delinquent time on accounts receivable by 60%.

In cash control, she set up and managed an investment portfolio which increased after-tax profits on invested funds by $25,000 annually.

Because this woman is now employed with a company you probably know, I must keep her name confidential until a mutual interest is established. She has 20 years of corporate accounting and financial experience, has an accounting degree from the University of Georgia, and has taken continuing education courses in computer use, tax procedures, accounting, and speed reading.

If you would like to meet with this person or further discuss her background and experience, please call me at the above number after 5:00 P.M. or during the weekend. I might add that this letter is personal. I will not receive a commission or fee of any kind as a consequence of employment that might result.

Sincerely,

H. Lee Rust

[The *Jobsearch* Workbook continues on page 154.]

FINANCIAL ACCOUNT EXECUTIVE

New opportunity for person with good agency/financial experience. Someone with background in servicing a sizable bank advertising account, in marketing financial services, or in a financial advertising operation would be ideal. Fine growth potential. Midwest. 4A agency. Profit sharing plan. Young full-service team. Need your résumé and income range.

AD COUNSEL JOURNAL
P.O. Box 65267, Atlanta, Ga. 47165

Advertisement response letter for an anonymous search.

H. LEE RUST
3404 East Briarcliff Road
Birmingham, Alabama 35223
Telephone (205) 967-9728

February 21, 1990

Ad Counsel Journal
Post Office Box 65267
Atlanta, Georgia 47165

Dear Sir:

I have a business associate and friend who is a leader of an innovative marketing organization in a $1.2-billion bank holding company. He managed the 10th anniversary celebration of a major subsidiary that drew 25,000 people through ten branches in one day.

Because you advertised for a financial account executive, I thought you would be interested in some of his other accomplishments.

He led a task force which was used to solve special marketing problems for both the holding company and its bank subsidiaries.

He wrote print ads and brochure copy for a Campus Plan Account promotion which opened 2,000 new accounts in the first six months.

For a new, small-town bank, he created and directed the grand opening promotion that drew traffic equal to 10% of the town's population.

He personally sold bank services and solicited new accounts, exceeding his annual quota by over $60,000.

Because you probably know this man's current employer, I cannot disclose his name until a mutual interest is established. However, a marketing degree and four years with an in-house bank agency have prepared him to respond to the needs of your advertised position.

If you would like to meet with him or further discuss his background and experience, please call me at (205) 669-0711 or, after 5:00 P.M., at the above number. I might add that this letter is being written as a personal favor. I will not receive a commission or fee of any kind should you reach agreement on his employment.

Cordially,

H. Lee Rust

Example of stationery and envelope used in a jobsearch. Stick to a business format with block letters in 8½" by 11" size. Personal stationery will not do.

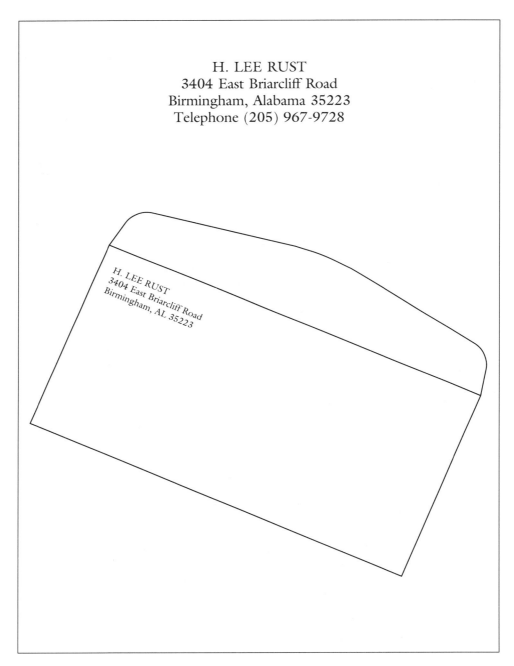

H. LEE RUST
3404 East Briarcliff Road
Birmingham, Alabama 35223
Telephone (205) 967-9728

H. LEE RUST
3404 East Briarcliff Road
Birmingham, AL 35223

This list is only a sample of the useful books available at most public libraries. Don't neglect this source of information, which is readily available and easy to access.

Business Reference Books
Available at Public Libraries

Million Dollar Directory
Middle Market Directory
Principal International Businesses
    Dun & Bradstreet
    New York, New York   Phone (212) 608-9170
Businesses are listed alphabetically, geographically, and by Standard Industrial Classification (SIC) code. Names of company officers are also shown.

Standard & Poor's Corporation Records
    Standard & Poor's
    New York, New York   Phone (212) 208-8000
A synopsis of corporate information and financials.

Standard Industrial Classification Code Manual
Listing of business types by code numbers established as a standard by the government.
Directory of Occupational Titles
List of standard occupations by title.
Franchise Opportunities Handbook
Listing of franchises available in the U.S. with brief synopsis of each, indexed by category.
    U.S. Government Printing Office
    Washington, D.C.   Phone (202) 738-3238

Ulrich's International Periodicals Directory
    R.B. Bowker Company
    New York, New York   Phone (212) 645-9700

Encyclopedia of Business Information Sources
Lists source books, periodicals, organizations, directories, handbooks, and bibliographies by category, topic, and geographical location.
Encyclopedia of Associations
Listing of U.S. trade and other associations by key words.
Directory of European Associations
Listing of European trade and other associations by category number.
    Gale Research Company
    Detroit, Michigan   Phone (313) 961-2242

Guide to American Directories
    B. Klein Publications
    Coral Springs, Florida   Phone (305) 752-1708

Listing by category of over 8,000 industrial, mercantile, and professional directories including sources and prices.

Thomas Register of American Manufacturers
    Thomas Publishing Company
    New York, New York   Phone (212) 290-7200
Company listings by products manufactured; no names of individuals.

Who's Who in Finance and Industry
Who's Who in Business and Finance
    Macmillan Publishing Co., Inc., Directory Division
    New York, New York   Phone (212) 702-2000

Business Periodicals Index
    The H. W. Wilson Company
    Bronx, New York   Phone (212) 588-8400
A subject index to articles that have appeared in over a hundred business magazines. This index is published monthly and is usually available as far back as ten years.

Listed below is only a sampling of special trade directories also found in libraries. These books usually show corporate officers' names.

The Polk Bank Directory
The Advertiser's Red Book
The Packaging Marketplace
Martindale-Hubbel Law Directory
Securities Dealers of North America
International Directory of Importers
Pharmaceutical and Cosmetics Firms, U.S.A.
Worldwide Directory of Computer Companies
Consultants and Consulting Organizations Directory
Directory of Foreign Manufacturers in the United States
E/MJ Directory of Mining and Metal Processing Operations

Don't let concerns over your livelihood impede your Jobsearch efforts. Complete this personal net worth form and the cash flow and Jobsearch expense estimate to plan for any time you might be out of work. Don't forget to include your spouse's net worth and income.

Personal Net Worth

Name: _____   Date: _____, 19___

ASSETS

Cash on hand and in bank .... _____

Savings account balance .... _____

Other savings, IRA accounts, etc. .... _____

Accounts and notes receivable .... _____

Stocks and bonds, readily saleable .... _____

Stocks and bonds, closely held .... _____

Cash value of life insurance .... _____

Real estate owned, home .... _____

Real estate owned, other .... _____

Automobiles owned .... _____

Personal property and household furnishings .... _____

Personal property, other .... _____

Other assets .... _____

Total Assets .... _____

LIABILITIES

Bills on hand .... _____

Notes payable .... _____

Student loans .... _____

Real estate mortgage, home .... _____

Real estate mortgage, other .... _____

Auto loan balance .... _____

Installment purchase loan balances .... _____

Other debts .... _____

Total Liabilities .... _____

Net Worth .... _____

Total Liabilities and Net Worth .... _____

11

This monthly cash flow projection will help plan for time spent without a salary.

Monthly Cash Flow Projection

Name: _____   Date: _____, 19___

Month	1	2	3	4
Beginning cash balance				
Income				
Disbursements				
Ending cash balance				

INCOME

Month	1	2	3	4
Salary				
Severance benefits				
Other company payments				
Unemployment compensation				
Spouse's income				
Dividends				
Interest income				
Rental income				
Tax refund				
Cash from savings				
Cash from loans				
Cash from life insurance				
Repayment of debts owed me				
Other income				
_____				
Total income				

Monthly Cash Flow Projection
Disbursements

Name: _____   Date: _____

Month	1	2	3	4
Bills on hand				
Mortgages				
Auto loan payments				
Installment loan payments				
Utilities				
Telephone				
Automobile expense				
Insurance premiums				
Food				
Clothing				
Drugs and medical				
Household items				
Personal items				
Laundry and dry cleaning				
Dues and subscriptions				
Taxes				
Gifts				
Education				
Child care or domestic services				
Recreation and entertainment				
Micellaneous				
Jobsearch expense				
Total disbursements				

This Jobsearch expense estimate will allow you to budget these items in your monthly expense whether you have a job or conduct your search without employment.

Jobsearch Expense Estimate

Name: _____   Date: _____

Jobsearch stationery   _____
Résumé photographs   _____
Subscriptions   _____
Reference books   _____
Other information   _____
Secretarial services   _____
Computer typing services   _____
Copying expense   _____
Postage   _____
Long-distance telephone calls   _____
Local travel and parking   _____
Other travel   _____
Other expenses   _____

_____   _____
_____   _____
_____   _____
_____   _____
_____   _____
_____   _____
_____   _____

                          Total expenses   _____

This listing of direct job-related accomplishments is the most important form in your Jobsearch. It includes the items you have to sell; complete it with care.

Direct Job-Related Accomplishments

Name: _____   Date: _____

Title, Company Name, City, and State

_____ 1._____
Period in Years
_____

2._____
_____

3._____
_____

4._____
_____

5._____
_____

Title, Company Name, City, and State

_____ 1._____
Period in Years
_____

2._____
_____

3._____
_____

4._____
_____

5._____
_____

Direct Job-Related Accomplishments

Name: _____   Date: _____

Title, Company Name, City, and State
_____ 1._____
Period in Years
_____

2._____

_____

3._____

_____

4._____

_____

5._____

_____

Title, Company Name, City, and State
_____ 1._____
Period in Years
_____

2._____

_____

3._____

_____

4._____

_____

5._____

_____

Direct Job-Related Accomplishments

Name: _____   Date: _____

Title, Company Name, City, and State

_____ 1._____
Period in Years

_____

2._____

_____

3._____

_____

4._____

_____

5._____

_____

Title, Company Name, City, and State

_____ 1._____ _____
Period in Years

_____

2._____

_____

3._____

_____

4._____

_____

5._____

_____

This list of indirect job-related accomplishments includes those items related to your responsibilities but not a part of your everyday tasks.

Indirect Job-Related Accomplishments

Name: _____   Date: _____

_____
Title, Company Name, City, and State

_____ 1. _____
Period in Years

_____

2. _____

_____

3. _____

_____

_____
Title, Company Name, City, and State

_____ 1. _____
Period in Years

_____

2. _____

_____

3. _____

_____

_____
Title, Company Name, City, and State

_____ 1. _____
Period in Years

_____

2. _____

_____

3. _____

_____

Your list of educational accomplishments should include not only significant courses or lab work but also extracurricular activities, particularly those related to your major course of study and those that show your work habits or interests. Also include continuing education.

Educational Accomplishments

Name: _____   Date: _____

Degree Received, Institution, City, and State
_____ 1._____
Period in Years

_____

2._____

_____

3._____

_____

4._____

_____

5._____

_____

Degree Received, Institution, City, and State
_____ 1._____
Period in Years

_____

2._____

_____

3._____

_____

4._____

_____

5._____

_____

Personal or civic accomplishments include any and everything outside your work or educational experience.

Personal or Civic Accomplishments

Name: _____ Date: _____

Your Title (if any), Organization, City, and State

_____ 1. _____
Period in Years

_____

2. _____

_____

3. _____

_____

Your Title (if any), Organization, City, and State

_____ 1. _____
Period in Years

_____

2. _____

_____

3. _____

_____

Your Title (if any), Organization, City, and State

_____ 1. _____
Period in Years

_____

2. _____

_____

3. _____

_____

You're not looking for just a job; you're embarking on the next segment of your career. Work toward a goal over a reasonable span of time. Take advantage of your Jobsearch to start or continue your career planning process.

Career Goals

Name: _____   Date: _____

Goal	Immediate	In 5 years	In 10 years
Position			
Salary			
Perquisites (perks)			
Percent equity			
Scope of authority			
Number of subordinates, direct			
Number of subordinates, indirect			
Independence			
Structured environment			
Work hours vs. private time			
Travel			
Percent time working with – People			
– Data			
– Things			
Security			
Challenge			
Professional recognition			
Civic recognition			
Personal recognition			

18

It's difficult to make a sale without knowing your marketing targets. By identifying the potential buyers of your skills, you can package your accomplishments and experiences to appeal specifically to those markets.

Marketing Targets

Name _____   Date _____

I. Industry _____
   Size of organization _____
   Type of organization _____
   Geographic area _____
   Position and responsibilities _____
   Personal preference _____
   Career preference _____

II. Industry _____
   Size of organization _____
   Type of organization _____
   Geographic area _____
   Position and responsibilities _____
   Personal preference _____
   Career preference _____

III. Industry _____
   Size of organization _____
   Type of organization _____
   Geographic area _____
   Position and responsibilities _____
   Personal preference _____
   Career preference _____

IV. Industry _____
   Size of organization _____
   Type of organization _____
   Geographic area _____
   Position and responsibilities _____
   Personal preference _____
   Career preference _____

Use this personal résumé form to create the first rough draft of your résumé. This is an important sales tool in your Jobsearch.

Personal Résumé Form

Name: _____

Address: _____

_____

Telephone: Home: _____

Office: _____

Photo
[optional]

Civil Status: _____

_____

Children: _____

Education: High School _____

_____

_____

College _____

_____

_____

Graduate School _____

_____

Continuing Education _____

_____

_____

Professional Highlights:

_____

_____

_____

_____

Personal Résumé Form

Professional History:

_____

_____   _____

                _____

                _____

                _____

                _____

                _____

                _____

                _____

_____

_____   _____

                _____

                _____

                _____

                _____

                _____

                _____

                _____

Personal Résumé Form

Professional History:

_____

_____   _____

                _____

                _____

                _____

                _____

                _____

                _____

                _____

                _____

                _____

_____

_____   _____

                _____

                _____

                _____

                _____

                _____

                _____

                _____

                _____

                _____

Personal Résumé Form

Professional Organizations: _____

_____

_____

_____

Military Service: _____

_____

_____

_____

Special Items of Interest: _____

_____

_____

_____

_____

_____

_____

_____

_____

References: _____

_____

_____

_____

_____

[The *Jobsearch* Workbook continues on page 176.]

This résumé was used by an accountant in a search for a financial officer's position. By expanding her search, she became the legal administrator for a major law firm, a position she didn't even know existed before starting her search.

PERSONAL RESUME
March 1990

NAME: NAFF, KARILYN G.

ADDRESS: 1674 North Park Drive
Atlanta, Georgia 30341

TELEPHONE: (404) 936-7511

Photo [optional]

CIVIL STATUS: Born November 6, 1936, Decatur, Georgia; married.

CHILDREN: Two daughters, both graduates of the University of Georgia.

EDUCATION: **University**—Graduated in 1958 from the University of Georgia, School of Commerce and Business Administration, with a Bachelor of Science degree; majored in Accounting.

Continuing Education—Have completed university courses in Income Tax Procedure, Principles of Management, and Computer Programming as well as other courses in computer use, accounting, and speed reading.

PROFESSIONAL HIGHLIGHTS: As Treasurer or Controller of four companies ranging in size from $5 million to over $43 million in annual sales, implemented and designed systems for conversion of all accounting functions to computer application including work with minicomputers, service bureaus, large systems, and conversion from one computer to another. Designed and established an inventory control system at a franchise operation which reduced inventory requirements by 35% or $500,000. In cash control, set up and managed an investment portfolio which increased after tax profits by $25,000. Designed a credits control system for a grocery distributor which reduced credits issued by $2,500 per week. Cut delinquent account period by one-half for installment sales at a multi-cemetery operation.

PROFESSIONAL HISTORY:
Chicken Quick Food Company, Inc., Atlanta Georgia   **1986–1990**
Joined this $12-million-gross-sales franchise food operation as Treasurer and Controller after a 9-month break in financial statements. Brought all records up to date and completed annual audit and 10–K SEC filing in less than three months working with predominantly new staff. Replaced old computer with a functionally interrelated network including design of the new system for all accounting functions. Recognized need and set up a formal Buyer's Guide showing inventory movement, source, and delivery information. This allowed a 50% reduction in purchasing staff. Established

a system for cash control and accounts payable which reduced cash balance from $85,000 to $40,000 annually. Designed and wrote accounting systems for franchises.

Cooperative Grocers of North Georgia, Inc., Atlanta, Georgia   **1983–1986**
As Controller of this $43 million cooperative food distributor, put accounts payable and general ledger on computer. Implemented rigid inventory control system which reduced inventory losses by $30,000 the first year which reduced inventory level by $1/4 million. This also improved accuracy of inventory records allowing gradual reduction in physical inventory count period from monthly to semiannually. Became Controller and set up complete accounting systems for three new subsidiary acquisitions in advertising, radio broadcasting, and maintenance.

Zigler Foods Company, Inc., Tallahassee, Florida   **1982**
As Treasurer and Controller of this wholesale grocery company, converted over 150 computer programs from an IBM to a Data General system in less than four weeks. Set up a retail accounting system for company stores and revamped the billing, inventory control, and purchase order systems. After establishing a computer accounting system, contracted with a local television station to process its daily program analysis producing additional revenue of $27,000 per year with no increase in costs.

Mark Memorial Services, Inc., Atlanta, Georgia   **1967–1981**
Treasurer and Controller of this $5 million cemetery company with operations in five Southeastern cities. Set up and operated accounting system for both the home office and all local offices. Personally wrote 80% of the programs to computerize accounts. Set up installment sales accounting procedures including an automatic delinquent notice system which reduced average delinquent time by one-half from 20 to 10 days.

Civil Service, Atlanta and College Park, Georgia   **1958–1967**
Served as Accountant, City Clerk, and Treasurer for the Atlanta Board of Health and the City of College Park, Georgia.

OTHER: Was a founder and first treasurer of the accounting fraternity at the University of Georgia.

REFERENCES: Mr. K. R. Greenfield, Manager, Atlanta Data Center, Compushare, Inc., Atlanta, Georgia, (404) 938-6811.

Mr. Michael Strong, Vice-President, Southern National Bank of Atlanta, Atlanta, Georgia, (404) 577-3681.

Mr. Earle Barker, CPA, Howard, Barker and McDowell, Atlanta, Georgia, (404) 233-5967.

This résumé was used by a statistics expert to find a position in his field of study, an esoteric niche not needed by many businesses. He succeeded against substantial odds.

PERSONAL RESUME
February 1990

NAME: MARQUE, Ronald J.
(Pronounced "Mark")

Photo
[optional]

ADDRESS: Apartment 4, Terrace Court
Chicago, Illinois 47092

TELEPHONE: (312) 221-9130

CIVIL STATUS: Born May 30, 1962, Pottstown, Pennsylvania; married; no children.

LANGUAGES: Both English and French spoken, read, and written fluently.

EDUCATION: Graduated from the University of Illinois in 1985 with a Master of Business Administration degree in Finance and Econometrics. In addition to usual business courses, studied business applications of statistics including queuing theory, Markov chains, and variance and regression analysis. Studied econometric modeling, investment analysis, and corporate finance and planning.

Received a Bachelor of Arts degree in Political Science with a minor in Economics also from the University of Illinois in 1983.

Continuing Education: Completed the American Institute of Real Estate Appraisers initial course on real estate appraising.

PROFESSIONAL HIGHLIGHTS: For a $500 million mortgage company, instituted and computerized regression analysis for loan closings and interest rate movements with 88% accuracy in gross amounts and 100% accuracy in predicting trends. As head of the marketing department, produced $600,000 of profit in mortgage sales while the money market fluctuated through two complete reversals. Made discount decisions in conjunction with the president that resulted in an increase in production of 100.9%. Analyzed and originated the sale of mortgage-backed securities, producing profits of up to $57,000 per security. Reorganized the marketing department, resulting in an 18% decrease in total expense and 80% decrease in overtime.

PROFESSIONAL HISTORY:

Ingel Mortgage Company, Inc., Chicago, Illinois   **1987–1990**

As head of the marketing department, sold a two-year inventory of $5.5 million of mortgages with poor payment histories. Sold over $1 million of problem Florida condominiums with a $27,000 profit. Renegotiated a $5 million commitment that was in jeopardy. Analyzed and corrected a mortgage portfolio of an acquired subsidiary to meet GNMA requirements. Set up computer control of GNMA tandem commitments for $86 million of mortgages. Analyzed and underwrote all conventional loans from ten company branches.

1986–1987

As collection department head, decreased delinquency to under 4% for the first time in three years. Reorganized workload of seven staff members for optimum effectiveness. Reorganized delinquent files and created computer print out cards for improved accuracy and quick retrieval.

American Financial Services, Grove Heights, Illinois   **1985–1986**

As customer service representative for this small loan service company, was able to collect over $200,000 of accounts that had been written off as bad debts. Had best delinquency ratio on consumer accounts and under 1% on dealer accounts. Responsible for analyzing and closing both second mortgage and personal secured loans.

Barbara Corporation, Pottstown, Pennsylvania   **Summers: 1980–1984**

As a machinist in the largest plant of this industrial manufacturer, ran eight different metal-working and milling machines on a universal-joint production line. Worked seven days a week through each summer to earn 65% of college expenses.

PROFESSIONAL ORGANIZATIONS: Association of MBA Executives

REFERENCES: Mrs. Connie H. Thomason, Vice-President, Ingel Mortgage Company, Chicago, Illinois, (312) 251-2447.

Mr. Ralph G. Brown, Manager, CIT Financial Services, Grove Heights, Illinois, (312) 823-3100.

Mr. Michael Padalarno, Vice–President, Ingel Mortgage Company, Chicago, Illinois, (312) 251-2447.

Ms. Shookler had spent virtually all of her career in sales of women's apparel and wanted to stay there. This résumé emphasized her accomplishments in that field.

PERSONAL RESUME
April 1990

NAME: SHOOKLER, Lois B.

ADDRESS: 365 Poinsettia Drive
Wilmington, Delaware 19804

TELEPHONE: (302) 879-6685

CIVIL STATUS: Born September 10, 1950, Chicago, Illinois; married.

CHILDREN: One daughter, age 19.

PROFESSIONAL HIGHLIGHTS:

As sales representative or assistant manager for four consumer product companies ranging in size from $14 million to $150 million in annual sales, had nine consecutive years of sales increases. Won three individual sales awards. Worked closely with outside consulting firm on improved reporting system and developed new merchandising programs that resulted in doubling department exposure in major accounts. Successfully opened seventy-one accounts for a new product line in less than two years. Took over a territory and increased sales 48% in the first five months while adding 37 new accounts. Screened and then field-trained 12 salesmen for the Middle Atlantic region with resultant increase in sales of over 25%.

PROFESSIONAL HISTORY:

Woman's World, Inc., New York, New York   **1988–1990**

As territory salesman for Delaware, Maryland, and southern New Jersey with this national apparel company, sold merchandise to 168 medium to better specialty shops and department stores including 90 of the 97 key accounts in cities of 50,000 population and above. Increased territory sales 10% for fiscal 1989, against a 3% company increase. Re-established line into major position at the first and third largest department store chains in the area and increased volume 32% in second largest chain.

Balanchine, Inc., Wilmington, Delaware   **1987–1988**

As assistant store manager in the second largest branch of this major Delaware department store chain, supervised 108 salespeople and service clerks. Personally handled all customer complaints. Suggested and implemented relocation of sportswear and cosmetic departments, contributing to the growth of this store from fifth to second largest in the chain. Took personal supervision of intimate apparel department, resulting in its becoming the largest in sales compared with 21 other stores.

Poyner, Gross, Inc., Wilmington, Delaware   **1986–1987**
   As President and minority stockholder of this new commercial and
   residential decoration service company, was responsible for initial
   organization and for establishing bank credit lines. Personally generated
   $65,000 sales volume in first four months. Recruited and trained four
   office and sales employees.

Elen Shoreman, Inc., New York, New York   **1981–1985**
   In three Middle Atlantic states as salesman for complete intimate and
   career apparel lines, increased annual sales from $536,000 to $925,000
   in two years. Saw potential new market and opened eleven military
   exchanges for the foundation line. Worked with cross-selling of mixed
   product lines and introduced a completely new line for the firm.

Rothman's, Inc., Division of ITC, Inc., New York   **1970–1980**
   Increased sales from $286,000 to $636,000 in an already developed
   market as territory salesman in Delaware and southern New Jersey. Led
   the Middle Atlantic region in sales two of the three years it led the nation.
   Also handled sales interviews and screening for all applicants in Trenton
   and Wilmington.

EDUCATION: Attended Joliet College, Joliet, Illinois, 1967–1970, with
   continuing education in Psychology and Commercial Law at night.
   Completed the Xerox Corporation Sales Training Course.

REFERENCES: Mr. John Barton, Executive Vice-President, Rothman's, Inc.,
   New York, New York, (212) 782-1444.

   Ms. Bernice Strutz, Merchandise Manager, Lowe's Department Store,
   Wilmington, Delaware, (302) 263-0344.

   Mr. Milton Blatt, V/P National Sales Manager, Elen Shoreman, Inc., New
   York, New York, (212) 867-9700.

Mr. Harlen used his experience as pastor of a community church to embark on a fund raising career. His Jobsearch effort was directed toward this charity market. Note this is a functional rather than chronological form of résumé.

PERSONAL RESUME
April 1990

NAME: HARLEN, Carter M.

ADDRESS: 3230 West Valley Drive
New Orleans, Louisiana 70132

TELEPHONE: (504) 977-8815, home;
(504) 964-2340, office

CIVIL STATUS: Born March 15, 1954, New Orleans, Louisiana; U.S. Citizen; married.

CHILDREN: One son, 12; one daughter, 9.

EDUCATION:
Graduated in 1975 from Anderson College, Anderson, Michigan, with a Bachelor of Science degree. Major subjects included Social Studies and Education; minors were in English and Psychology.

GRADUATE SCHOOL:
Anderson School of Theology, Anderson, Michigan, 1976.

CONTINUING EDUCATION:
University of Notre Dame, South Bend, Indiana, summer 1980; completed course in Public Relations and Administration for Colleges and Universities.

Robert Sharpe Institute, Memphis, Tennessee, 1980 and 1981; completed Estate Planning and College Development courses.

PROFESSIONAL HIGHLIGHTS:
Established the development department for a Midwestern liberal arts college and served as its development and alumni officer. Raised over $5 million in deferred gifts for endowment and organized special campaigns to build a new administrative building costing $4.5 million. Served as executive director for a permanent, fund raising organization of 13 Midwestern graduate seminaries. Increased member schools from 7 to 13 and set up a corporate fund campaign that increased gifts from businesses by 95%. Served as pastor of a community church and vice-chairman for research and development of a state board of church extensions. Served as president of a real estate development corporation.

PROFESSIONAL EXPERIENCE:
Fund Raising

As development and alumni director at Anderson College, Anderson, Michigan, reorganized entire department and instituted business procedures for all functions. Established gift records and prospect files and increased regular contributions over three times. Planned, contracted, and raised funds for a $4.5 million building. Assisted with estate planning as a major fund-raising technique with potential bequests exceeding $7 million.

As executive director of the Accredited Theological Schools of Michigan and Indiana, planned, organized, and implemented multiseminary fund-raising activities that increased the number of contributors by 65%. Increased school foundation membership and total contributed dollars and obtained largest single gift in the organization's history.

Was planning and development consultant for Sanford Southern College, Lake City, Florida, and for an international church radio and television commission. Established a five-year, long-range plan for the college including fund-raising and deferred-giving programs that increased gift income 40%.

Ministry

Pastored a community church, increasing its regular attendance by 267%, its annual regular income by 375%, and its net assets by 350%.

As vice-chairman of a state board of church extensions, was responsible for research and development. Made logistical studies for six areas and provided consultant services to churches for design, construction, financing, and fund raising.

Business

Owner/president of a land development company in Central Florida, purchased and sold 497 building lots; purchased, developed, and sold a seven-unit shopping plaza.

PROFESSIONAL ORGANIZATIONS:
American College Public Relations Association; American Alumni Council; New Orleans Board of Realtors; Church of God, Anderson, Michigan, Ordained Minister

REFERENCES: Dr. John Dickhaught, President, Methodist Theological School of Michigan, Columbus, Michigan, Telephone (313) 363-1247

Dr. Hilda Rich, Director, Motivation Center, Inc. New Orleans, Louisiana, Telephone (504) 933-2416

Dr. John Knight, President, United Theological Seminary, Alpena, Michigan, Telephone (313) 279-5717

Jerrold Brooks found himself caught in a restructuring layoff after twenty-three years with only one company. He was able to extract the major accomplishments from those twenty-three years to become vice-president of manufacturing for a Howard & Sharpe competitor. Note this is also a functional form of résumé.

PERSONAL RESUME
January 1990

NAME: BROOKS, Jerrold A.

ADDRESS: 1216 Thornhill Drive
Dallas, Texas 75221

TELEPHONE: (214) 871-1496

CIVIL STATUS: Born April 12, 1942, Columbus, Ohio; married.

CHILDREN: One daughter, age 13; three sons, ages 4, 11, and 15.

EDUCATION:

University—Graduated from the University of Ohio in 1964 with a Bachelor of Science degree in Business Administration; majored in Production Management. Minor subjects included Engineering, Accounting, and Statistics.

Continuing Education—Mechanical Engineering, University of Texas, night school from 1968 to 1974; have also completed courses and seminars in Quality Control, Packaging, Textiles, Purchasing, Time and Motion Study, Accounting, Investments, Real Estate, and Public Speaking.

PROFESSIONAL HIGHLIGHTS:

In 23 years with Howard & Sharpe, a $50 million, five-plant manufacturer of children's through juniors' sports and outerwear, served variously as vice-president or manager over Marketing, Merchandising, Packaging, Manufacturing, Engineering, Quality Control, and Purchasing. Significant accomplishments included performing most new product and trend research while serving on a four-man merchandising committee for 15 years; determined each style that was adopted for a given line. Sales increased from $5.5 million to $50 milllion and profits from $500,000 to $2,800,000. Set up and managed first Southern plant. Designed, built, and managed a 100-man packaging department; developed packaging design and procedures for the entire diversified product line. Developed work-flow systems in outerwear plant, producing savings of $150,000 per year. Originated quality control program for the entire company, reducing losses and returns by $300,000 per year. Developed company reorganization and cost reduction program in 1974 that saved over $700,000 in two years.

PROFESSIONAL EXPERIENCE:

Merchandising and Marketing: From selling on the road to recruiting and managing the entire sales force, having participated in all areas of sales, advertising, garment design, and merchandising. Put company into jacket and car coat field, increasing outerwear sales $300%. Developed entry into permapress field with resultant 70% increase in sportswear sales over two years. Pursued and negotiated highly profitable Army contracts with annual sales of $1 million. Handled customer service with large discount chains, increasing sales 20%. Was responsible for sales projections and costing for a complete, diversified line.

Packaging: Originated, developed, and directed a "total" finishing and packaging program for all five plants from 1975–1987. Designed every package in the diversified line in coordination with marketing/ merchandising plans. Responsible for all labeling, tagging, logo design, brand coordination, advertising gimmicks, and promotional programs. Developed color hanger concept for selection of coordinated sets at retail level.

Production and Engineering: Developed and set up a complete perma-press line, including all material handling. Supervised design and construction for four major plant expansions, including layout of all production machinery. Improved methods of pattern making, fit control, spreading, and cutting, which saved $500,000 in three years. Started and managed two new plant facilities. Originated, designed, and set up quality control laboratory. Have worked with time studies, production costs and rates, cost formulas, production control, and planning. Have operated all machines and entire production facilities personally.

Purchasing: Managed purchasing effort over a five-year period with peak annual level of $12 million. Negotiated contracts with major textile suppliers, saving $250,000 in one year measured against going market prices and purchases of similar goods and quantities in previous year. Organized complete quality "spec" system used in large contracts, backed up by fabric inspection system at plants and lab. This improved quality of fabrics and garments and saved $80,000 in fabrics, $20,000 in trim, and up to $100,000 per year on customer returns. Familiar with textile market trends, price movements in greige goods, blends, cottons, and other fibers, as well as dyeing, printing, and finishing markets.

Administration: Managed building construction and real estate; headed budget committee and cost accounting departments. Did research in cost control and overhead reduction, resulting in increased profits of 3% to 4% in one year due only to savings produced. Set up traffic department with freight scheduling and cost control, saving in excess of $75,000 per year. Participated in or managed all administrative functions of the company.

REFERENCES: Mr. Samuel Bayer, President, Warner Thread Company, New York, New York, (212) 938-0424.

Mr. Sam Norwood, Vice-President, Howard & Sharpe, Dallas, Texas, Office (214) 925-3771; Home (214) 870-2142.

Mr. Alan Sherman, President, Sherman Plastics Company, New York, New York, (212) 760-8870.

Ms. Parsons was stuck in a law position studying title abstracts every day. From a job offering little useful experience for other forms of legal work, she secured a position in the real estate acquisition department of a major utility.

PERSONAL RESUME
May 1990

NAME: PARSONS, Janet C.

ADDRESS: 2701 Flagstone Road
         Kansas City, Missouri 64112

TELEPHONE: (816) 533-2069

Photo
[optional]

CIVIL STATUS: Born September 30, 1949, in Valley View, Kansas; married.

CHILDREN: One son, age 11; twin daughters, age 13.

EDUCATION:
Graduate—Received law degree, L.L.B., from the University of Missouri in 1974; admitted to the Missouri Bar that same year.

University—Graduated from Cornell University in 1971 with a Bachelor of Arts degree in Political Science.

Continuing Education—Have taken over 20 university and bar sponsored courses and seminars in various aspects of continuing legal education but predominantly related to real estate. Completed real estate brokers test requirements and am licensed as a Missouri real estate broker.

PROFESSIONAL HIGHLIGHTS:
Nine years of general law practice as a sole practitioner and managing partner in Salina, Missouri, followed by five years of corporate experience predominantly related to real estate matters as senior title attorney with Associates Title Insurance Company in Kansas City, Missouri.

In general practice, formed over a dozen corporations; handled 15 real estate litigation cases; negotiated settlements and tried various tort claims; acted as a trustee in bankruptcy and served as general guardian and general administrator of Columbia County, Missouri. In corporate experience, am usually assigned the more difficult real estate title cases and examinations. As only lawyer in office with trial experience, have handled or been consulted on all cases involving claims in Missouri. Prepare and administer escrow contracts, solicit new business, and disburse construction funds.

PROFESSIONAL HISTORY:
Associates Title Insurance Company, Kansas City, Missouri   **1985–Present**
As senior title attorney in this forty-person office with five lawyers, have examined over 4,000 real estate titles of up to $50 million value. Make

186

decisions concerning insurability and underwriting and draft insurance contracts and binders. Have handled claims concerning a wide variety of real estate related disputes resulting in both negotiated settlements and court trials. Work daily with between three to eight private and outside corporate attorneys on real estate and real estate related matters. Evaluate hazards, set limits, draft and administer escrow accounts. Responsible for disbursement of multimillion-dollar construction funds; have settled disputes over and established safeguards against mechanics' and materialmen's liens; meet regularly with real estate agents, bank and lending institutions' loan officials, developers, and other lawyers to discuss real estate projects and to solicit business. Have worked with property sales, transfers, trades, leases, development, zoning, uses, condemnations, and mineral rights.

General Law Practice, Salina, Missouri   **1974–1985**
General practice in this small city serving a population of 80,000 with 30 to 40 lawyers. Was general guardian and general administrator for the county from 1974 to 1982. Handled over thirty estates in this capacity including both sale and purchase of real estate for wards. In corporate work, formed, amended, merged, and dissolved over a dozen corporate charters. Handled over fifteen cases of real estate litigation including judicial sales, bankruptcy, bills to quit title, condemnation for both state and defendants, boundary disputes, foreclosures, and liens. Drafted and negotiated wide variety of contracts including labor union contracts. Tried and won a trademark infringement and unfair business practices suit. Have negotiated, tried, and won a number of tort cases.

PROFESSIONAL ORGANIZATIONS:
President of the Columbia County Bar Association in 1979–1981. Currently a member of the American, Missouri, and Kansas City Bar Associations and the Sigma Delta Kappa legal fraternity.

SPECIAL ITEM OF INTEREST:
Conducted Real Estate Seminar for the University of Missouri Continuing Legal Education Program.

REFERENCES: Mr. James M. Spence, Jr.; Pelham, McDaniel and Jones, Kansas City, Missouri, (816) 824-9523.

Mr. Elton G. Brown, III; Circuit Judge, Maclenny, Missouri, (314) 752-7389.

Mr. Thomas O. Paulson; Hughes, Coretti, Forrester, Rudd and Hensley, Kansas City, Missouri, (816) 251-5050.

Jeff McCauli had done little other than wire houses until he used this résumé to join the electrical department at Disney World, a position giving him experience valuable toward forming his own electrical contracting firm, his eventual career goal.

PERSONAL RESUME
June 1990

NAME: McCauli, Jeffrey D.

ADDRESS: 2599-B South Garden Road, Orlando, Florida 32812

TELEPHONE: (407) 895-6173

CIVIL STATUS: Born May 22, 1965 in Detroit, Michigan, Divorced, no children

EDUCATION:
Graduated with Honor Certificate from Delta High School, Muncie, Indiana in 1984. High School courses included two basic electrical studies. Attended one year of Southern College, Orlando, Florida, studying computer maintenance and repair. Took apprenticeship classes in electrical construction and maintenance through the Florida Homebuilders Association at Mid-Florida Technical Institute. Completed Electrical Code classes given by Tom Henry, author and professor in electrical theory. Took first-year electrical apprenticeship classes at Winter Park Adult Education Extension Center. Completed self study and passed both the Journeyman Electrician's Exam and the Master Electrician's Exam, passing both on the first effort.

PROFESSIONAL HIGHLIGHTS:
Licensed Master Electrician with the City of Orlando, which has reciprocal agreements with most Central Florida jurisdictions; hold Journeyman's Electrician License in Orange, Osceola, and Seminole Counties, Florida; passed both Master and Journeyman's Electrical Examinations on first attempt; know electrical code requirements for the National Electrical Code published by the National Fire Protection Agency and used nationwide; have worked in electrical construction for the past four years rising from helper to the youngest project manager ever employed by Construction Electric Co.; am routinely assigned complete, custom home, electrical installations with no supervision; familiar with reading electrical drawings and specifications, making revisions, and completing electrical construction to comply with both drawings and code requirements.

PROFESSIONAL HISTORY:
Construction Electric Co. of Florida, Orlando, Florida   **July 1985 to present**
Electrical Contractors and Engineers
> Began as an electrical apprentice working in new home construction; rose
> to project supervisor assigned to the largest, custom built projects
> including 400 amp service residences; make decisions as to new homes
> wiring layout and construction techniques; revise plans to comply with
> Electrical Code requirements; can take plans to a single home and
> complete all wiring installation without assistance; read, revise, and up-
> date electrical construction drawings and specifications; have wired over
> 400 homes.

Air Containers Incorporated, Orlando, Florida   **Feb 1985 to June 1985**
Builders of specialized containers for air transport
> Assisted in the manufacture of wooden and other parts as well as the
> assembly of over 500 air freight containers principally for the transport
> of human bodies; responsible for compliance of orders with purchase
> requests; also made product deliveries throughout Florida.

Ace Auto Garage, Orlando, Florida   **July 1984 to Feb 1985**
Automotive repair shop
> Worked as an auto mechanic repairing every aspect of both American and
> Foreign automobiles specializing in Cadillacs; tasks included dealing with
> customers, locating and purchasing parts, making the repairs, and testing
> the completed vehicles. Repaired over 1,000 cars, working on as many as
> 10 in one day.

Michigan's Merchant Mart, Flint, Michigan   **Feb 1984 to June 1984**
Furniture company specializing in office equipment
> General helper and furniture mover for this $1 million plus annual sales
> business.

During High School
> Worked at various temporary jobs including newspaper delivery, billing,
> and collections for the Flint (Michigan) Journal; household maintenance
> and repairs; and child care.

REFERENCES: Frank Russel, President, Automotive Products, Inc. Longwood,
Florida (407) 838-9947

Tom Bird, General Manager, Construction Electric Co. of Florida, Orlando,
Florida (407) 866-4157 (Do not contact without prior notification.)

Robert Gardner, Apprentice at Construction Electric Co. (407) 363-1844
(home number)

Susan Abrams was a college graduate with no work experience in her field of study. By concentrating heavily on her educational work and using summer jobs to demonstrate her dedication and work ethic, she was successful in starting her engineering career.

PERSONAL RESUME
February 1990

NAME: ABRAMS, Susan Marie

ADDRESS (School): Post Office Box 7611
Gainesville, Florida 34576   Telephone: (904) 267-5412

ADDRESS (Parents): 976 Austin Terrace
Orlando, Florida 32872   Telephone: (407) 329-4658

CIVIL STATUS: Born July 29, 1968 in Detroit, Michigan

EDUCATION:
Graduated from Mount Morris High School, Orlando, Florida. During high school, participated for three years in the Engineering Club and served as Treasurer in Senior year. Have just completed a Bachelor of Engineering Degree concentrating on Fluid Dynamics at the University of Florida, Gainsville, Florida. Lab work included both liquid and gaseous laminar and chaotic flow experiments on applications to shapes from turbine blades to solid bodies. Received Best of Class award for a study of computer application to the formula evaluation of laminar/turbulent flow changes. Graduated in the top half of the class but maintained a 3.5 average in all courses related to Fluid Dynamics major. Plan to continue formal education in night school working toward a Masters Degree in Fluid Dynamics.

PROFESSIONAL HIGHLIGHTS:
Educational skills include computer use from PC's to mini's with program development for a wide variety of fluid flow evaluations. Analyzed fluid flow through valves, pipes, and mechanical equipment as well as over and around solid bodies with a concentration on the moment of turbulence and design changes to extend laminar flow.

Work skills include wide contact with the public in a service and selling environment as well as attention to detail in busy fast food restaurant. Have worked three of four summers during college career in jobs as diverse as playing "Goofy" in the Disney World Magic Kingdom to counter clerk at Burger King. Was chosen Employee of the Week three times at Burger King and once at Belk's Department Store. At Burger King, personally served up to 350 customers per shift. After working as a stock clerk at Belk's one summer, was asked to return as a cashier during two Christmas vacations. Handled cash and credit card purchases of up to $7,000 per day with only four exception reports totaling less than $10.00 in a total of 60 days. Have never missed a day of work or reported late.

WORK HISTORY:

Summers:

1990 **Disney World,** Orlando, Florida

Awarded a job at this Theme Park against 6 applications for each opening. Assigned to the cartoon character squad, dressed daily as "Goofy", and entertained both children and adults throughout the Fantasy Land section of the park. Met several thousand people each day using only pantomime to communicate.

1989 **Burger King,** Orlando, Florida

Served as a counter clerk at this local fast food restaurant chain handling over a customer per minute during busy lunch periods. Assisted in the food preparation section during slack periods making both hamburgers and salads. Was encouraged to return the next summer as assistant night manager.

1988 **Belk's Department Store,** Orlando, Florida

Worked as a stock clerk at Belk's receiving incoming goods, maintaining inventory, and delivering stock to four separate departments. Handled over 20 freight receipts per day containing up to 1,000 items of merchandise. Participated twice in manual inventory counts of over 5,000 items without error. Asked to return during two Christmas vacations, 1988 and 1989, to work as a counter clerk and cashier. Handled up to 250 customers per shift.

ORGANIZATIONS:

Member of the Engineering Club at both Mount Morris High School and the University of Florida. Joined the American Society of Mechanical Engineers during junior year and participated in two seminars on Fluid Flow Dynamics during Spring breaks, 1989 and 1990. Submitted a paper on Chaotic Flow Characteristics to the ASME Journal.

REFERENCES: Lawrence B. Clark, Chairman of Mechanical Engineering, University of Florida, Gainesville, Florida (904) 776-5543

Charlene M. Siciliano, Director of Personnel, Burger King, Orlando, Florida (407) 834-2996

Doris O'Conner, Ladies Wear Manager, Belk's Department Store, Orlando, Florida (407) 667-1000

My son Felix wants to be a rock star but happily also realizes he needs to make a living. He used this résumé to get a part-time job during college composing music for an ad agency. This job became full time when he graduated. He's still working toward rock star status. This is a modified functional form of résumé useful when you have little relevant work experience but related educational background.

PERSONAL RESUME
September, 1989

NAME: RUST, Felix Henry

ADDRESS (School):
38 Hemingway Avenue, Apt. 42
Boston, Massachusetts 02119   Telephone: (617) 249-7411

ADDRESS (Father):
6071 Park Place Gardens
Orlando, Florida 32812   Telephone: (407) 240-5544

CIVIL STATUS: Born August 6, 1969 in Los Angeles, California, single, parents divorced, raised by father.

LANGUAGES: English and French, both spoken and read fluently.

EDUCATION:
Began school in the Mt. Brook, Alabama public school system, transferred to the Altamont School in fifth grade through freshman high school, completed high school at William R. Boone High School, Orlando, Florida.

Began college at George Washington University, Washington, D.C. After a year in the business curriculum, chose a music major and transferred to that department. Transferred to the Berklee College of Music, Boston, Massachusetts in January, 1989. Currently completing a professional music major with voice as principal instrument and minors in composition and piano.

MUSICAL HIGHLIGHTS:
Have written and performed 18 original rock music songs including producing studio tapes, singing, and playing all instruments used. Performed professionally as keyboardist with a local rock group in Washington, D.C. during two school semesters including concerts in over 20 clubs with audiences of up to 200. Have working knowledge of most musical forms, compose for five different instruments, write lyrics, and perform on four instruments as well as sing. Began piano lessons at age 10 but quickly switched to trombone in the fifth grade. Played in the high school bank five years before beginning synthesizer and piano lessons again at age fifteen. At George Washington University studied piano,

192

guitar, saxophone, and voice. Was the keyboardist and back-up singer with a local rock band appearing in area nightclubs. Transferred to Berklee on the recommendation of principal music professor. Began as a piano principal with a song writing major. Decided to concentrate on voice to improve performance delivery and switched to that principal this year.

Musical interests and influences range from Bach, Chopin, and Prokofiev to Queen, Iron Maiden, and Metallica. Songs written and copyrighted range from jazz to hard rock. Submitted performance tape to over 200 recording and music publishing companies. Continue to write and perform a wide range of music concentrating on rock and rock derivatives.

PERSONAL HIGHLIGHTS:
Have held 5 different part-time jobs from newspaper delivery to sales clerk in a classical music store. Earned 25% of college expenses. Following an eclectic scope of interest, was awarded the French Prize at The Altamont School; passed the Series 7 General Securities Examination at age 16 to become the youngest licensed stock broker in the United States; was elected President of the Student Counsel during senior year at Boone High School; was Master of Ceremony at all school functions during last two high school years; passed scuba diving certification in 1985; and completed instruction, received license, and parachute jumped in 1986.

WORK HIGHLIGHTS:
Throughout school career have held a variety of part-time jobs beginning as a paperboy during eighth grade, starting with a 200-paper route and ending with over 500. Made ice cream during one summer, delivering and selling in the morning and making ice cream to order in the afternoons. Spent the summer of 1985 studying for the Series 7 General Securities Examination and worked during the summer of 1986 as a stockbroker making up to 100 calls per day. During the 1987 school year, worked part-time as a salesman at the Banana Republic clothing store in Washington, D.C. Was a counterman at J. Buildner & Sons delicatessen during one semester selling as well as making sandwiches, salads, and cold plates. Began working as a salesperson in the Classical Music Department of Tower Records in Boston, was promoted to Security after two months.

REFERENCES: Jim Levy, Head of the Jazz Department, George Washington University, Washington, D.C. (301) 770-5966

Charles Sorrento, Voice Professor, Berklee College of Music, Boston, Mass. (617) 986-9877

H. Lee Rust, father, President of Same Day Express, Inc., Orlando, Florida (407) 240-7877

It's not good enough that you think your references are good ones. You must KNOW they are good. Use this reference check questionnaire to have their responses checked.

Reference Check Questionnaire

Reference's name _____ Date _____

Title _____

Company_____ City _____

Telephone number _____ State _____

1. How long have you known him? _____

2. In what capacity have you known him? _____

3. How did he perform in his job? _____
    _____

4. Is he a hard worker? _____

5. How intelligent is he? _____

6. How original or imaginative? _____

7. How aggressive? _____

8. How egotistical? _____

9. How versatile? _____

10. How much potential does he have? _____
    _____

11. How does he get along with superiors and subordinates? _____
    _____

12. Does he take criticism well? _____
    _____

13. Can he be demanding of his subordinates? _____
    _____

14. Does he have a sense of humor? _____

15. Does he tolerate frustration well? _____

16. Is he honest? _____

17. What are his weaknesses or negative points? _____
    _____

18. Would you consider hiring him yourself? _____

General comments concerning this call and the reference _____
_____

This letter was used to communicate with a reference used in Karilyn Naff's résumé.

Karilyn G. Naff
1674 North Park Drive
Atlanta, Georgia 30341
Telephone (404) 936-7511

March 15, 1990

Mr. K. R. Greenfield
Manager
Compushare, Inc.
2117 First Avenue, North
Atlanta, Georgia 30308

Dear Kirk:

I enjoyed seeing you again after so many months and particularly appreciate your willingness to be a reference in my current job campaign. As promised, I enclose a copy of my résumé.

My objective is to find a position as treasurer or vice-president of finance with a medium-size to large manufacturing company. I feel my experience with distributors is readily transferable to other companies that have large inventory and data processing operations.

I will keep you informed of my progress. If convenient, you might call to advise me of any companies that contact you. This will help me plan my strategy.

My best regards to Nancy and the children.

Yours truly,

Karilyn G. Naff

Enclosure

Use this personal contacts list to compile the contacts which might help with your Jobsearch as well as record appropriate follow-up.

Personal Contacts List

Name _____   Date_____

Name _____   Date contacted _____ by letter,
_____   phone, meeting _____
Title _____   Follow-up _____
Company _____   _____
Address _____   _____
City and state _____   _____
Telephone _____

_____   _____
_____   _____
_____   _____
_____   _____
_____   _____
_____   _____

_____   _____
_____   _____
_____   _____
_____   _____
_____   _____
_____   _____

_____   _____
_____   _____
_____   _____
_____   _____
_____   _____

_____   _____
_____   _____
_____   _____
_____   _____
_____   _____

This letter was used to confirm a meeting with a personal contact. Note that it defines Lois Shookler's job targets as well as the single most significant accomplishment she has to sell.

Lois B. Shookler
365 Poinsettia Drive
Wilmington, Delaware 19804
Telephone (302) 879-6685

April 15, 1990

Mr. William M. Morris
Head Buyer
Waldon Department Stores, Inc.
1345 5th Avenue, North
Wilmington, Delaware 19899

Dear Bill:

Thank you for your time last Wednesday and your kind offer of assistance in my search for a new job.

As we discussed, I am now ready to move out of territory work into sales management. With my depth of experience in the apparel field, I can make a contribution to any clothing or related manufacturer interested in increasing sales in the Delaware, Maryland, and New Jersey area.

In particular, my knowledge of the 97 key accounts in this area and my sales training experience should be of interest. The enclosed copy of my résumé includes some of my other sales accomplishments.

Following your suggestion, I plan to contact Roger Harris of Simon and Harris next week. I would appreciate your passing my résumé on to other potentially interested companies or advising me of contacts I might make. I will let you know what Mr. Harris says and will keep you advised of my progress.

Cordially,

Lois B. Shookler

LBS/js
Enclosure

Lois Shookler used this letter to confirm a telephone conversation with a personal contact who could not offer immediate help. The follow-up letter, however, kept the subject on Glen Brunstein's mind. He called later with a suggestion of a company to contact.

Lois B. Shookler
365 Poinsettia Drive
Wilmington, Delaware 19804
Telephone (302) 879-6685

April 15, 1990

Mr. Glen S. Brunstein, President
Made-to-Form, Inc.
1400 Madison Avenue
New York, New York 10010

Dear Glen:

Confirming our telephone conversation yesterday, I enclose my résumé. Your assistance in my job search should be of great help.

I am now interested in moving out of direct sales into a position as regional sales manager for an apparel firm. My preference is to stay in the Wilmington area where I can make maximum use of my contacts with over 160 retail outlet buyers.

Although you had no immediate suggestions, please look over my résumé and keep my availability in mind. I will plan to call you again in about two weeks to advise you of my progress and check on any ideas you may have.

Yours truly,

Lois B. Shookler

LBS/js
Enclosure

This letter was used to send a résumé to a contact introduced by another party.

Lois B. Shookler
365 Poinsettia Drive
Wilmington, Delaware 19804
Telephone (302) 879-6685

April 20, 1990

Ms. Elaine R. Erdman
Senior Vice-President
Lovejoy Clothes, Inc.
1791 Peachtree Street
Richmond, Virginia 23224

Dear Ms. Erdman:

Confirming our telephone conversation yesterday, I enclose my résumé.

As Mr. Roger Harris explained to you, I am looking for a regional sales manager's position with an apparel company. Your firm may be in a position to use a woman with my background and experience.

As you will see in my résumé, I have a history of increasing territory sales in both difficult and well-established markets. During 1989 I led company sales for Woman's World with a 10% increase versus a 3% increase nationwide. I also trained Middle Atlantic region salesmen for Rothman's and increased territory over 25%.

I will call you late next week to schedule a personal interview. I am in Richmond frequently and could meet with you at your convenience.

Yours truly,

Lois B. Shookler

Enclosure

REGIONAL SALES MANAGER

We are looking for a person with strong sales background in the apparel field to head up one of our major regions. Supervisory and sales training experience are required. Reply with your résumé and salary history to Box 147, Woman's Wear Journal. Our employees know of this search. We are an equal opportunity employer.

Note that this ad response letter begins with an accomplishment in the first sentence. That single accomplishment should motivate the recipient to read the entire letter.

Lois B. Shookler
365 Poinsettia Drive
Wilmington, Delaware 19804
Telephone (302) 879-6685

April 28, 1990

Box 147
c/o Woman's Wear Journal
964 Avenue of the Americas
New York, New York 10010

Dear Sirs:

As sales representative or assistant manager for four national apparel and department store companies, I have 20 years of experience including a continuous record of year-to-year volume increases and a 93% penetration of total key accounts in my territory.

> As a territory salesperson for Woman's World, Inc., I successfully opened seventy-one accounts for a new leisure-wear line in less than two years.

> I took over another territory and increased sales 48% in the first five months while adding thirty-seven new outlets.

> For the Middle Atlantic region, I screened and then field-trained twelve new salespeople with a resultant increase in sales of over 25% for intimate apparel.

> I suggested and implemented relocation of sportswear, lingerie, and cosmetics departments in a department store branch of Balanchine, Inc., moving this outlet from fifth to second largest in the chain.

> During this period, I supervised 108 department store salespeople.

> I saw a potential new market and opened eleven military exchanges for a foundation line of Elen Shoreman, Inc.

I am 40 years old, married, with one daughter, age 19. Though I have a slight preference for the Middle Atlantic region or the Northeast, I am more attracted by professional challenge.

I would like to discuss further details of my experience with you in a personal interview and can be reached at the above number.

Yours truly,

Lois B. Shookler

FINANCIAL ANALYST

Requirements include advanced mathematics, familiarity with computer techniques, 2 to 5 years experience in corporate financial analysis, and a college degree, MBA preferred. Salary to $30,000, potential for advancement, and excellent benefits. Send your resume in confidence to:

Northwest Instruments Company
P.O. Box 2515
Portland, Oregon 97201

We Are an Equal
Opportunity Employer

Ronald Marque had little experience in his target field. He therefore emphasized his education in the first paragraph of this ad response letter and rewrote his accomplishments in mortgage sales to relate to financial analysis. Refer to his résumé in Form 21.

Ronald J. Marque
Apartment 4, Terrace Court
Chicago, Illinois 47092
Telephone (312) 221-9130

February 11, 1990

Mr. Brian M. Cooper, Vice-President, Finance
Northwest Instruments Company
P.O. Box 2515
Portland, Oregon 97201

Dear Mr. Cooper:

For a $500-million mortgage company, I instituted and computerized a regression analysis for loan closings and interest rate movements with 88% accuracy in gross amount and 100% accuracy in predicting trends. I am an MBA graduate in Econometrics. In addition to usual business courses, I studied the application of statistics including queuing theory, Markov chains, variance and regression analysis, as well as modeling, investment analysis, and corporate planning.

Because you advertised for a financial analyst with this type of experience and training, I thought you would be interested in some of my other accomplishments.

> For the management of the Ingel Mortgage Company, I analyzed and wrote reports on a system to predict sales volume for cash management, a history and evaluation of unsold mortgage loans, and an audit report on the portfolio of an acquired subsidiary.

> Using internal rate of return, discounted cash flow, payback and lease vs. buy, I performed a number of capital investment case studies ranging in size from $10,000 to $600,000.

> I analyzed and originated the sale of mortgage-backed securities, producing profits of up to $57,000 per security.

> As a department head, I reorganized the mortgage marketing function, resulting in an 18% decrease in total expense and an 80% decrease in overtime with no loss of efficiency.

I am married with no children and have worked for two mortgage and finance companies. My objective is to find a position outside the mortgage field where I can make better application of my training and recent business experience.

I would like to discuss further details of my background and accomplishments with you in a personal interview. After 5:00 P.M. I can be reached at the above number, or at (312) 967-4960 during working hours.

Sincerely,

Ronald J. Marque

VICE-PRESIDENT AND
GENERAL MANAGER

The largest women's tailored-suit and dress manufacturer in the United States needs a "hands on" executive to take full profit-and-loss responsibility over its Columbus, South Carolina division. Minimum 10 years apparel experience including both marketing and production. Salary commensurate with experience.
You must submit your complete resume and salary requirements in order to be considered.

Reply to: P.O. Box 19711
New York, N.Y. 10022
We Are an Equal Opportunity
Employer

For this ad response letter, Jerrold Brooks found the company's name by calling several friends to inquire about the identity of the largest tailored-suit manufacturer in the United States with a division in Columbus.

Jerrold A. Brooks
1216 Thornhill Drive
Dallas, Texas 75221
Telephone (214) 871-1496

Mr. Richard A. Graffner, Jr., President   February 6, 1990
Liberty Tailored Wear, Inc.
P.O. Box 19711
New York, New York 10022

Dear Mr. Graffner:

As a vice-president of Howard & Sharpe, a children's and infant's apparel company, I performed new product and trend R&D while serving on a four-man merchandising committee for 15 years. Sales went from $5.5 million to $50 million and profits from $500,000 to $2.8 million.

Because you advertised for a vice-president and general manager over your Columbus, South Carolina division, you may be interested in the scope of my experience and accomplishments.

I started up and managed two new plant facilities and improved methods of pattern making, fit control, spreading, and cutting. This saved $400,000 in three years.

I organized and implemented a complete quality system including fabric inspection and labs. This improved quality, saving $80,000 in fabrics, $20,000 in trim, and up to $100,000 per year in customer returns.

With total responsibility over the marketing function, I changed to a more diversified and high-styled line in sportswear in order to compete with cheap imports. Sales rose 40% in two years.

I have worked with time studies, production costs and rates, cost estimating formulas, production control, and production planning.

I am 47 years old and have a Business Administration degree with continuing education in Mechanical Engineering, Packaging, Textiles, Quality Control, and Accounting.

Although I do not have a current résumé, I will be glad to prepare one to give you at an interview. I would like to meet with you to discuss my background in detail and will plan to call you late next week to see if a convenient time can be arranged.

Sincerely,

Jerrold A. Brooks

CORPORATE TREASURER

ICC has a key management opportunity for an individual with broad financial experience and specific expertise in treasury and corporate finance functions.

You will direct worldwide treasury activities. Primary responsibilities will be cash forecasting and managing bank relations, foreign currency exposure management, development of corporate financing strategies, and management of nonbenefit insurance programs.

This position requires a BS degree (MBA preferred) and 7 years exeprience in both controllership and treasury roles. Multinational responsibility is a prerequisite. The ideal candidate is currently earning 40 to 75K annually. This individual may be chief financial officer of a $50-million to $200-million company or treasurer or assistant treasurer of a $200-million-plus organization.

ICC is a multidivision, international electronics manufacturer headquartered in Los Angeles, CA. We reported record sales of $400 million, up 20% over last year.

For immediate and confidential consideration, please send your résumé including salary history to: Doug Hooper, Director of Corporate Staffing, 464 West Street, Los Angeles, CA 94142. We are an equal opportunity employer m/f.

ICC CORPORATION

Robert Blair didn't have the multinational experience called for in this ad. He simply did not mention it in this reply letter but referred directly to all other requirements. He added a paragraph emphasizing his qualifications in the areas requested and listed additional experience that should be of interest to the company.

Robert V. Blair
4177 Kennis Drive
Syracuse, New York 13209
Telephone (315) 881-0884

Mr. Doug Hooper   February 12, 1990
Director of Corporate Staffing
ICC Corporation
464 West Street
Los Angeles, California 94142

Dear Mr. Hooper:

I have been vice-president finance of a $50-million company and assistant treasurer of a $400-million multidivision company. Because you advertised for a corporate treasurer with this type of background, you might be interested in some of my other accomplishments.

Cash Forecasting and Management. For Delta Materials Company, I developed and implemented changes in a cash management system which produced a permanent reduction of "required cash balances" of well over $2 million.

Bank Relations. I built rapport with bank contacts nationwide, which allowed the doubling of credit lines from $28 million to $57 million.

Corporate Financing. For Transport Systems, Inc., I negotiated private debt placements that increased long-term financing from $15 million to $38 million. I took part in the company's first public debt offering of $60 million and am also experienced in most other forms of financing.

In addition to the above areas specifically mentioned in your advertisement, I have 13 years of experience in data processing, sales, and sales management with IBM Corporation. As Buffalo branch manager, I exceeded revenue and earnings objectives by 20%.

I am a Certified Public Accountant and holder of the Certificate in Management Accounting. I graduated from the University of Wisconsin in 1964 with a degree in Economics and Business with an Accounting major. I am 47 years old, married, and have one daughter, age 13.

I would like to meet with you to discuss further details of my career.

Sincerely,

Robert V. Blair

VP–INTERNATIONAL

In return for an opportunity to DOUBLE OUR INTERNATIONAL BUSINESS within three to five years, the successful candidate for our position of V.P.—International will send us a résumé describing:

- concrete accomplishments
- prior P&L responsibility
- solid familiarity from within the controls industry
- responsible line experience in two or more of:
  marketing
  manufacturing
  engineering
- finance experience (plus)
- international experience (a must)
- geographic limitations (if any)
- compensation history and requirements

This position reports to the president of a firm in a turnaround situation already on the upswing. This is not a job for someone who wants to preside gracefully over an already secure commercial empire, but for an executive whose history, not just his/her cover story, reveals a productive response to risk and challenge. You should currently earn between fifty and seventy–five thousand dollars.

We are an equal opportunity employer.
Reply to Box H-72, *The New York Times*

This ad response by Robert S. Thomason was slightly modified in that it responds to the listed requirements by repeating the entire list except for compensation history. The result for this Jobsearch client was an immediate request for an interview. Bob learned that his letter was the only one of over 500 that responded point by point to the qualifications requested.

Robert S. Thomason
1921 Forest Run Drive
Great Falls, Virginia 23322
Telephone (703) 755-6421

Box H-72, c/o The New York Times   April 2, 1990
Post Office Box 361400
New York, New York 10023

Gentlemen:

In response to your New York Times advertisement of March 25, 1990, for a new vice-president-international, I think you will be interested in the following aspects of my career:

Concrete accomplishments: As president, I returned a brick manufacturing company to profitability in two years, starting from a $600,000 loss.

Prior P&L responsibility: I have been president of two separate corporations grossing in excess of $7 million per year.

Familiarity with controls industry: In both Europe and the United States, I purchased and installed industrial controls in new plant projects.

Responsible line experience in:
Marketing. I set up, staffed, and managed a sales group in Europe for an engineering and construction company, including direct sales effort on my part, and produced $50 million in project sales in the second year.

Manufacturing. I was president of one capital- and one labor-intensive company as well as construction superintendent for industrial plants.

Engineering. I am a graduate mechanical engineer and have served as both project manager and project engineer for industrial contracts.

Finance experience: I set up both accounting and cost control systems, and have negotiated commercial bank and SBA loans and open lines of credit.

International experience: I've served four years in Europe with a European firm having minority American participation, doing both Eastern and Western European work; I read and speak French fluently. My wife is a French citizen.

I am 38 years old, a graduate of Yale University, with one child, age 7. At your convenience, I am available for an interview.

Yours truly,

Robert S. Thomason

DESIGN ENGINEER

Westinghouse is expanding its power turbine division. We are seeking engineers with turbine blade design and wind tunnel evaluation experience. Our salary and benefit programs are competitive. We are an equal opportunity employer. Reply with your résumé and salary requirements to:

Ellen G. Brownlee
Westinghouse Electric Company, Inc.
Turbine Division
1000 Westinghouse Center
Pittsburgh, Pennsylvania 47991

This ad response emphasizes educational versus work-related experience for Susan Abrams, a first-time job seeker. It also serves as a cover letter for her résumé (Form 27), the exception for first-time job seekers who should send a résumé when responding to a help wanted ad.

Susan Marie Abrams
976 Austin Terrace
Orlando, Florida 32872
Telephone (407) 240-6040

June 24, 1990

Ms. Ellen G. Brownlee
Westinghouse Electric Company, Inc.
Turbine Division
1000 Westinghouse Center
Pittsburgh, Pennsylvania 47991

Dear Mrs. Brownlee,

In response to your advertisement in the Journal of Mechanical Engineering, my educational background in fluid flow, computer application to fluid dynamics analysis, and laminar/turbulent transitions might be of interest to your company.

In particular, I have done extensive lab work in the fields of liquid and gaseous flow characteristics with a specialty in the point of change between laminar and chaotic flow functions. This experience, coupled with my computer analysis work during college, might be well suited to the blade evaluation and design function described in your ad.

If appropriate, I would like to meet with you to discuss the contribution I might make to your organization. In that regard, enclosed is a copy of my résumé. I am available to meet at your convenience and can be reached at the above number.

I look forward to hearing from you and to the possibility of working with you and your associates.

Sincerely,

Susan M. Abrams

encl.

Jerrold Brooks immediately confirmed a telephone call with this letter enclosing his résumé but highlighting his major accomplishments. Note the qualification to his salary level in the sentence following the salary number.

Jerrold A. Brooks
1216 Thornhill Drive
Dallas, Texas 75221
Telephone (214) 871-1496

February 16, 1990

Mr. Richard A. Gaffner, Jr.
President
Liberty Tailored Wear, Inc.
Post Office Box 19711
New York, New York 10022

Dear Mr. Gaffner:

Thank you for your telephone call and interest in my background experience. As you requested, I enclose a copy of my résumé.

My accomplishments during a 23-year history with Howard & Sharpe have prepared me to take on the general manager's position that we discussed. In particular, my quality control experience outlined under Production and Engineering will allow me to make an immediate contribution to the customer-return and customer-complaint problems you mentioned.

At Howard & Sharpe my current salary is $50,000 with an incentive bonus that was $10,000 last year. Although one of my reasons for considering a job change is a salary increase, an acceptable salary will depend more upon the challenge of the position and the future potential.

After you have had an opportunity to review the enclosed information, I would like to meet with you to discuss the position and the contributions I can make. I look forward to receiving your call after your trip to the West Coast next week.

Sincerely,

Jerrold A. Brooks

Enclosure

These two situations wanted ads were placed by Jobsearch clients in trade newsletters likely to be read by executives of tartet companies.

Jerrold Brooks (Form 24) placed this ad in the *Garment Trade Daily* newsletter.

> GENERAL MANAGER/VP MFG—23 years experience in every aspect of ready-to-wear manufacturing, marketing, and sales including new product development and merchandising. Respond to GTD #640.

Janet Parsons (Form 25) placed this ad in *The Real Estate Lawyer,* a newsletter distributed to all lawyers registered in the *Martendale-Hubbel Law Directory* with a real estate specialty.

> REAL ESTATE LAW—14 years experience; Missouri Bar and licensed real estate broker; trail work, title claims, insurance, and right-of-way; seeks real estate litigation-related position. 2701 Flagstone Rd., Kansas City, MO 64112, (816) 533-2069.

This mail marketing letter was sent by a Jobsearch client to large, national companies taken from the Dun & Bradstreet directories. It was directed toward a vice-president-finance or treasurer's position. Note that this letter from Bob Blair is directed toward a corporate treasurer's position in a smaller company. Also note Bob's advertisement response (Form 38).

Robert V. Blair
4177 Kennis Drive
Syracuse, New York 13209
Telephone (315) 881-0884

Name, Title   January 25, 1990
Company Name
Street Address
City, State, Zip Code

Dear Mr./Ms. _____:

As assistant treasurer of Delta Materials Company, I developed and implemented major changes in the cash management system which produced a permanent reduction of "required cash balances" amounting to over $2 million. Subsequently, I became vice-president-finance with Transport Systems, Inc., and applied the same techniques with similar results.

If you need a financial executive with this type of imagination, you may be interested in other highlights of my career:

>   Realizing the need, I created an investment policy and used it to manage a short-term portfolio that reached a high of $45 million.

>   After setting as an objective a 25% reduction in days to collection I established a plan and coordinated efforts to achieve this goal.

>   I organized and participated in preparations for a $60 million public debt offering that opened a new source of financing for the company.

>   In 13 years of experience with data processing, sales, and sales management with IBM Corporation, I became Buffalo branch manager and exceeded revenue and earnings objectives by 20%.

I am 47 years old, married, and have one daughter, age 13. I graduated from the University of Wisconsin in 1964 with a Bachelor of Arts degree in Economics and Business. I am a Certified Public Accountant and holder of the Certificate in Management Accounting.

I would like to meet with you to discuss further the contribution I could make to your firm. I will call to arrange a convenient time to meet.

Sincerely,

Robert V. Blair

This mail marketing letter was sent to the owners and presidents of small to medium-size companies taken from the chamber of commerce directory. In this letter Bob defined Certificate in Management Accounting because it would not be known to officials in small companies. Note the reference to Bob's Buffalo trip.

Robert V. Blair
4177 Kennis Drive
Syracuse, New York 13209
Telephone (315) 881-0884

Name, Title   January 25, 1990
Company Name
Street Address
City, State, Zip Code

Dear Mr./Ms. _____:

I have held sales and sales management positions with IBM Corporation, including Buffalo branch manager with profit-and-loss responsibility for a $5-million operation, which exceeded revenue and earnings objectives by 20%.

If you need a general manager with this type of experience, you may be interested in certain highlights of my career:

As owner, I formed a new company including financing, supervision of construction, selection and hiring of personnel, advertising, marketing, and management. I brought sales to a $550,000 yearly level in four months.

As assistant treasurer of Delta Materials, a large public company, I built and maintained rapport with bank contacts, which allowed the doubling of credit lines in just three days.

Serving as a vice-president for a $50-million company, I designed a materials control system for two divisions to eliminate stock outages and reduce investment in inventory by 30%.

I am 47 years old, married, and have one daughter, age 13. I graduated from the University of Wisconsin in 1964 with a Bachelor of Arts degree in Economics and Business. My major was in Accounting with a minor in Industrial Management. I am a holder of the Certificate in Management Accounting, a recognition of proficiency in both management and financial skills.

I plan to be in Buffalo during the week of March 1 and would like to meet with you at that time. If you will call me, we can arrange a convenient time to meet.

Sincerely,

Robert V. Blair

This mail marketing letter was sent to college and university presidents in the target area. Note the difference in wording and in the choice of the accomplishments in Carter's letter directed toward charities (Form 46).

Carter M. Harlen
3230 West Valley Drive
New Orleans, Louisiana 70132
Telephone (504) 977-8815

April 5, 1990

Name, Title
University Name
Street Address
City, State, Zip Code

Dear _____:

As planning and development director at a 1,000-student liberal arts college, I analyzed the space needs, layout, and design for a new administration building and then raised $4.5 million to build it.

If you need this type of fund raising talent, you might be interested in some of my other accomplishments:

For Anderson College I established a college development department and raised over $5 million in deferred gifts.

I reorganized the alumni department and increased regular contributions over three times.

As a result of my efforts in planning, organizing, and implementing a multischool fund raising activity, corporate contributions increased by 95% and total contributors by 65% for the accredited theological schools of Michigan and Indiana.

I developed a long-range, fund-raising plan for Sanford Southern College, increasing its gifts by 130% over a four-year period.

After taking a series of courses in Estate Planning, I applied this expertise to establish various trusts and bequests for several charitable organizations.

I am 36 years old and have a Bachelor of Science degree in Social Studies and Education with postgraduate work in Public Relations, Administration, and College Development. I am interested in a planning and development position with an educational institution in the New Orleans area.

I would like to meet with you to discuss my qualifications and their application to your organization and can be reached at (504) 964-2340, or after 5:00 P.M. at (504) 977-8815.

Sincerely,

Carter M. Harlen

This mail marketing letter is similar to the preceding one but is directed toward charities.

Carter M. Harlen
3230 West Valley Drive
New Orleans, Louisiana 70132
Telephone (504) 977-8815

April 5, 1990

Name, Title
Organization Name
Street Address
City, State, Zip Code

Dear _____:

At a nonprofit charitable institution where I was development director, I planned a capital donation program and raised $4.5 million to build a new administration building.

Because you may need this type of fund-raising talent, you might be interested in some of my other accomplishments:

I planned, organized, and implemented a multi-institutional fund-raising activity and increased corporate contributions by 95% and total contributors by 65%.

I set up a five-year, long-range fund-raising and deferred-giving plan that increased gift income by 40%.

For a charitable institution, I established a college development department and raised over $5 million in deferred gifts.

As a consultant, I developed a long-range fund-raising plan for a Southern college, increasing its gifts by 130% over a four-year period.

After taking a series of courses in Estate Planning, I applied this expertise to establish various trusts and bequests for several charitable organizations.

I am 36 years old and have a Bachelor of Science degree in Social Studies and Education with postgraduate work in Public Relations Administration. I am interested in a planning and development position with a charitable or civic organization in the New Orleans area.

I would like to meet with you to discuss my qualifications and their application to your organization and can be reached at (504) 964-2340, or after 5:00 P.M. at (504) 977-8815.

Sincerely,

Carter M. Harlen

This mail marketing letter was sent to local companies and to vice-presidents of sales or marketing in national companies with Columbus distributorships. Note Bill Larson did not have a university degree but attended college. His age, which was 54, is not mentioned. However, the ages of his children would indicate it was between 44 and 54.

William M. Larson
2631 Mountain View Drive
Columbus, Ohio 43221
Telephone (614) 876-0548

Name, Title   March 25, 1990
Company
Street Address
City, State, Zip Code

Dear _____:

As general manager or sales manager for Philco distributors in seven locations, I was sent to problem areas. In each case, I increased both sales and profits, reorganized the salespersons and dealer groups, introduced training programs, and turned a smooth-running operation over to my successor.

If sales or distribution is a problem for your company, you should be interested in some of my specific accomplishments:

> For a local appliance and electronics distributor, I organized a special products division, selected lines, established marketing plans, and created $2.4 million in sales with a 22.3% gross profit.

> At Philco in Columbus, I reorganized bookkeeping, billing, ware-housing, and inventory control and reduced operating expense by 5%. At the same time, I increased total sales volume while items representing $897,000 in previous annual sales were being removed from the lines offered.

> I started my career in retail sales with Sears, Roebuck and Company, setting sales records in three different departments in four years.

I am married and have two daughters, 19 and 22. I studied Business Administration at Marshall University, with continuing education in both company and university sponsored sales management courses and seminars.

I would like to meet to discuss my background and the contribution that I might make to your company. I will call to arrange a convenient time.

Sincerely,

William M. Larson

This letter was used by Susan Abrams in her mail marketing campaign, which included 175 companies. Again, because she was a first-time job seeker with no directly related work accomplishments, she included a copy of her résumé (Form 27).

Susan Marie Abrams
976 Austin Terrace
Orlando, Florida 32872
Telephone (407) 240-6040

June 10, 1990

Mr. George C. Snyder
Stoddard Valve Company
5145 Curry Ford Rd.
Seattle, Washington 98776

Dear Mr. Snyder:

My educational background in fluid flow, computer application to fluid dynamics analysis, and laminar/turbulent transitions might be of interest to your company.

I am looking for an engineering position with a company dealing in the fields of liquid and gaseous flow characteristics. With a specialty in the point of change between laminar and chaotic flow functions, I might contribute to your design section in the areas of computer analysis or turbulence prevention techniques.

If appropriate, I would like to meet with you to discuss this further. In that regard, enclosed is a copy of my résumé. I am available to meet at your convenience and can be reached at the above number.

I look forward to hearing from you and to the possibility of working with you and your associates.

Sincerely,

Susan M. Abrams

This letter was used by my son in his mail marketing campaign for a part-time position during college. He wanted to use his music background and not make hamburgers in a fast food restaurant. As a first-time job seeker, he also enclosed his résumé (Form 28).

Felix H. Rust
38 Hemingway Avenue, Apt. 42
Boston, Massachusetts 02119
Telephone (617) 249-7411

September 2, 1989

Ms. Iris S. Greenbaum
Greenbaum Advertising, Inc.
1789 North West 17th Street
Boston, Massachusetts 02103

Dear Ms. Greenbaum,

My music composition and lyric writing experience might be of interest to your advertising agency.

I am looking for a part-time position with an agency that might need jingles, original background music, or music adaptation on a sporadic basis. I can work on an as-needed basis with flexible hours that can be tailored to your needs.

If appropriate, I would like to meet with you to discuss the contribution I might make to your organization. In that regard, enclosed is a copy of my résumé together with a cassette tape of songs I have both written and performed. I am available to meet at your convenience and can be reached at the above number.

I look forward to hearing from you and to the possibility of working with you and your associates.

Sincerely,

Felix H. Rust

encl.

Compare this mail marketing letter with Lois Shookler's ad response (Form 35). She had never been a manufacturer's representative but could phrase her accomplishments to give herself credibility in this field.

Lois B. Shookler
365 Poinsettia Drive
Wilmington, Delaware 19804
Telephone (302) 879-6685

Mr. Lawrence Harbringer   April 22, 1977
Vice-President, Sales
Young Fashions, Inc.
714 Monte Verde Avenue
San Mateo, California 96074

Dear Mr. Harbringer:

I introduced a new career apparel and lounge-wear line in Delaware, New Jersey, and Maryland, putting it into seventy-one accounts.

Because you might need a manufacturer's representative with this kind of talent, some of my other accomplishments might interest you.

After taking over lines for an intimate apparel company, I increased sales 48% in the first five months while adding thirty-seven new accounts.

I saw a potential new market and opened eleven military exchanges for a foundation line.

In seventeen years of territory sales experience in apparel, I have a continuous record of year-to-year volume increases and a far above average rapport with the key accounts in my region. I sell ninety of the ninety-seven largest accounts in cities of 50,000 or more people.

I am 40 years old, married, with one daughter, age 19. I travel my territory working out of a fully equipped mobile sales office. For new lines, I would expect a $500 per week draw against a minimum of 7% commission as well as an 80% delivery guarantee for commissions against firm orders.

I would welcome a personal meeting to discuss your line and the contribution I can make to your sales. I can be reached at the above number over the weekends or by message during the week after 3:00 P.M.

Sincerely,

Lois B. Shookler

This third-party mail marketing letter was used to explore an entrepreneurial venture as part of a more conventional Job-search.

H. Lee Rust
3404 East Briarcliff Road
Birmingham, Alabama 35223
Telephone (205) 967-9728

January 11, 1990

Mr. Gerry Wiggers
President
Industrial Materials, Inc.
2222 South Fourth Avenue
Birmingham, Alabama 35210

Dear Mr. Wiggers:

I have a business associate and friend who is interested in purchasing all or an equity position in an industrial supplies distributor or manufacturer's representative firm. Because this individual is now employed with a company you probably know, I must keep his name confidential until an interest in further discussions is established.

He is 35 years old and has a background in industrial engineering and construction with experience in industrial sales and purchasing. He is a native of Birmingham and is bright, aggressive, and one of the hardest workers that I know.

If you are interested in converting some of your years of work into equity, he may offer you such an opportunity. If you are interested in expanding your company, he can bring both capital and an additional, aggressive sales hand into your venture.

If you would like to discuss this possibility further, please call me at the above number after 5:00 P.M. or during the weekend. I might add that this letter is personal. I will not receive a commission or fee of any kind as a result of agreements you might reach.

Sincerely,

H. Lee Rust

This letter responds to a request for completion of an employment application. Note that both Bill's résumé and reference to a series of accomplishments are included with the letter.

William M. Larson
2631 Mountain View Drive
Columbus, Ohio 43221
Telephone (614) 876-0548

April 4, 1990

Ms. Marion W. Bircher
Vice-President of Personnel
Hitachi Television, Inc.
Post Office Box 1796
San Francisco, California 94371

Dear Ms. Bircher:

As requested in our telephone conversation of March 15, and subsequent letter, my completed employment application is enclosed. In order to give you more information about my past experience and accomplishments, I have also attached a copy of my résumé.

In particular, you might note the history of sales and profit increases I created for Philco during 23 years of steadily increasing responsibilities.

After you have had an opportunity to review the enclosed information, I would like to meet with you to discuss the contribution I can make to Hitachi. I look forward to hearing from you in the next few weeks.

Sincerely,

William M. Larson

Enclosures

Karilyn Naff used this letter to confirm a telephone conversation with an employment agency and send them her résumé. Note that she defines her job objectives and refers to accomplishments in her résumé.

Karilyn G. Naff
1674 North Park Drive
Atlanta, Georgia 30341
Telephone (404) 936-7511

April 13, 1990

Mr. Richard M. Wilson
General Manager
Financial Placement, Inc.
Post Office Box 3796
Memphis, Tennessee 38101

Dear Mr. Wilson:

Confirming our telephone conversation yesterday, I enclose my personal résumé.

As we discussed, I am seeking a position as controller of a firm grossing in excess of $20 million annually, or as treasurer of a smaller company. I have a definite preference for a large city in the Southeast. My minimum salary requirement is $40,000. You may use this figure for your own reference, but I prefer that salary not be discussed with a potential employer.

As you will see in my résumé, I have a broad background in financial management, with a history of implementing controls that increased profits. The four companies for which I have worked were all in different industries. This has exposed me to a wide variety of problems and methods of solution. I have also worked with many types of computers and computer control systems.

I would appreciate your sending my résumé to any firms that retain you to fill appropriate vacancies and advising me of their names. Because I am conducting a broad search on my own, I do not want my résumé sent to firms that do not have a specific job opening. I will keep you advised of my availability.

Thank you for your kind assistance.

Sincerely,

Karilyn G. Naff

Encl.

This is a letter to an employment agency that works in the apparel industry. Again, both job objectives and accomplishments are highlighted together with salary requirements.

Jerrold A. Brooks
1216 Thornhill Drive
Dallas, Texas 75221
Telephone (214) 871-1496

February 5, 1990

Hoffman Associates
200 Fifth Avenue
Suite 1555
New York, New York 10017

Dear Sirs:

I have a 23-year career history with an apparel manufacturer that grew from $5.5 million to $50 million gross annual sales. During this period I served as vice-president or manager over marketing, merchandising, packaging, manufacturing, engineering, quality control, and purchasing.

Perhaps you know of a company that could use this scope of experience. In this regard, I enclose a copy of my résumé outlining a few of my more significant accomplishments.

My objective is to find a position as vice-president of marketing or merchandising with a large company or as president or general manager of a smaller company or division. My preference would be to stay in an industry associated with apparel, textiles, or packaging.

I am not limited by location and would consider the challenge of complete responsibility over an unprofitable operation. My minimum salary requirement is in the $60,000 range and will depend upon location and potential. You may use this figure for your own reference. My preference is that you do not discuss salary with a protential employer.

Please advise me of any opportunities I might investigate, or send my résumé to companies that might be interested. Your assistance will be appreciated.

Sincerely,

Jerrold A. Brooks

Enclosure

This form is used to define a single-target Jobsearch.

SINGLE-TARGET JOBSEARCH

Date _____

Name of Company _____

Headquarters address _____

City, state, zip code _____

Telephone number _____

Description of industry or industries _____

_____

Size of company: Annual gross sales _____

Number of employees _____

Type of company _____

Position desired _____

Responsibilities _____

_____

Location desired _____

Division or subsidiary if different from headquarters _____

Reasons for treating this as a single target_____

_____

Reasons you wish to work for this company_____

_____

Reasons this company might hire you _____

_____

Inside sources of information _____

_____

Outside sources of information _____

_____

Other contacts in a position to help _____

_____

_____

In regard to this letter from Ronald Marque, note his résumé (Form 21) and his ad answer (Form 36). His effort with this local company was only one part of a job campaign that was national in scope.

Ronald J. Marque
Apartment 4, Terrace Court
Chicago, Illinois 47092
Telephone (312) 221-9130

April 23, 1990

Ms. Sandra G. Chardier
Vice-President, Finance
American Food Machinery, Inc.
Post Office Box 4000
Chicago, Illinois 47092

Dear Ms. Chardier:

I enjoyed meeting you last Monday and appreciate the preliminary interest you had in the possible use of regression analysis and econometric modeling for investment and other management decisions at American Food Machinery.

Following your suggestion, I set up a meeting with John Chandler on Monday of next week. I will use the information he gives me on past capital investments to perform several different decision analyses. I will compare these projected results with the actual current return. This will allow me to test my theory that such financial tools would be of benefit to American Food Machinery.

Then I will update the report I gave you. This should be completed by April 30. I will call you late next week to find a convenient time to discuss the results with you.

As you know, I am particularly interested in American Food Machinery and the possibility of joining your department as financial analyst. My report should demonstrate the contribution that I can make.

Thank you for your assistance.

Sincerely,

Ronald J. Marque

This short letter simply confirms an appointment. Even if this short, the cardinal rule says always confirm a contact with a letter.

Karilyn G. Naff
1674 North Park Drive
Atlanta, Georgia 30341
Telephone (404) 936-7511

April 5, 1990

Mr. Carlos Aslego
Vice-President, Finance
Morris Products Company
7514 Highway 31, South
Hapeville, Georgia 30354

Dear Mr. Aslego:

Confirming our telephone conversation yesterday, I will meet you at 10:30 A.M. on April 18 at the Morris Products plant.

I am most interested in the controller's position with your company and look forward to discussing it with you and Mr. Wakefield.

Thank you for your consideration.

Yours truly,

Karilyn G. Naff

This letter was used to decline a job interview due to geographic preferences. Lois Shookler did, however, qualify her decision pending the completion of her search.

Lois B. Shookler
365 Poinsettia Drive
Wilmington Delaware 19804
Telephone (302) 879-6685

April 20, 1990

Mr. Wilson B. Myers
President
Merchandise Sales, Inc.
2712 South 20th Street
Hartford Conneticut 06607

Dear Mr. Myers:

Thank you for your interest in me and my background. I was impressed by the recent growth of your company and your description of its future plans. Although I would like to participate in such an aggressive organization, my intention is to remain in the Wilmington area.

My current job search should be completed in another four weeks. If I have not found a suitable position in Wilmington by then, I will call you to arrange a meeting.

Meanwhile, I wish you the best of luck with your expansion plans.

Sincerely,

Lois B. Shookler

This letter confirms a telephone conversation that had negative results. It leaves the options open and schedules a follow-up call made by Carter Harlen.

Carter M. Harlen
3230 West Valley Drive
New Orleans, Louisiana 70132
Telephone (504) 977-8815

April 19, 1990

Ms. Brooks Stanford
Administrative Director
Crippled Children's Hospital
1900 Greenfield Avenue
New Orleans, Louisiana 70157

Dear Ms. Stanford:

Confirming our telephone conversation yesterday, I am most interested in the planning and development position we discussed. Although you hope to find a candidate with direct hospital experience, if you do not, I would like to be considered.

My fund-raising experience with educational institutions should be readily transferable to your hospital building program. In addition, my business and construction background would also be of use.

I will plan to call you in about a month to check on your progress in filling the position. Meanwhile, if you wish to talk with me further, I will be available at your convenience.

Thank you for your kind consideration.

Sincerely,

Carter M. Harlen

This fax letter was used by Susan Abrams to contact a business-man who would not return her calls.

FAX LETTER

To: _____ Mr. Ladd D. Morris _____

Company: __ Lansom Industries _____

Fax Number: ___ (414) 785-8300 _____

From: ___ Susan M. Abrams _____

Date: _____ September 23, 1988 _____ Time: ___ 9:00 am ___

Total number of pages including this cover sheet: ____ 1 _____

— —

*** If there are any problems with this transmission, please call as soon
as possible:

(205) 834-2882   (800) 826-0042

— —

We are transmitting from:

Toshiba 30100 Facsimile Machine

Fax number: (205) 830-6154

— —

Dear Mr. Morris,

I have been unable to reach you since my letter of August 30 but
am most interested in the position we discussed. Would you please
call me when convenient at (205) 974-1396. I look forward to
talking with you further.

Sincerely,

Susan M. Abrams

— —

Review these questions and your responses prior to an interview. These are the form of general questions an experienced interviewer might ask. Add additional questions in the blank spaces that relate to your background.

INTERVIEW QUESTIONS TO EXPECT

1. Did you bring a résumé?
2. What salary do you expect to receive?
3. What was your salary in your last job?
4. Why do you want to change jobs or why did you leave your last job?
5. What do you identify as your most significant accomplishment in your last job?
6. How many hours do you normally work per week?
7. What did you like and dislike about your last job?
8. How did you get along with your superiors and subordinates?
9. Can you be demanding of your subordinates?
10. How would you evaluate the company you were with last?
11. What were its competitive strengths and weaknesses?
12. What best qualifies you for the available position?
13. How long will it take you to start making a significant contribution?
14. How do you feel about our company—its size, industry, and competitive position?
15. What interests you most about the available position?
16. How would you structure this job or organize your department?
17. What control or financial data would you want and why?
18. How would you establish your primary inside and outside lines of communication?
19. What would you like to tell me about yourself?
20. Were you a good student?
21. Have you kept up in your field? How?
22. What do you do in your spare time?
23. At what age do you want to retire?
24. What are your greatest strengths and weaknesses?
25. What is your job potential?
26. What are your career goals?
27. Do you want to own your own business?
28. How long will you stay with us?
29. What did your father do? Your mother?
30. What do your brothers and sisters do?
31. Are you a member of a church or synagogue? Do you attend regularly?
32. Do you participate in civic affairs?

33. What professional associations do you belong to?
34. What is your credit standing?
35. What are your personal likes and dislikes?
36. How many children do you have?
37. Would you describe your family as a close one?
38. How aggressive are you?
39. What motivates you to work?
40. Is money a strong incentive for you?
41. Do you prefer line or staff work?
42. Would you rather work alone or in a team?
43. What do you look for when hiring people?
44. Have you ever fired anyone?
45. Can you get along with union members and their leaders?
46. What do you think of the current economic and political situation?
47. How will government policy effect our industry or your job?
48. Will you sign a noncompete agreement or employment contract?
49. Why should we hire you?
50. Do you want the job?
51. _____
52. _____
53. _____
54. _____
55. _____
56. _____
57. _____
58. _____
59. _____
60. _____
61. _____
62. _____
63. _____
64. _____
65. _____
66. _____
67. _____
68. _____
69. _____
70. _____

Use these questions to more fully participate in your interview and control its content and direction. Again, add questions in the blanks that relate to your job or educational background.

INTERVIEW QUESTIONS TO ASK

1. What is the first problem that needs attention of the person you hire?
2. What other problems need attention now?
3. What has been done about any of these to date?
4. How has this job been performed in the past?
5. Why is it now vacant?
6. Do you have a written job description for this position?
7. What are its major responsibilities?
8. What authority would I have? How would you define its scope?
9. What are the company's five-year sales and profit projections?
10. What needs to be done to reach these projections?
11. What are the company's major strengths and weaknesses?
12. What are its strengths and weaknesses in production?
13. What are its strenghts and weaknesses in its products or its competitive position?
14. Whom do you identify as your major competitors?
15. What are their strengths and weaknesses?
16. How do you view the future for your industry?
17. Do you have any plans for new products or acquisitions?
18. Might this company be sold or acquired?
19. What is the company's current financial strength?
20. What can you tell me about the individual to whom I would report?
21. What can you tell me about other persons in key positions?
22. What can you tell me about the subordinates I would have?
23. How would you define your management philosophy?
24. Are employees afforded an opportunity for continuing education?
25. What are you looking for in the person who will fill this job?
26. _____
27. _____
28. _____
29. _____
30. _____
31. _____
32. _____
33. _____
34. _____
35. _____

This form is used to keep a written record of interviews. You will refer to this as you complete your follow-up and any additional interviews.

INTERVIEW RECORD

Company _____ Date _____

Contact's name _____ Title _____

Other contacts _____ Title _____

_____ Title _____

Address _____ Phone _____

Products _____

Gross Annual Sales _____ Profits _____

Past five years sales growth _____% Past five year profits growth _____%

Number of employees _____ Years in business _____

Title of position discussed _____

Responsibilities _____

Questions and comments:

_____

_____

_____

_____

_____

_____

_____

_____

_____

_____

_____

_____

_____

General impressions of interview _____

_____

_____

_____

Follow-up _____

_____

This is a follow-up letter to a personal interview. Note it refers to an important part of the interview discussion and relates an accomplishment to this item. Ronald Marque also kept the initiative for the next follow-up call.

Ronald J. Marque
Apartment 4, Terrace Court
Chicago, Illinois 47092
Telephone (312) 221-9130

March 26, 1990

Mr. Charles G. Westmoreland
Industrial Products Manufacturing Co.
Post Office Box 6713–A
Kansas City, Kansas 66117

Dear Mr. Westmoreland:

I want to confirm my interest in the financial analyst's position we discussed this morning.

Because most of your current investment decisions are based on pay back period and return on investment only, I feel I could contribute some new techniques that would give additional, useful data. The work I have done with business statistics and econometric modeling should also be applicable to analyzing new markets for Industrial Products Manufacturing Co.

In my last position I did an econometric model of residential housing demand and mortgage company competition in Chicago which showed a growing market segment attracting little attention from other firms. We used this information to sell over $50 million worth of loans.

After you have talked with other candidates, I would like to meet with you to discuss my background and the future plans of IPM in more detail. I will call you late this month to arrange a convenient time.

Thank you for your interest and consideration.

Sincerely,

Ronald J. Marque

Jerrold Brooks confirmed an interview with this letter again emphasizing a related accomplishment, showing enthusiasm for the job, and maintaining the initiative for follow-up.

Jerrold A. Brooks
1216 Thornhill Drive
Dallas, Texas 75221
Telephone (214) 871-1496

February 28, 1990

Mr. Conway M. Green
President
Martex, Inc.
Post Office Box 740
Greenville, North Carolina 27601

Dear Mr. Green,

I enjoyed our discussion this week. You have done an impressive job with Martex, including your five-year expansion plans.

I would like to participate in this next phase of your growth. My merchandising experience during Howard & Sharpe's expansion years has given me the background to anticipate some of the problems your firm might face. As you know, I put Howard & Sharpe into perma press, creating a new $2-million market. I also designed its plans to enter the discount chain market. Evaluating the Martex line and identifying new markets would be an attractive challenge.

I look forward to our next discussion at the New York fall show. As soon as I arrive I will call your hotel to set a lunch date.

Sincerely,

Jerrold A. Brooks

This letter confirms a job offer and some of the important compensation details. It also sets a definite date for the response.

Robert S. Thomason
1921 Forest Run Drive
Great Falls, Virginia 23322
Telephone (703) 775-6421

April 15, 1990

Mr. Martin B. Fairchild
President
Techmark Controls, Inc.
Post Office Box 179
Greenwich, Connecticut 04703

Dear Martin:

I enjoyed meeting you and Sam Burtcher this week and appreciate the job offer you extended to me. It is attractive; the job is challenging.

My understanding is that the position of Vice-President, International would carry a base salary of $60,000 per year with an incentive bonus to be worked out mutually after the first year of operation. It will be based on a percentage of before tax profits generated by overseas sales. An automobile, moving expenses, and two trips to the United States per year for my family are included in addition to Techmark's standard benefit package.

I will discuss this move with my wife, complete my investigation of one other pending prospect, and get back in touch with you by April 27.

Thank you again for the confidence you have shown in me.

Sincerely,

Robert S. Thomason

This letter confirms a job offer with a salary too low for consideration.

Jerrold A. Brooks
1216 Thornhill Drive
Dallas, Texas 75221
Telephone (214) 871-1496

March 5, 1990

Mr. Richard A. Graffner, Jr.
President
Liberty Tailored Wear, Inc.
Post Office Box 19711
New York, New York 10022

Dear Mr. Graffner,

Our meeting last week was a pleasure even though we could not reach agreement on my joining your company. Liberty Tailored Wear is an interesting firm. You have assembled an impressive group of executives.

If you are unsuccessful in finding an executive who meets your requirements for Vice-President of Marketing at your price, I would like to discuss this position again. Although my salary requirements may appear high, I can make a commensurate contribution to Liberty.

Thank you again for your kind consideration.

Sincerely,

Jerrold A. Brooks

This letter followed a largely social dinner but confrimed the expectation of a job offer and set the time for a response.

Jerrold A. Brooks
1216 Thornhill Drive
Dallas, Texas 75221
Telephone (214) 871-1496

March 14, 1990

Mr. Conway M. Green
President
Martex, Inc.
Post Office Box 740
Greenville, North Carolina 27601

Dear Conway:

My wife and I appreciate the dinner you arranged for us. Meeting your wife and the wives of your associates was also an unexpected pleasure.

I look forward to receiving your offer next week, as I am most interested in the position with Martex.

You will hear from me prior to the end of the month. Meanwhile, I send my best regards.

Sincerely,

Jerrold A. Brooks

This form is used to record job offers in detail. This information will be needed to compare competing offers.

RECORD OF JOB OFFER

Date _____

Company _____

Contact and title _____

Address _____

_____ Telephone _____

Position _____

Responsibilities _____

Location _____

Starting salary _____

Benefits:	Comments	Value
Vacations	_____	_____
Holidays	_____	_____
Group insurance, hospital	_____	_____
Life	_____	_____
Accident	_____	_____
Major medical	_____	_____
Disability	_____	_____
Dental	_____	_____
Sick leave	_____	_____
Automobile	_____	_____
Expense account	_____	_____
Pension	_____	_____
Profit sharing or bonus	_____	_____
Stock options	_____	_____
Other	_____	_____

Total value, salary and benefits _____

Comments on moving expenses and other items _____

_____

Follow up _____

_____

Use this form to compare competing job offers, but don't use a mathematical average in the ratings. Some elements of a potential job are much more important than others.

EVALUATION OF JOB OFFERS

Name _____ Date _____

Item	I	II	III	IV
Position _____	_____	_____	_____	_____
Title _____	_____	_____	_____	_____
Responsibilities _____	_____	_____	_____	_____
Authority _____	_____	_____	_____	_____
Industry _____	_____	_____	_____	_____
Company, size and type _____	_____	_____	_____	_____
Company, style and character ___	_____	_____	_____	_____
Location _____	_____	_____	_____	_____
Salary _____	_____	_____	_____	_____
Benefits _____	_____	_____	_____	_____
Promotion potential _____	_____	_____	_____	_____
Salary potential _____	_____	_____	_____	_____
Equity potential _____	_____	_____	_____	_____
Work hours _____	_____	_____	_____	_____
Travel _____	_____	_____	_____	_____
Security _____	_____	_____	_____	_____
Challenge _____	_____	_____	_____	_____
Professional risk_____	_____	_____	_____	_____
Variety and interest_____	_____	_____	_____	_____
Contacts with– People _____	_____	_____	_____	_____
– Data_____	_____	_____	_____	_____
– Things _____	_____	_____	_____	_____
Personal relationships _____	_____	_____	_____	_____
Internal politics _____	_____	_____	_____	_____
Recognition– Professional _____	_____	_____	_____	_____
– Civic _____	_____	_____	_____	_____
– Personal _____	_____	_____	_____	_____
Contribution to career goals ____	_____	_____	_____	_____
Spouse's preference_____	_____	_____	_____	_____
Overall preference _____	_____	_____	_____	_____

This letter was used to accept a job offer and establish a date for reporting to work.

Robert S. Thomason
1921 Forest Run Drive
Great Falls, Virginia 23322
Telephone (703) 755-6421

April 28, 1990

Ms. Gail B. Fairchild
President
Techmark Controls, Inc.
Post Office Box 179
Greenwich, Connecticut 04703

Dear Gail,

Confirming our telephone conversation yesterday, I wish to accept the position of Vice-President, International with Techmark Controls. The conditions of employment are as outlined in my letter of April 10 except for the addition of an overseas housing allowance of $300 per month.

I will report to your Greenwich office on May 16 and will be ready to leave for Brussels with my family on June 15.

I look forward to working with you and your associates. The position is an attractive opportunity and challenge.

Sincerely,

Robert S. Thomason

This letter was used to decline a job offer.

Robert S. Thomason
1921 Forest Run Drive
Great Falls, Virginia 23322
Telephone (703) 755-6421

April 27, 1990

Mr. Fred M. Langford
President
Overseas Oil, Inc.
Post Office Box 6000
Houston, Texas 77025

Dear Mr. Langford,

I have accepted the position of Vice-President, International with Techmark Controls. Although I was strongly interested in the position with Overseas Oil, I felt I could better use my industrial and sales experience in the process controls industry.

I want to thank you and your associates for your offer and your kind consideration.

Sincerely,

Robert S. Thomason

Ms. Naff sent this letter to all of her personal contacts and others who assisted with her search. Your Jobsearch isn't complete until this letter is in the mail.

Karilyn G. Naff
1674 North Park Drive
Atlanta, Georgia 30341
Telephone (404) 936-7511

April 27, 1990

Mr. K. R. Greenfield
Manager
Compushare, Inc.
2117 First Avenue, North
Atlanta, Georgia 30308

Dear Kirk,

I have just accepted the position of controller with Morris Products in Hapeville. Your assistance and excellent reference helped make this move possible.

If I can ever reciprocate, please call me.

Thank you again. Drop in to see me on your next visit to Hapeville.

Cordially,

Karilyn G. Naff

Index

[Boldface numbers **(14)** refer to items in the Jobsearch Workbook section beginning on page 145.]

[Boldface numbers **(14)** refer to items in the Jobsearch Workbook section beginning on page 145.]

[Boldface numbers **(14)** refer to items in the Jobsearch Workbook section beginning on page 145.]

[Boldface numbers **(14)** refer to items in the Jobsearch Workbook section beginning on page 145.]

[Boldface numbers **(14)** refer to items in the Jobsearch Workbook section beginning on page 145.]

[Boldface numbers **(14)** refer to items in the Jobsearch Workbook section beginning on page 145.]

[Boldface numbers **(14)** refer to items in the Jobsearch Workbook section beginning on page 145.]

[Boldface numbers **(14)** refer to items in the Jobsearch Workbook section beginning on page 145.]